Henry William Lovett Hime

The Outlines of Quaternions

Henry William Lovett Hime

The Outlines of Quaternions

ISBN/EAN: 9783337312435

Printed in Europe, USA, Canada, Australia, Japan

Cover: Foto ©ninafisch / pixelio.de

More available books at **www.hansebooks.com**

THE OUTLINES OF QUATERNIONS

BY

LIEUT.-COLONEL H. W. L. HIME

(LATE) ROYAL ARTILLERY

LONDON
LONGMANS, GREEN, AND CO.
AND NEW YORK: 15 EAST 16th STREET
1894

CONTENTS

PART I

SUBTRACTION AND ADDITION OF VECTORS

CHAPTER I

FIRST PRINCIPLES OF VECTORS

SECTION 1
The Nature of a Vector

ART.		PAGE
1°.	Definition of a vector	1
2°.	A vector implies an operation of transference. . . .	1
3°.	Actual and null vectors	2
4°.	A vector implicitly involves three numbers . . .	2
5°.	Distinction between a vector and a radius vector . .	2
6°.	Opposite, coinitial, successive, coplanar, and diplanar vectors	2

SECTION 2
Equality and Inequality of Vectors

7°.	Definition of equal vectors	2
8°.	Example of equal vectors	3
9°.	All equal vectors are denoted by the same symbol . . .	3

SECTION 3
Subtraction and Addition of Two Vectors

10°.	Definition of the difference of any two vectors . . .	3
11°.	,, ,, ,, sum of two successive vectors . .	4
12°.	,, ,, ,, ,, ,, any two vectors	4

ART.		PAGE
13°.	$a = -(-a); \ -(+a) = +(-a) = -a$	4
14°.	Directions can be assigned to the sides of a plane triangle such that the sum of two sides shall be equal to the third	4
15°.	Sum and difference of two coinitial sides of a parallelogram	5

SECTION 4
Addition and Subtraction of Vectors in general.

16°.	Definition of the sum of any number of vectors	5
17°.	The subtraction and addition of vectors are associative and commutative operations	5

SECTION 5
Coefficients of Vectors

18°.	$xa \pm ya = (x \pm y)a; \ x(ya) = (xy)a = xya$	6
19°.	The quotient of two parallel vectors is a number	6
20°.	Parallel vectors have the same ratio as their lengths	7
21°.	$x(a \pm \beta) = xa \pm x\beta$	7

SECTION 6
Scalars, Unit-Vectors, and Tensors

22°.	Definition of a scalar	8
23°.	,, ,, ,, unit-vector and a tensor	8
24°.	Distinction between a scalar and a tensor	8

CHAPTER II
ON POINTS AND VECTORS IN A GIVEN PLANE

SECTION 1
Linear Equations connecting Two Vectors

25°.	If $pa + q\beta = 0$, and p and q have real and actual values, then $a \parallel \beta$	10
26°.	If $pa + q\beta = 0$, and a and β are oblique; then $p = 0, q = 0$	10

SECTION 2
Linear Equations connecting Three Vectors

27°.	If $la + m\beta + n\gamma = 0$, a, β, γ are coplanar	11
28°.	If $la + m\beta + n\gamma = 0$, and a, β, γ terminate in a straight line; then $l + m + n = 0$	12

CONTENTS

ART.		PAGE
29°.	Anharmonic and harmonic section of vectors	13
30°.	(a) Investigation of the equation $l\alpha + m\beta + n\gamma = 0$, when $l + m + n \neq 0$	14
	(b) The equation of the six segments	15
	(c) On the sign of geometric figures	15
31°.	Investigation of the equation $\alpha + \beta + \gamma = 0$	16

CHAPTER III

ILLUSTRATIONS IN COPLANAR VECTORS

32°.	Illustrations	19

CHAPTER IV

ON POINTS AND VECTORS IN SPACE

SECTION 1

The Mean Point

33°.	Definitions of the simple and complex mean points	25
34°.	The position of the mean point depends absolutely upon the configuration of the system	25
35°.	The sum of the vectors drawn from the mean point to all the points of the system is zero	26
36°.	The projection of the mean point is the mean point of the projected system	26

SECTION 2

Linear Equations connecting Four Noncoplanar Vectors

37°.	Vector-diagonal of a parallelopiped	27
38°.	If $h\alpha + l\beta + m\gamma + n\delta = 0$, and $\alpha, \beta, \gamma, \delta$ terminate in a plane; then $h + l + m + n = 0$	28
39°.	Equation of a plane in terms of its intercepts on the Cartesian axes of coordinates	29

PART II

DIVISION AND MULTIPLICATION OF TWO VECTORS

CHAPTER I

FIRST PRINCIPLES OF QUATERNIONS

SECTION 1
Definitions

ART.		PAGE
1°. (a)	Definition of a quaternion	30
(b)	„ „ a^{-1}	30
(c)	$\frac{\beta}{a} = \beta a^{-1}$; $\beta a = \frac{\beta}{a^{-1}}$	30
(d)	If $q = \frac{\beta}{a}$, $qa = \beta$; if $q' = \beta a$, $q'a^{-1} = \beta$	30
(e)	Definition of the angle of a quaternion	31
(f)	„ „ „ plane of a quaternion	31
(g)	„ „ „ coplanar quaternions	31
(h)	„ „ „ diplanar quaternions	31
(i)	$\frac{\delta}{a} \pm \frac{\gamma}{a} = \frac{\delta \pm \gamma}{a}$, &c.	31
(j)	Miscellaneous definitions	31

SECTION 2
The Nature of a Quaternion

		PAGE
2°. (a)	Nature of the symbol $\frac{\beta}{a}$	31
(b)	„ „ „ symbol βa	32
3°.	The operation of tension	33
4°.	„ „ „ version	33
(a)	The nature of a versor	33
(b)	Positive and negative rotation	34
(c)	Symbolic expression of a versor	34
(d)	A versor implicitly involves three numbers	36
5°.	A quaternion implicitly involves four numbers	36

CHAPTER II

THE PROPERTIES OF A SYSTEM OF THREE MUTUALLY RECTANGULAR UNIT-VECTORS, i, j, k

ART.		PAGE
6°.	Definition of the function of a unit-vector, in the first power, as a versor	37
7°.	$ij = k$; $ij \neq ji$; $j(-k) = -jk$	37
8°.	$i(j \pm k) = ij \pm ik$	38
9°.	$\dfrac{i}{j} = -k$; $\dfrac{j}{i} = k$	38
10°.	$ijk = i^2 = j^2 = k^2 = -1$; $ijk \neq ikj$; $-j^2 \neq (-j)^2$ . .	39
11°.	Real geometric signification of $\sqrt{-1}$	40
12°.	$\dfrac{1}{i} = -i$	41
13°.	$\dfrac{1}{a} = \dfrac{-U\alpha}{T\alpha}$. Graphic representation of a vector and its reciprocal	41
14°.	$i\dfrac{1}{i} = \dfrac{1}{i}i$	42

CHAPTER III

THE VARIOUS FORMS OF A QUATERNION

SECTION 1

A Quaternion as the Product of a Tensor and a Versor

15°.	$q = TqUq = UqTq$	43
16°.	$U(Uq) = Uq$	44

SECTION 2

A Quaternion as the Sum of a Scalar and a Vector

17°.	$q = Sq + Vq$	44
18°.	Recapitulation of the formulæ of 17°	48
19°.	On the symbol, $\cos\theta + \epsilon\sin\theta$	49
20°.	The sum of a scalar and a vector is a quaternion . .	49
21°.	Vector multiplication is not commutative . . .	50
22°.	$S\alpha\beta = \frac{1}{2}(\alpha\beta + \beta\alpha)$; $V\alpha\beta = \frac{1}{2}(\alpha\beta - \beta\alpha)$ . . .	50
23°.	If $Vq = 0$, the constituent vectors are parallel . .	50
24°.	The square of a vector is a negative scalar . .	51

ART.		PAGE
25°.	If $Sq = 0$, the constituent vectors are at right angles	51
26°.	$V\alpha\beta$ represents the vector-area of the parallelogram whose coinitial sides are a and b	51

Section 3

A Quaternion as the Power of a Vector

27°.	Definition of the function of a unit-vector, in any power, as a versor	52
28°.	The versors of the four quaternions of 17° as the powers of unit-vectors	52
29°.	$\epsilon^{-i} = \dfrac{1}{\epsilon^i}$; $\epsilon^{-i} \neq -\epsilon^i$; $-\epsilon^i \neq (-\epsilon)^i$	53
30°.	The algebraic laws of indices apply to versors and quaternions	54
31°.	Geometric interpretation of Moivre's theorem	55
32°.	$\eta^{2i} = \pm 1$; $\eta^{2i+1} = \pm \eta$	56
33°.	The power of a vector is a quaternion. The amplitude of a quaternion	56
34°.	Every quaternion may be represented by the power of a vector	57

Section 4

Quadrinomial Form of a Quaternion

35°.	$q = w + xi + yj + zk$	57
36°.	(a) Second proof that vector multiplication is not commutative	58
	(b) Vector multiplication is distributive	58
	(c) ,, ,, ,, associative	59
37°.	$(\alpha \pm \beta)^2 = \alpha^2 \pm 2S\alpha\beta + \beta^2$, &c., &c.	60
38°.	$\dfrac{\alpha}{\beta}\gamma \neq \dfrac{\alpha\gamma}{\beta}$; $\dfrac{\alpha}{\beta}\beta = \dfrac{\alpha\beta}{\beta}$; $\dfrac{\alpha}{\beta}\dfrac{\beta}{\gamma} \neq \dfrac{\alpha\beta}{\beta\gamma}$	60
39°.	Functions of a quaternion in quadrinomial form	61

CHAPTER IV

EQUALITY AND INEQUALITY OF QUATERNIONS

40°.	(a) Definition of equal quaternions	63
	(b) On the equality of two tensors	63
	(c) ,, ,, ,, ,, ,, versors	63

ART.		PAGE
41°.	If $\frac{a}{\beta} = \frac{\gamma}{\delta}$, then $\frac{\delta}{\beta} = \frac{\gamma}{a}$	64
42°.	Any two geometric quotients can be reduced to a common denominator	64
43°.	No two diplanar quaternions can be equal	65
44°.	If an equation contain scalar and vector terms, the sums of the scalar and vector terms on either side are respectively equal	65

CHAPTER V
THE VARIOUS KINDS OF QUATERNIONS

45°.	Collinear quaternions	66
46°.	Reciprocal „	66
47°.	Opposite „	67
48°.	Conjugate „	68
49°.	Miscellaneous formulæ and theorems	69

CHAPTER VI
THE POWERS OF QUATERNIONS

50°.	$q^n = T^n q (\cos n\theta + \epsilon \sin n\theta)$	74
51°.	Investigation of the value of q^2	74

CHAPTER VII
ADDITION AND SUBTRACTION OF QUATERNIONS

52°.	Σq = a quaternion	77
	Δq = „ „	77
53°.	$\Sigma S q = S \Sigma q$; $\Sigma V q = V \Sigma q$; $\Sigma K q = K \Sigma q$, &c., &c. . .	77
54°.	$\Sigma T q \neq T \Sigma q$, &c.	78
55°.	$\Sigma \angle q \neq \angle \Sigma q$, &c.	79
56°.	$\Sigma U q \neq U \Sigma q$, &c.	80

CHAPTER VIII
MULTIPLICATION AND DIVISION OF TWO QUATERNIONS

SECTION 1
Diplanar Quaternions

57°.	$q_1 q_2$ = a quaternion	81
	$\frac{q_1}{q_2}$ = „ „	81

ART.	PAGE
58°. $T\frac{q_1}{q_2} = \frac{Tq_1}{Tq_2}$; $Tq_1q_2 = Tq_1Tq_2$. A theorem of Euler.	81
59°. $Uq_1q_2 = Uq_1Uq_2$; $U\frac{q_1}{q_2} = \frac{Uq_1}{Uq_2}$.	82
60°. $Sqr \neq SqSr$; $Vqr \neq Vrq$; $qr \neq rq$	83
61°. $\angle qr = \angle rq$; $SUqr \neq SUqSUr$	84
62°. $Kqr = KrKq$	84
63° (a) Quaternion multiplication is not commutative	84
(b) „ „ „ distributive	84
(c) „ „ „ associative	84

Section 2
Coplanar Quaternions

64°. $qr = rq$	85
65°. $qKq = Kq \cdot q$, &c.	85

Section 3
Right Quaternions

66°. $Sv_1v_2 = \frac{1}{2}(v_1v_2 + v_2v_1)$; $Vv_1v_2 = \frac{1}{2}(v_1v_2 - v_2v_1)$; $Kv_1v_2 = v_2v_1$.	85
67°. Product of two right quaternions at right angles to each other is a third right quaternion at right angles to both.	85

Section 4
Circular Vector-Arcs

68°. Definition of equal vector-arcs	86
69°. Addition of vector-arcs is equivalent to multiplication of quaternions.	87
70°. Addition of diplanar vector-arcs is non-commutative	87
71°. Geometric meaning of the inequality, $qq' \neq q'q$	88
72°. Addition of coplanar vector-arcs is commutative	88
73°. Geometric meaning of the equation, $Kq'q = KqKq'$.	89
74°. Composition of two right rotations	89
75°. Conical rotation, and the operator $q(\quad)q^{-1}$.	90

CHAPTER IX
FORMULÆ

76°. 92°. } Various Formulæ	93

CHAPTER X

INTERPRETATION OF QUATERNION EXPRESSIONS

ART.   PAGE

93°. Geometric meaning of $S\alpha\beta\gamma = 0$ 99

94°.   ,,   ,,   ,, $S\alpha\beta\gamma$, when $S\alpha\beta\gamma \gtrless 0$ . . . 99

95°. If $S\alpha\beta\gamma \lessgtr 0$, $S\alpha\beta\gamma = -(x_1 y_2 z_3)$ 100

96°. Geometric meaning of $V\alpha\beta\gamma$, when $S\alpha\beta\gamma = 0$ 101

97°.
109°. } Equations of various loci 102

CHAPTER XI

DIFFERENTIATION OF VECTORS AND QUATERNIONS

SECTION 1

General Principles

110°. Definition of the differential of any variable . . . 111

111°. Differential of the square of a scalar 113

112°.   ,,   ,, an area 114

SECTION 2

Differential of a Vector

113°. General formula for the differential of a vector . . . 115

114°. Differential of $\rho = \dfrac{t^2 a}{2}$ 116

SECTION 3

Differential of a Quaternion

115°. General formula for the differential of a quaternion . . 117

116°. Differential of $Q = q^2$ 117

SECTION 4

Miscellaneous Examples

117°–129°. $qr = qdr + dq \cdot r$, &c. &c. . . . 118

CHAPTER XII

EQUATIONS

SECTION 1
Scalar Equations

ART.		PAGE
130°.	A vector cannot be determined by two scalar equations	124
131°.	,, ,, can always be determined by three scalar equations	124
132°.	,, ,, cannot be eliminated by fewer than four scalar equations	126

SECTION 2
Linear Vector Equations

133°. Definition of the general form of a linear vector equation . 126
134°. Conjugate and self-conjugate functions 127
135°. Properties of ϕ 127
136°. Definition of the inverse function ϕ^{-1} 128
137°. A method of solving linear vector equations . . . 128

CHAPTER XIII

ILLUSTRATIONS IN QUATERNIONS

SECTION 1
138°–140°. Plane trigonometry 130

SECTION 2
141°–156°. Spherical trigonometry . 132

SECTION 3
157°–158°. The triangle. 146

SECTION 4
159°–169°. The circle . . 148

SECTION 5
170°–192°. Conic sections 155

Section 6

ART.
193°–196°. Various curves 169

Section 7

197°–201°. The plane 176

Section 8

202°–206°. The tetrahedron 177

Section 9

207°–216°. The sphere 179

Section 10

217°–219°. The cone 184

Table of the pages of the Figures.

FIG.	PAGE	FIG.	PAGE	FIG.	PAGE	FIG.	PAGE
1	3	13	41	25	87	37	162
2	6	14	44	26	91	38	165
3	7	15	47	27	99	39	169
4	11	16	49	28	101	40	170
5	14	17	54	29	114	41	172
6	16	18	57	30	115	42	173
7	27	19	64	31	130	43	175
8	31	20	67	32	132	44	179
9	32	21	71	33	140	45	180
10	33	22	74	34	147	46	186
11	37	23	78	35	150		
12	38	24	86	36	156		

List of Works referred to in the following pages.

1. *Lectures on Quaternions.* By Sir W. R. Hamilton. Dublin, 1853.
2. *Elements of Quaternions.* By Sir W. R. Hamilton. Dublin, 1866.
3. *Introduction to Quaternions.* By Professors P. Kelland and P. G. Tait. London, 1873.
4. *Kurze Anleitung zum Rechnen mit den Hamilton'schen Quaternionen.* By Professor J. Odstrčil. Halle a. S., 1879.
5. *Elements of Quaternions.* By Professor A. S. Hardy. Boston, U.S., 1881.
6. *Mathematical Papers.* By Professor W. K. Clifford. London, 1882.
7. *Elementary Treatise on Quaternions.* By Professor P. G. Tait. 3rd. ed., Cambridge, 1890.
8. *Theorie der Quaternionen.* By Dr. P. Molenbroek. Leiden, 1891.

NOTE.

$\neq$ means, 'is not equal to.'

c ,, $\dfrac{2}{\pi}$, when in the exponent of a vector.

THE
OUTLINES OF QUATERNIONS

PART I

SUBTRACTION AND ADDITION OF VECTORS

CHAPTER I

FIRST PRINCIPLES OF VECTORS

SECTION 1

The Nature of a Vector

1°. Definition.—*A Vector is any quantity which has Magnitude and Direction* (Clifford).

It follows that a straight line, $\overline{AB}$, considered as having not only *length* but *direction*, is a vector. Its initial point, A, is called its Origin; and its final point, B, is called its Term.

With the exception of three special vectors (i, j, k, Pt. II., 6°), vectors will be denoted in these pages either by a symbol combining their initial and final letters, such as $\overline{AB}$, or by a small letter of the Greek alphabet, in order to distinguish them from the ordinary straight lines of geometry, such as AB or *a*.

2°. A vector, $\overline{AB}$, may be conceived as having for its function to transport (*vehere*, to carry) a particle from A to B. A vector thus implies an *operation*, and represents *translation in a certain direction for a certain distance*.

B

3°. When its origin and term, A and B, are distinct points, $\overline{AB}$ is said to be an Actual Vector; but when, as a limit, these points coincide, it is said to be a Null Vector.

Actual is used as opposed to *null*; *real* as opposed to *imaginary*.

4°. In order to determine the position of any point in space, B, in relation to any other point, A, three numbers must be known. Let A be the centre of the earth (supposed to be a perfect sphere), and B any point upon its surface. Then, in order to be able to draw a straight line from A to B we must know, first, the Latitude of B; secondly, its Longitude; and thirdly, the Radius of the Earth.

Every vector, then, implicitly involves three numbers; one indicating its *length*, and two its *direction*.

5°. A vector is not to be confounded with the radius vector of Algebraic Geometry. The latter represents *length* only, and implies but *one* number. It is, in fact, one of the three numbers contained in a vector.

6°. *Opposite* Vectors, such as $\overline{AB}$ and $\overline{BA}$, are sometimes called Vector and Revector.

Coinitial Vectors are vectors whose origins coincide.

If there be any series of vectors such that the origin of the second coincides with the term of the first, the origin of the third with the term of the second, &c., &c., these vectors are called *Successive* Vectors.

Coplanar Vectors are those that lie in the same plane.
Diplanar Vectors are those that lie in different planes.

We will have hereafter to consider vector arcs; but at present the only vectors considered are rectilinear.

Section 2

Equality and Inequality of Vectors

7°. *Definition.*—*Two given vectors are equal to each other when (and only when) the origin and term of the one can be brought to coincide simultaneously with the corresponding points of the other, by motion of translation, without rotation.*

As a consequence of this definition, no two vectors are equal unless they have, first, *equal lengths*, and, secondly, *similar directions*—the phrase 'similar directions' meaning '*parallel directions* with the *same sense.*' Similarly, 'contrary (or opposite) directions' means 'parallel directions with contrary (or opposite) sense.'

The meaning of the word 'parallel' is extended, so as to include lines which form parts of one common straight line.

8°. If two equal vectors, $\overline{AB}$ and $\overline{CD}$, do not form part of one common straight line, they may be regarded as the opposite sides of a parallelogram, ACDB, fig. 1.

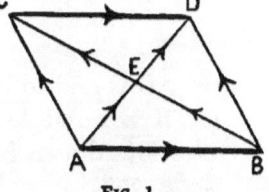

Fig. 1.

9°. Since the operation implied by a vector—transference in a certain direction for a certain distance—is the same, whatever point in space be selected as the origin of motion; all equal vectors are denoted by the same vector-symbol. Thus, if $\overline{AB} = \overline{CD}$, and if $\overline{AB}$ be denoted by β, $\overline{CD}$ is also denoted by β. It follows that a (Hamiltonian) vector has no particular position in space.

Section 3

Subtraction and Addition of Two Vectors

10°. *Definition.*—*When a first vector, $\overline{AB}$, is subtracted from a second vector, $\overline{AC}$, which is coinitial with it, or from a third vector, $\overline{A'C'}$, which is equal to that second vector, the remainder is that fourth vector, $\overline{BC}$, which is drawn from the term B of the first to the term C of the second vector* (*Hamilton*).

In symbols, fig. 1,
$$\overline{A'C'} - \overline{AB} = \overline{AC} - \overline{AB} = \overline{BC}.$$

The foregoing definition is perfectly general, and includes the case in which the vectors are parallel, *i.e.* in which $\angle CAB = \pi$, or zero.

If $\overline{AC}$ be a null vector, the equation $\overline{AC} - \overline{AB} = \overline{BC}$ becomes
$$-\overline{AB} = \overline{BA}.$$
Similarly,
$$-\overline{BA} = \overline{AB}.$$

Therefore, *the minus sign reverses the direction of a vector*; and if $\overline{AB}$ is represented by a, $\overline{BA}$ will be represented by $-a$.

11°. Since, by 10°,
$$\overline{AC} - \overline{AB} = \overline{BC},$$
and also $\qquad -\overline{AB} = \overline{BA};$
therefore, $\qquad \overline{AC} + \overline{BA} = \overline{BC};$

where $\overline{AC}$ is said to be added to $\overline{BA}$.

Or, if $\overline{BA}$ and $\overline{AC}$ be successive vectors, 6°, their sum is a vector, $\overline{BC}$, drawn from the origin of the first, B, to the term of the second, C.

Hence, $\qquad \overline{BA} + \overline{AB} = \overline{BB} = 0 \quad \ldots \ldots \quad (1)$

12°. We have now to consider the sum of two non-successive vectors.

Definition.—*If there be two successive vectors, $\overline{AC}$ and $\overline{CD}$, and if a third vector, $\overline{C'D'}$, be equal to the second, but not successive to the first; the sum obtained by adding the third to the first is that fourth vector, $\overline{AC}$, which is drawn from the origin of the first to the term of the second (Hamilton).*

In symbols, fig. 1,
$$\overline{C'D'} + \overline{AC} = \overline{CD} + \overline{AC} = \overline{AD}.$$

This definition holds good when the vectors are parallel, *i.e*, when $\angle ACD = \pi$ or zero.

If $\overline{CD}$ be a null vector,
$$+ \overline{AC} = \overline{AC}; \text{ or}, + \overline{AB} = \overline{AB}.$$

13°. By 10° and 12° we have:
$$\overline{AB} = -\overline{BA} = -(\overline{BA}) = -(-\overline{AB}); \text{ or}, a = -(-a);$$
$$\overline{BA} = +(\overline{BA}) = +(-\overline{AB}); \text{ or}, -a = +(-a);$$
$$-\overline{AB} = -(\overline{AB}) = -(+\overline{AB}); \text{ or}, -a = -(+a).$$

Also, since
$$\overline{AC} - \overline{AB} = \overline{BC},$$
and $\qquad \overline{AC} = \overline{BC} + \overline{AB};$

it follows that a vector may be tranferred from one side of an equation to the other by changing its sign.

14°. Since $\qquad \overline{BC} + \overline{AB} = \overline{AC},\ 12°,$

it follows that directions can be assigned to the sides of any triangle, considered as vectors, such that the sum of two of the vector-sides will be equal to the third.

15°. If $\overline{AC}$, fig. 1, be a vector equal to $\overline{BD}$, but not successive to $\overline{AB}$, we have, by definition,

$$\overline{AC} + \overline{AB} = \overline{BD} + \overline{AB} = \overline{AD}.$$

But since $AC = BD$, ACDB is a parallelogram. It follows that the sum of any two coinitial sides, $\overline{AC}$ and $\overline{AB}$, of any parallelogram, ACDB, is the intermediate and coinitial diagonal, $\overline{AD}$.

We have also, by definition, $\overline{AC} - \overline{AB} = \overline{BC}$; or, the difference between any two coinitial sides, $\overline{AC}$ and $\overline{AB}$, of any parallelogram, ACDB, is the non-coinitial diagonal, $\overline{BC}$.

We have, by definition, $\overline{CD} + \overline{AC} = \overline{AD} = \overline{BD} + \overline{AB}$; or, if $\overline{AC} = \beta$ and $\overline{AB} = \alpha$,

$$\alpha + \beta = \beta + \alpha.$$

We have, similarly, $\overline{AC} - \overline{AB} = \overline{BC} = \overline{DC} + \overline{BD}$; or,

$$\beta - \alpha = -\alpha + \beta.$$

It follows that the sum, or difference, of any two vectors has a value which is independent of their order.

Section 4

Addition and Subtraction of Vectors in general

16°. To obtain the sum of three vectors, we have merely to add the third to the sum of the first and second, obtained as in 12°.

In general, the sum of any number of vectors is formed by adding the last to the sum of all that precede it. Thus, fig. 2, $\quad \overline{AD} = \overline{CD} + \overline{AC} = \overline{CD} + \overline{BC} + \overline{AB}.$

17°. From fig. 2,

$$\overline{BD} + \overline{AB} = \overline{AB} + \overline{BD}\,(15°) = \overline{AD} = \overline{CD} + \overline{AC} = \overline{AC} + \overline{CD};$$

or,

$$(\gamma + \beta) + \alpha = \alpha + (\beta + \gamma) = \gamma + (\beta + \alpha) = (\beta + \alpha) + \gamma$$

6 ADDITION AND SUBTRACTION OF VECTORS IN GENERAL

Similarly,
$$-a + (-\gamma - \beta) = -\gamma + (-a - \beta), \&c., \&c.$$

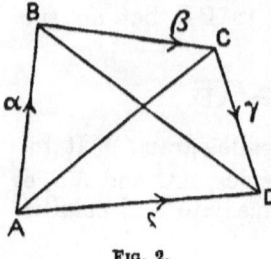

Fig. 2.

As these processes may be carried on to any extent with similar results, we may infer that the addition and subtraction of vectors are commutative and associative operations; that is, the sum, or difference, of any number of vectors has a value which is independent of their *order* and of the *mode of grouping* them.

Section 5
Coefficients of Vectors

18°. The coefficients of vectors obey the ordinary laws of algebra.

Let $\overline{AB} \ldots \overline{YZ}$ be a series of m successive and equal vectors. Then, if $\overline{AB} = a$ and $\overline{AZ} = \beta$,
$$\overline{AZ} = \beta = a + a + a \ldots m \text{ times} = ma = m\overline{AB} \quad \ldots (1)$$
Similarly,
$$\overline{ZA} = -\beta = -(ma) = -ma = -m\overline{AB} \quad \ldots (2)$$
If $\overline{AH} = \gamma$ be another parallel vector, such that
$$\gamma = na = n\overline{AB};$$
then, $\quad \dfrac{1}{n}\gamma = a = \dfrac{1}{m}\beta; \quad \beta = \dfrac{m}{n}\gamma; \quad \gamma = \dfrac{n}{m}\beta.$

If x and y be *any* two numbers,
$$xa \pm ya = (x \pm y)a; \quad x(ya) = (xy)a = xya.$$
It will presently be shown that
$$x(\delta \pm \epsilon) = x\delta \pm x\epsilon,$$
where δ and ϵ are any two vectors.

19°. The equations, $\overline{ZA} = -\overline{AZ} = -m\overline{AB}$ and $\overline{AH} = n\overline{AB}$, connecting the three parallel vectors, $\overline{ZA}, \overline{AB},$ and $\overline{AH}$, in the last article, may be written in the form:
$$\dfrac{\overline{ZA}}{\overline{AB}} = -m; \quad \dfrac{\overline{AH}}{\overline{AB}} = n;$$

and since $\overline{ZA}$, $\overline{AB}$, and $\overline{AH}$ may be *any* parallel vectors, we conclude that the quotient of two parallel vectors is a *number*, which is *positive* when they have the *same*, and *negative* when they have contrary sense, 7°.

Conversely, it is easy to show that if the quotient of two vectors be a number, the vectors are parallel; with the same sense if the number be positive, and with contrary sense if it be negative.

20°. The positive or negative number, m, obtained by the division of one parallel vector by another, is evidently the ratio of their lengths. For the equation $\overline{AZ} = m\overline{AB}$, merely asserts that if a moving point be transferred from A, in the *direction* of $\overline{AB}$, for a *distance* equal to m times $\overline{AB}$, it will reach Z; which simply means that the *length* of $\overline{AZ}$ is m times the length of $\overline{AB}$. Similarly, $\overline{ZA}$ is $-m$ times the length of AB, or m times the length of $-\overline{AB}$; that is, m times the length of $\overline{AB}$ measured in the contrary direction.

If in the equations $\overline{AZ} = m\overline{AB}$, $\overline{AH} = n\overline{AB}$, we suppose $\overline{AB}$ to be the unit of length, then m will be *the length* of $\overline{AZ}$, and n *the length* of $\overline{AH}$. The equations,

$$\frac{\overline{AZ}}{\overline{AH}} = \frac{m}{n}; \quad \frac{\overline{ZA}}{\overline{AH}} = \frac{-m}{n},$$

therefore, express the proposition that parallel vectors have the same ratio as their lengths, or as the *lines* that represent them.

21°. Let $\overline{OB}$ and $\overline{AO}$ be any vectors, fig. 3. Take the line $A'O = mAO$. Then, since parallel vectors are proportional to their lengths, if the vector AO be a, the vector $A'O$ will be ma. Join AB, and produce OB to meet $A'B'$, drawn parallel to AB. We know from Euclid that $OB' = mOB$; hence, if $\overline{OB} = \beta$, $\overline{OB'} = m\beta$. Similarly, $\overline{A'B'} = m\overline{AB}$. But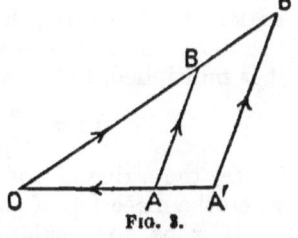

Fig. 3.

$\overline{A'B'} = \overline{A'O} + \overline{OB'}$, and $\overline{AB} = \overline{AO} + \overline{OB}$. Therefore,

$$ma + m\beta = m(a + \beta).$$

It can be similarly proved that $ma - m\beta = m(a - \beta)$,

and that $\frac{1}{m}\alpha \pm \frac{1}{m}\beta = \frac{1}{m}(\alpha \pm \beta)$. Hence, in general, if x be any number, and if α and β be any vectors,
$$x(\alpha \pm \beta) = x\alpha \pm x\beta.$$

Section 6
Scalars, Unit-Vectors, and Tensors

22°. The positive or negative number, m, obtained by dividing one parallel vector by another, is called a Scalar (*scala*, a scale). Scalars are the real quantities of algebra, and as such are combined with each other according to the ordinary laws of algebra.

23°. In equation (1) of 18°,
$$\overline{AZ} = m\overline{AB},$$
where m is a positive scalar, let the length of $\overline{AB}$ be unity, m being consequently the length of $\overline{AZ}$, 20°. In this case, still representing $\overline{AZ}$ by β, $\overline{AB}$ will be denoted by the symbol, $U\beta$; read *Unit-Vector* of β—*i.e.*, the vector of unit length with the same direction as β; while m will be denoted by the symbol, $T\beta$; read, *Tensor* of β (*tendere*, to stretch). Hence we have,
$$\left. \begin{array}{c} \beta = T\beta U\beta \, ; \\ T\beta = \dfrac{\beta}{U\beta} \, ; \qquad U\beta = \dfrac{\beta}{T\beta} \end{array} \right\} \quad . \quad . \quad (1)$$

24°. Since $T\beta$ is the ratio of two vectors with similar directions, β and $U\beta$, or $-\beta$ and $-U\beta$, it is *always* positive. Consequently, when multiplied into a vector, it alters the length of the vector, but cannot reverse its direction. A scalar, on the other hand, which may be either positive or negative, not only alters the length of any vector into which it is multiplied, but, when negative, reverses its direction.
$$T\rho = \frac{\rho}{U\rho} = \frac{-\rho}{-U\rho} = T(-\rho); \quad . \quad . \quad . \quad (1)$$
hence, the value of the tensor of a vector remains unchanged when the direction of the vector is reversed.

If x be any scalar, the unit-vector of $x\rho$ is obviously $\pm U\rho$, according as x is positive or negative. Hence,
$$T(x\rho) = \frac{x\rho}{\pm U\rho} = \pm x\frac{\rho}{U\rho} = \pm xT\rho, \quad . \quad . \quad . \quad (2)$$
according as $x \gtrless 0$.

SCALARS, UNIT-VECTORS, AND TENSORS

In general, $TS = \pm S$, according as $S \gtrless o$; or, the tensor of scalar is that scalar taken positively. The tensor of a tensor is the tensor itself; or, $TT = T$.

If x and y be any scalars,
$$S(x\rho + y) = y;$$
because $x\rho$ is a vector, and a vector has no scalar part, just as a scalar has no vector part. The scalar of a scalar is the scalar itself; consequently, the scalar of a tensor (which is a positive scalar) is the tensor itself. In symbols,
$$SV = o;\ VS = o;\ SS = S;\ ST = T\ .\ \ .\ \ . \quad (3)$$

For shortness' sake, we will frequently write d for the tensor of a vector δ, or $\overline{OD}$; m for the tensor of $\mu = \overline{OM}$, a for the tensor of $a = \overline{OA}$, &c., &c.

CHAPTER II

ON POINTS AND VECTORS IN A GIVEN PLANE

SECTION 1

Linear Equations connecting Two Vectors

25°. Since any number of vectors, which are not coinitial, may be made so by translating them until their origins coincide in some common point, O ; we will for the future suppose, unless the contrary be stated, that all the vectors under consideration, a, β, &c., are thus drawn from one common origin, O.

This point, O, is called the *Origin of the System*; and each particular vector, say $\overline{OA}$, is called *the vector of its own term*, A.

Let $\overline{OA} = a$, $\overline{OB} = \beta$, be any two given parallel vectors. Then, by 19°, they are connected together by an equation of the form

$$\beta = ma \quad \ldots \quad \ldots \quad \ldots \quad (1)$$

which expresses the collinearity of the three points, O, A, and B.

If β be a variable vector, ρ, and m a variable scalar, x, this equation may be written,

$$\rho = xa \quad \ldots \quad \ldots \quad \ldots \quad (2)$$

which expresses that the locus of the variable point, B, is the indefinite straight line passing through the points O and A.

The equation, $\beta = ma$, assumes a more symmetric form if we suppose $m = \dfrac{-p}{q}$. Then,

$$pa + q\beta = 0 \quad \ldots \quad \ldots \quad \ldots \quad (3)$$

26°. If a and β are oblique vectors, and if we have $pa + q\beta = 0$; then, $p = 0$ and $q = 0$. For otherwise we should have, $\beta = \dfrac{-p}{q} a = ta = \gamma$, say, where γ is *some* vector with the same direction as a; or, two vectors with different directions would be equal, which is contrary to definition. This principle may also be stated as follows:—If a and β are oblique vectors, and if we have an equation of the form,

$$xa + y\beta = ta + v\beta\ ;$$

then $\qquad x = t$ and $y = v$.

Section 2

Linear Equations connecting Three Vectors

27°. We have shown that if two oblique vectors, a and β, be connected by an equation of the form, $la + m\beta = 0$, then $l = 0$, and $m = 0$. Let us now suppose two such vectors to be connected by the equation, $la + m\beta + n\gamma = 0$, where n is some third actual scalar, and γ is some third vector, situated in we know not what plane.

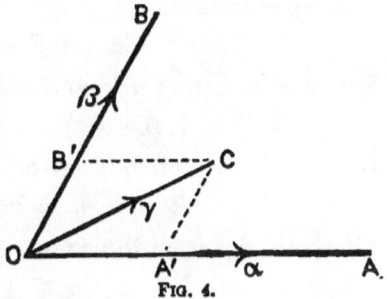

Fig. 4.

Let $\overline{OB} = \beta$, $\overline{OA} = a$, fig. 4, be the two given vectors. Then, since

$$la + m\beta + n\gamma = 0,$$

$$\gamma = -\frac{l}{n}a - \frac{m}{n}\beta.$$

Take $\overline{OA'} = \dfrac{-l}{n}a$, and $\overline{OB'} = \dfrac{-m}{n}\beta$; let $\overline{OC}$ represent γ, and draw $\overline{B'C}$ and $\overline{A'C}$.

We have now, $\qquad \overline{OC} = \overline{OA'} + \overline{OB'}$;
but, 11°, $\qquad \overline{OC} = \overline{OA'} + \overline{A'C}$;
therefore, $\qquad \overline{OB'} = \overline{A'C}$.

Therefore, the figure $OB'CA'$ is a parallelogram, and is consequently plane.

Therefore, if three coinitial vectors are connected by an equation of the form

$$la + m\beta + n\gamma = 0,$$

12 LINEAR EQUATIONS CONNECTING THREE VECTORS

where l, m, n are actual scalars; then a, β, γ are coplanar; and the converse.

28°. If $\quad la + m\beta + n\gamma = 0,$
what must be the relation between the scalars l, m, n, in order that the points A, C, B, fig. 4, may be collinear?

Let $\overline{OA} = a$, $\overline{OB} = \beta$, $\overline{OC} = \gamma$. If A, B, C are collinear, then, by 19°, $\dfrac{AC}{AB} =$ some scalar $= p$, say. Now, $\overline{AC} = \gamma - a$, and $\overline{AB} = \beta - a$; hence, $p = \dfrac{\gamma - a}{\beta - a}$; or,

$$(1-p)a + p\beta - \gamma = 0.$$

But, by condition,

$$la + m\beta + n\gamma = 0.$$

Hence, eliminating γ from these two equations,

$$(l + n - np)a + (m + np)\beta = 0.$$

But a and β are oblique vectors; therefore, 26°,

$$l + n - np = 0;\ m + np = 0.$$

Eliminating p from these two equations, we get

$$l + m + n = 0 \quad \ldots \ldots \quad (1)$$

the required relation.

Conversely, if three vectors be connected by an equation of the form $la + m\beta + n\gamma = 0$, with the condition,

$$l + m + n = 0;$$

then the three vectors terminate in a straight line.

If we eliminate successively the scalars l, m, n, from the two equations

$$la + m\beta + n\gamma = 0,$$
$$l + m + n = 0;$$

we get

$$m(-a + \beta) + n(\gamma - a) = 0,$$
$$n(-\beta + \gamma) + l(a - \beta) = 0,$$
$$l(-\gamma + a) + m(\beta - \gamma) = 0.$$

Therefore,

$$\frac{l}{m} = \frac{BC}{CA};\ \frac{m}{n} = \frac{CA}{AB};\ \frac{n}{l} = \frac{AB}{BC};$$

or, $\quad l : m : n = BC : CA : AB \quad \ldots \ldots \quad (2)$

LINEAR EQUATIONS CONNECTING THREE VECTORS 13

The same two equations give us

$$a = \frac{m\beta + n\gamma}{m + n}; \quad \beta = \frac{n\gamma + la}{n + l}; \quad \gamma = \frac{la + m\beta}{l + m} \quad . \quad . \quad . \quad (3)$$

The third equation of (3) may be put in words as follows: If we are given any two vectors, $\overline{OA} = \alpha$, $\overline{OB} = \beta$, and if there be a third coinitial vector, $\overline{OC} = \gamma$, such that

$$(l + m)\gamma = la + m\beta;$$

then, C, the term of γ, lies upon the straight line AB, which it cuts in the ratio $l : m$.

29°. If, while α and β remain constant, we suppose γ to be a variable vector and $l : m$ to be a variable ratio; this last equation may be written,

$$\rho = \frac{x\alpha + y\beta}{x + y};$$

which expresses that the locus of the variable point C, the term of ρ, is the indefinite straight line AB; which line it cuts, so that

$$\frac{AC}{CB} = \frac{y}{x}.$$

If C' be another variable point on the line AB, and if its vector be

$$\rho' = \frac{x'\alpha + y'\beta}{x' + y'},$$

we have, in like manner,

$$\frac{AC'}{C'B} = \frac{y'}{x'}.$$

We now define (ABCD) by the following equation:

$$(ABCD) = \frac{AB}{BC} \frac{CD}{DA};$$

where A, B, C, D are any four collinear points.

In the present case, therefore, we have

$$(ACBC') = \frac{AC}{CB} \frac{BC'}{C'A} = \frac{yx'}{xy'}.$$

When $(ACBC') = -1$, the range becomes harmonic, and $\frac{yx'}{xy'} = -1$; or, $\frac{y}{x} = -\frac{y'}{x'}$. Substituting this value of the

14 LINEAR EQUATIONS CONNECTING THREE VECTORS

ratio $y' : x'$ in the equation for ρ', given above, we have

$$\rho = \frac{x\alpha + y\beta}{x + y}\;;\; \rho' = \frac{x\alpha - y\beta}{x - y}\;;$$

where the points C and C′ are the harmonic conjugates to the points A and B. When C and C′ vary together owing to the variation of $y : x$, they form divisions in involution upon the indefinite straight line AB, the double points of the involution being A and B.

30°. (a). Suppose we have, $l\alpha + m\beta + n\gamma = 0$, with the condition

$$l + m + n \neq 0\;;$$

then the three vectors are still coplanar, 27°, but they no longer terminate in a straight line. Their terms are now the corners of a triangle, ABC, fig. 5.

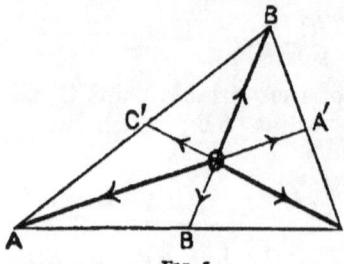

FIG. 5.

To find the values of the vectors of the points
A′ = OA . BC,
B′ = OB . CA,
C′ = OC . AB,
and the ratios of the segments
BA′ : A′C, &c.

Let $\overline{OA'} = \alpha'$, $\overline{OB'} = \beta'$, $\overline{OC'} = \gamma'$.

Since α and α', β and β', γ and γ', are respectively parallel vectors, they are connected together by equations of the form,

$$\alpha = x^{-1}\alpha',\; \beta = y^{-1}\beta',\; \gamma = z^{-1}\gamma' \quad \ldots \quad (1)$$

Substituting these values of α, β, γ, successively, in the given equation, we get

$$\left.\begin{array}{l} lx^{-1}\alpha' + m\beta + n\gamma = 0 \\ l\alpha + my^{-1}\beta' + n\gamma = 0 \\ l\alpha + m\beta + nz^{-1}\gamma' = 0 \end{array}\right\} \quad \ldots \ldots \quad (2)$$

But α', β, γ; α, β', γ; α, β, γ', are coinitial vectors terminating, respectively, in the straight lines BC, CA, AB. Therefore, 28°,

$$\left.\begin{array}{l} lx^{-1} + m + n = 0 \\ l + my^{-1} + n = 0 \\ l + m + nz^{-1} = 0 \end{array}\right\}.$$

LINEAR EQUATIONS CONNECTING THREE VECTORS 15

Hence, $$x = \frac{-l}{m+n}; \quad y = \frac{-m}{n+l}; \quad z = \frac{-n}{l+m} \quad . \quad . \quad (3)$$

Substituting these values of x, y, z, in equation (1), we get

$$\alpha' = \frac{-l\alpha}{m+n}; \quad \beta' = \frac{-m\beta}{n+l}; \quad \gamma' = \frac{-n\gamma}{l+m} \quad . \quad . \quad (4)$$

Substituting the same values of x, y, z, in the equations of (2),

$$\alpha' = \frac{m\beta + n\gamma}{m+n}; \quad \beta' = \frac{n\gamma + l\alpha}{n+l}; \quad \gamma' = \frac{l\alpha + m\beta}{l+m} \quad . \quad . \quad (5)$$

Equations (4) and (5) give the sought values of the vectors of the points A', B', C'.

Comparing the equations of (5) with the equations of (3), 28°, it is evident that

$$\frac{\overline{BC'}}{\overline{C'A}} = \frac{l}{m}; \quad \frac{\overline{CA'}}{\overline{A'B}} = \frac{m}{n}; \quad \frac{\overline{AB'}}{\overline{B'C}} = \frac{n}{l} \quad . \quad . \quad . \quad . \quad (6)$$

(b). If we multiply together the three ratios, equations (6), we get the equation of the Six Segments,

$$\frac{\overline{AB'}}{\overline{B'C}} \frac{\overline{BC'}}{\overline{C'A}} \frac{\overline{CA'}}{\overline{A'B}} = 1, \quad . \quad . \quad . \quad . \quad . \quad (7)$$

as the condition of concurrence of the lines AA', BB', CC'.

We have, also (6),

$$\begin{aligned} l : m &= BC' : C'A = OBC : OCA, \\ m : n &= CA' : A'B = OCA : OAB, \\ n : l &= AB' : B'C = OAB : OBC. \end{aligned} \quad . \quad . \quad (8)$$

Therefore, $\quad l : m : n = OBC : OCA : OAB;$

where OBC, &c., are the areas of the respective triangles.

(c). In such equations as those of (8), attention must be paid to the *signs* of figures, plane and solid.

Any plane figure is positive or negative according as the rotation of a particle round its periphery, as seen from a given aspect of the plane, is right-handed or left-handed. Thus, for any triangle ABC, we have

$$ABC = BCA = CAB = -BAC = -ACB = -CBA;$$

and as for a line we have

$$\overline{AB} + \overline{BA} = o;$$

so, for an area, we have
$$ABC + CBA = 0.$$

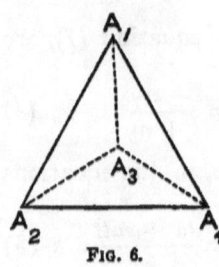

Fig. 6.

The case of solids is strictly analogous; the sign of the tetrahedron, fig. 6, being positive or negative according as the rotation of a particle round one of its faces is right-handed or left-handed, as seen from the opposite apex. Thus,
$$A_1A_2A_3A_4 = -A_1A_2A_4A_3$$
$$= -A_2A_1A_3A_4 = A_2A_3A_1A_4$$
$$= -A_2A_3A_4A_1, \&c., \&c.$$

In this case we have
$$A_1A_2A_3A_4 + A_2A_3A_4A_1 = 0.$$

31°. If $l = m = n$, the equation $l\alpha + m\beta + n\gamma = 0$ becomes
$$\alpha + \beta + \gamma = 0;$$
and the three vectors can obviously be made the sides of a triangle ABC, fig. 5, by 14°. In this case,
$$\overline{BC} = \alpha, \overline{CA} = \beta, \overline{AB} = \gamma.$$

Let $\overline{AA'}, \overline{BB'}$, be drawn, cutting $\overline{BC}$ and $\overline{CA}$ respectively in given ratios; and through their cross D (instead of O, fig. 5) draw a line from C cutting $\overline{AB}$ in C'. It is required to determine the ratios AD : DA'; BD : DB'; CD : DC'; and AC' : C'B.

Let the given ratios be
$$BA' : A'C = 1 - m : m;$$
$$CB' : B'A = n : 1 - n;$$
so that we have $\overline{A'C} = m\alpha$, and $\overline{CB'} = n\beta$.

(1) To determine AD : DA' and BD : DB'.

Since $BA' : A'C = 1 - m : m,$
by 28°
$$\overline{AA'} = m\gamma - (1-m)\beta$$
$$\quad = -m\alpha - \beta.$$

Similarly, $\overline{BB'} = \alpha + n\beta.$

Let $\overline{AD} = p\overline{AA'}; \overline{BD} = q\overline{BB'}.$

Then, $\overline{CA} + \overline{AD} = \overline{CD} = \overline{CB} + \overline{BD};$

or, $\beta - pm\alpha - p\beta = -\alpha + q\alpha + qn\beta;$
$$(1 - p - qn)\beta = (-1 + q + pm)\alpha.$$

LINEAR EQUATIONS CONNECTING THREE VECTORS 17

But, since a and β are not parallel, the coefficients of both must be zero, 26°. Therefore,

$$p = \frac{1-n}{1-mn}; \quad q = \frac{1-m}{1-mn}.$$

$$1 - p = \frac{n(1-m)}{1-mn}; \quad 1 - q = \frac{m(1-n)}{1-mn}.$$

Therefore,

$$\frac{AD}{DA'} = \frac{p}{1-p} = \frac{1-n}{n(1-m)}; \quad \frac{BD}{DB'} = \frac{q}{1-q} = \frac{1-m}{m(1-n)} \quad \ldots (1)$$

(2) To determine $CD : DC'$ and $AC' : C'B$.

Let $\overline{CC'} = x\overline{CD}; \quad \overline{AC'} = y\overline{AB} = y\gamma = y(-a-\beta)$.

Then, since $\overline{CC'} = \overline{CA} + \overline{AC'}$,

$$x\overline{CD} = \beta - ya - y\beta.$$

But, since $AD : DA' = (1-n) : n(1-m)$

$$\overline{CD} = \frac{n(1-m)\beta - (1-n)ma}{1-mn}.$$

Therefore,

$$xn(1-m)\beta - xm(1-n)a = (1-mn)(\beta - y\beta - ya),$$
$$\{xn(1-m) - (1-mn) + y(1-mn)\}\beta$$
$$= \{xm(1-n) - y(1-mn)\}a.$$

Equating the coefficients to zero,

$$x = \frac{1-mn}{m-2mn+n}; \quad y = \frac{m(1-n)}{m-2mn+n};$$

$$x - 1 = \frac{(1-m)(1-n)}{m-2mn+n}; \quad 1 - y = \frac{n(1-m)}{m-2mn+n}.$$

Therefore,

$$\left. \begin{aligned} \frac{CD}{DC'} &= \frac{1}{x-1} = \frac{m(1-n) + n(1-m)}{(1-m)(1-n)}; \\ \frac{AC'}{C'B} &= \frac{y}{1-y} = \frac{m(1-n)}{n(1-m)}. \end{aligned} \right\} \ldots (2)$$

Had the ratios been given in the form

$$BA' : A'C = m_1 : m_2; \quad CB' : B'A = n_1 : n_2;$$

c

we should have had

$$\frac{AD}{DA'} = \frac{n_2(m_1 + m_2)}{m_1 n_1}; \quad \frac{BD}{DB'} = \frac{m_1(n_1 + n_2)}{m_2 n_2} \quad . \quad (3)$$

$$\frac{CD}{DC'} = \frac{m_1 n_1 + m_2 n_2}{m_1 n_2}; \quad \frac{AC'}{C'B} = \frac{m_2 n_2}{m_1 n_1} \quad . \quad . \quad . \quad (4)$$

Knowing $\overline{AB}$, $\overline{AC}$, and the ratio $BA' : A'C$, we obtain $\overline{AA'}$ by (3) of 28°. $\overline{BB'}$ and $\overline{CC'}$ are similarly obtained. Again, knowing $\overline{AC}$, $\overline{AC'}$, and the ratio $CD : DC'$, we obtain $\overline{AD}$, and consequently $\overline{DA'}$. $\overline{BD}$, $\overline{DB'}$ and $\overline{CD}$, $\overline{DC'}$ are similarly obtained.

CHAPTER III

ILLUSTRATIONS IN COPLANAR VECTORS

32°. 1. The Mean Point of a triangle, M.
In the following illustrations, the successive sides of the triangle ABC—BC, CA, AB—will be represented by the vectors α, β, γ respectively, so that

$$\alpha + \beta + \gamma = 0.$$

The tensors of these vectors, or the lengths of the sides of the triangle, will be represented by a, b, c.

Let A′ and B′ be the middle points of BC and CA, and let AA′ and BB′ cross in M. Produce CM to meet AB in C′. Then, making $m = n = \frac{1}{2}$ in (1) of 31°, we get

$$\frac{AM}{MA'} = 2 \; ; \; \frac{BM}{MB'} = 2 \; ;$$

and (2) of 31°,

$$\frac{CM}{MC'} = 2 \; ; \; \frac{AC'}{C'B} = 1.$$

Therefore, the medians of a triangle meet in a point which trisects them. This point is called the Mean Point.

$$\overline{AM} = \tfrac{2}{3}\,\overline{AA'} = \tfrac{2}{3}\left(\frac{\gamma - \beta}{2}\right) = \frac{\gamma - \beta}{3} \quad \ldots \ldots \quad (1)$$

2. The Incentre, I, and the (b) Excentre, E_b.
I is the cross of AA′ and BB′, the bisectors of the angles CAB and ABC respectively. Produce CI to meet AB in C′. Then, proceeding by the method of 31°, we get

$$\frac{AI}{IA'} = \frac{b+c}{a} \; ; \; \frac{BI}{IB'} = \frac{c+a}{b} \; ; \; \frac{CI}{IC'} = \frac{a+b}{c} \; ; \; \frac{AC'}{C'B} = \frac{b}{a} \quad \ldots \quad (1)$$

The last equation shows that the internal angle-bisectors are concurrent.

By (3) of 28°,
$$\overline{AA'} = \frac{b\gamma - c\beta}{b + c}\,;\ \overline{BB'} = \frac{c\alpha - a\gamma}{c + a}\,;\ \overline{CC'} = \frac{a\beta - b\alpha}{a + b}\,.\quad (2)$$

These three equations are of the form
$$\rho = x\,(U\delta \pm U\epsilon) \quad \ldots \ldots \quad (3)$$

e.g.,
$$\overline{AA'} = \frac{bc}{b+c}\,(U\gamma - U\beta),$$

the negative sign showing that AA' is the bisector of the supplement of the angle between β and γ. Were the direction of β reversed, we would have
$$\overline{AA'} = \frac{bc}{b+c}\,(U\beta + U\gamma).$$

Equation (3), consequently, is the general expression for an angle-bisector, the tensors of the lines containing the angle being arbitrary.

By (3) of 28° and (1) of this article
$$\overline{AI} = \frac{b\gamma - c\beta}{a + b + c}\,;\ \overline{BI} = \frac{c\alpha - a\gamma}{a + b + c}\,;\ \overline{CI} = \frac{a\beta - b\alpha}{a + b + c}\ \ldots (4)$$

From (2) and (4),
$$IB' = \frac{b}{c+a} \cdot \frac{c\alpha - a\gamma}{a+b+c} \quad \ldots \ldots \quad (5)$$

E_b is the cross of the external angle-bisectors at C and A respectively. Let CE produced meet AB' in C''; AE meet BC in A''; and let the external angle-bisector at B meet CA in B''. Then,
$$\overline{AA''} = \frac{b\gamma + c\beta}{b-c}\,;\ \overline{BB''} = \frac{c\alpha + a\gamma}{c-a}\,;\ \overline{CC''} = \frac{a\beta + b\alpha}{a-b}\ \ldots (6)$$

Hence,
$$\overline{C''A} = \frac{b\gamma}{a-b}\,;\ \overline{C''B} = \frac{a\gamma}{a-b} \quad \ldots \ldots \quad (7)$$

Therefore, 29°,
$$(BC'AC'') = -1\,;$$

or, the sides of a triangle are cut harmonically by the internal and external bisectors of the opposite angles.

We also have
$$\frac{C''A'}{C''B'} = \frac{c+a}{b+c}\,;\ \frac{A''C'}{B'C'} = \frac{c+a}{b-c} \quad \ldots \ldots \quad (8)$$

Therefore, the points A', B', C'' and C', B', A'' are respectively collinear.

Again, $$\frac{A''C'}{C'B''} = \frac{c-a}{b-c}; \quad \ldots \quad (9)$$
or, the crosses of the external angle-bisectors with the opposite sides are collinear.

Let BE be drawn, and we have
$$\overline{BE} = \frac{ca - a\gamma}{c + a - b} = \frac{ca}{c + a - b}(U\alpha - U\gamma). \quad (10)$$

Therefore, BE bisects the angle ABC; BB' and BE coincide; and a line drawn from any corner of a triangle to the excentre of the opposite side passes through the incentre.

By subtraction of $\overline{BB'}$ from $\overline{BE}$, we have
$$\overline{B'E} = \frac{b}{c+a} \frac{ca - a\gamma}{c+a-b}.$$

Therefore, (4) and (5),
$$(BIB'E) = -1;$$

or, the internal angle-bisector is cut harmonically by the centres of the in- and excircles.

3. The Orthocentre, P.

By the methods explained in 31°,
$$\overline{AP} = \frac{\gamma \tan B - \beta \tan C}{\tan A + \tan B + \tan C}.$$

4. The Circumcentre, Q.

By 31°,
$$\overline{AQ} = \frac{(\tan C + \tan A)\gamma - (\tan A + \tan B)\beta}{2(\tan A + \tan B + \tan C)}.$$

5. The Midcentre, N.

Let M_1, M_2, M_3 be the middle points of the sides BC, CA, AB of the triangle ABC. Then the circumcentre, N, of the triangle $M_1 M_3 M_2$ is the midcentre of the triangle ABC.

$\overline{AN} = \overline{AM_1} + \overline{M_1N}$; which becomes, by 1 and 4,

$$\quad = \frac{\gamma - \beta}{2} + \frac{(\tan A + \tan B)\beta - (\tan C + \tan A)\gamma}{4(\tan A + \tan B + \tan C)}$$

$$\quad = \frac{(\tan A + 2\tan B + \tan C)\gamma - (\tan A + \tan B + 2\tan C)\beta}{4 \Sigma \tan s}$$

$$\quad = \tfrac{1}{2}\left\{\frac{(\tan C + \tan A)\gamma - (\tan A + \tan B)\beta}{2 \Sigma \tan s} + \frac{\gamma \tan B - \beta \tan C}{\Sigma \tan s}\right\}$$

$$\quad = \tfrac{1}{2}(\overline{AQ} + \overline{AP}), \text{ 4 and 3.}$$

Hence, $\overline{AQ} + \overline{AP} - 2\overline{AN} = 0$;
but $1 + 1 - 2 = 0$.

Therefore, 28°, the three coinitial vectors $\overline{AP}, \overline{AN}, \overline{AQ}$, terminate in a straight line which is bisected in N; or, the orthocentre, the midcentre, and the circumcentre are collinear, and N bisects $\overline{PQ}$.

The mean point, M, also lies upon the line PQ. For

$$2\overline{AQ} + \overline{AP} = \frac{(\tan C + \tan A)\gamma - (\tan A + \tan B)\beta}{\Sigma \tan s}$$
$$+ \frac{\gamma \tan B - \beta \tan C}{\Sigma \tan s};$$

$2\overline{AQ} + \overline{AP} = \gamma - \beta = 3\overline{AM}, 1$;
hence, $2\overline{AQ} + \overline{AP} - 3\overline{AM} = 0$;
but $2 + 1 - 3 = 0$;

therefore, the three coinitial vectors $\overline{AQ}, \overline{AP}, \overline{AM}$, terminate in a straight line which is trisected in M.

Therefore, the orthocentre, the midcentre, the mean point, and the circumcentre are collinear; and the line upon which they lie is bisected in N, and trisected in M.

Hence, $(PNMQ) = -1$.

6. Let I' be the point in which a line drawn from A through I, the incentre of ABC, cuts the line PQ. Then

$$\frac{PI'}{I'Q} = 2\cos A.$$

If $A = 60°$, $PI' = I'Q$; and I' is the midcentre of the triangle.

7. To find the vector-expressions for the isogonal and the isotomic of a given line.

Let δ be a vector drawn from the corner B of a triangle ABC, cutting CA in D so that $\frac{AD}{DC} = \frac{p}{r}$; and let $\angle ABD = \phi$.

Then, $\frac{p}{r} = \frac{AD}{DC} = \frac{c \sin \phi}{a \sin(B - \phi)}$,

and $\frac{\sin(B - \phi)}{\sin \phi} = \frac{cr}{ap}.$

Let δ', the isogonal of δ, cut CA in D'. Then,

$$\frac{AD'}{D'C} = \frac{c \sin(B - \phi)}{a \sin \phi} = \frac{c^2 r}{a^2 p}.$$

Therefore, $\delta = \dfrac{p\alpha - r\gamma}{p + r}$; $\delta' = \dfrac{c^2 r\alpha - a^2 p\gamma}{c^2 r + a^2 p}$ . . . (1)

If δ'' be the isotomic of δ,

$$\delta'' = \dfrac{r\alpha - p\gamma}{p + r} \quad \ldots \quad (2)$$

Let $p : r = c^n : a^n$. Then,

$$\delta_n = \dfrac{c^n \alpha - a^n \gamma}{c^n + a^n}; \quad \delta'_n = \dfrac{a^{n-2}\alpha - c^{n-2}\gamma}{c^{n-2} + a^{n-2}}.$$

Let $p : r = c^{n-2} : a^{n-2}$. Then,

$$\delta''_{n-2} = \dfrac{a^{n-2}\alpha - c^{n-2}\gamma}{c^{n-2} + a^{n-2}} \quad \ldots \quad (3)$$

Therefore, $\delta'_n = \delta''_{n-2}$;

or, the isotomic of δ_{n-2} is the isogonal of δ_n; a theorem which suggests a simple geometric construction for the successive centres of gravity of weights placed at the corners of the triangle proportional to the 0, 1, 2 . . . n^{th} powers of the opposite sides.

8. Suppose it be desired to obtain symmetric expressions for the vectors of the mean point, incentre, &c., &c., instead of the unsymmetric expressions obtained in the preceding illustrations. Let O be any point in the plane, and let

$$\overline{OA} = \alpha, \ \overline{OB} = \beta, \ \overline{OC} = \gamma.$$

Then the vector of the orthocentre, 3, may be written:

$$\overline{AP} = \dfrac{\gamma' \tan B - \beta' \tan C}{\Sigma \tan s};$$

where α', β', γ' are the vectors along the sides of ABC.

But, $\alpha' = \gamma - \beta$; $\beta' = \alpha - \gamma$; $\gamma' = \beta - \alpha$.
Therefore,

$$\overline{OP} = \alpha + \overline{AP} = \alpha + \dfrac{(\beta - \alpha)\tan B - (\alpha - \gamma)\tan C}{\Sigma \tan s}$$

$$\text{,,} \quad = \dfrac{\alpha \tan A + \beta \tan B + \gamma \tan C}{\Sigma \tan s} \quad \ldots \quad (1)$$

Similarly, for the circumcentre,

$$\overline{OQ} = \dfrac{(\tan B + \tan C)\alpha + (\tan C + \tan A)\beta + (\tan A + \tan B)\gamma}{2 \Sigma \tan s} \quad (2)$$

and for the midcentre,

$$\overline{ON} = \dfrac{(\Sigma \tan s + \tan A)\alpha + (\Sigma \tan s + \tan B)\beta + (\Sigma \tan s + \tan C)\gamma}{4 \Sigma \tan s} \quad \ldots \quad (3)$$

If G_n be the centre of gravity of weights placed at the corners of the triangle proportional to the nth power of the opposite sides,

$$\overline{OG}_n = \frac{a^n\alpha + b^n\beta + c^n\gamma}{a^n + b^n + c^n} \quad \ldots \ldots \quad (4)$$

If $n = 0$,

$$\overline{OG}_0 = \frac{\alpha + \beta + \gamma}{3}, \text{ the vector of the mean point} \ldots \quad (5)$$

If $n = 1$,

$$\overline{OG}_1 = \frac{a\alpha + b\beta + c\gamma}{a + b + c}, \text{ the vector of the incentre} \ldots \quad (6)$$

If $n = 2$,

$$\overline{OG}_2 = \frac{a^2\alpha + b^2\beta + c^2\gamma}{a^2 + b^2 + c^2}, \text{ the vector of the symmedian point} \ldots (7)$$

CHAPTER IV

ON POINTS AND VECTORS IN SPACE

Section 1

On the Mean Point

33°. *Definition.*—*If the sum, Σa, of m coinitial vectors, coplanar or non-coplanar,*

$$\overline{OA_1} = a_1, \quad \overline{OA_2} = a_2 \quad \ldots \quad \overline{OA_m} = a_m,$$

be divided by their number, m, the resulting vector,

$$\mu = \overline{OM} = \frac{\Sigma(\overline{OA})}{m} = \frac{\Sigma a}{m},$$

is the Simple Mean of those m vectors, and its term, M, is the Mean Point of the system of points, $A_1, A_2 \ldots A_m$.

If we are given such a system of points, $a_1, a_2 \ldots a_n$, and also a system of scalars, $p_1, p_2 \ldots p_n$; the vector

$$\gamma = \overline{OC} = \frac{p_1 a_1 + p_2 a_2 + \ldots p_n a_n}{p_1 + p_2 + \ldots p_n} = \frac{\Sigma p a}{\Sigma p}$$

is the Complex Mean of those n vectors, and its term, C, is the Centre of Gravity, or Barycentre, of the system of points, $A_1, A_2 \ldots A_n$, considered as loaded with the given weights, $p_1, p_2 \ldots p_n$ (Hamilton).

34°. The position of the mean point depends upon the configuration of the system, and is independent of the position of the arbitrary origin, O. For, let C be the mean point of a given system, $A_1 \ldots A_n$, with respect to an assumed origin, O; and let C' be the mean point of the same system with respect to another assumed origin O'; let $\overline{O'A_1}$, $\overline{O'A_2}$, &c., be represented by a'_1, a'_2, &c., and let γ be the mean vector with respect to O, γ' the mean vector with respect to O'. Then,

$$p_1 a_1 = p_1 \overline{OO'} + p_1 a'_1,$$
$$p_2 a_2 = p_2 \overline{OO'} + p_2 a'_2,$$
$$\cdots \cdots \cdots$$
$$p_n a_n = p_n \overline{OO'} + p_n a'_n;$$

or, $\quad \Sigma pa = \overline{OO'} \Sigma p + \Sigma pa'.$

But, by definition,

$$\Sigma pa = \gamma \Sigma p\;;\; \Sigma pa' = \gamma' \Sigma p\;;$$

therefore, $\quad \overline{OC} = \gamma = \overline{OO'} + \gamma' = \overline{OC'}.$

But the equal vectors, $\overline{OC}$, $\overline{OC'}$, have a common origin; therefore they must have a common term, or, $C = C'$. The position of the mean point has not been altered, therefore, by selecting O' instead of O as the origin of the system.

35°. The sum of the m vectors, $\rho_1, \rho_2 \ldots \rho_m$, drawn from the mean point to every point of the system, is zero.

By definition, $\quad \Sigma a = m\mu,$

i.e.,

$$a_1 + a_2 + a_3 + \ldots a_m = \mu + \mu + \mu + \ldots (m \text{ times}).$$

Therefore,

$$(a_1 - \mu) + (a_2 - \mu) + (a_3 - \mu) + \ldots (a_m - \mu) = 0.$$

But

$$a_1 - \mu = \rho_1\;;\; a_2 - \mu = \rho_2 \ldots a_m - \mu = \rho_m.$$

Therefore, $\quad \Sigma \rho = 0.$

Conversely, if C be such a point that the sum of the vectors drawn from it to each and every point of a given system is zero; then C is the mean point of the system.

36°. If any system of points, together with its mean point, be projected by parallel ordinates upon any plane, the projection of the mean point is the mean point of the projected system.

Let $A'_1 \ldots A'_n$ be the projections of the points $A_1 \ldots A_n$. Find M', the mean point of the projected system; draw MM', and let

$$\overline{MA_1} \ldots \overline{MA_n} = \rho_1 \ldots \rho_n\;;\; \overline{M'A'_1} \ldots \overline{M'A'_n} = \rho'_1 \ldots \rho'_n.$$

Then,
$$\rho'_1 = \rho_1 + \overline{A_1A'_1} - \overline{MM'}$$
$$\rho'_2 = \rho_2 + \overline{A_2A'_2} - \overline{MM'}$$
$$\cdot \quad \cdot \quad \cdot \quad \cdot \quad \cdot \quad \cdot \quad \cdot$$
$$\rho'_n = \rho_n + \overline{A_nA'_n} - \overline{MM'}.$$
$$\Sigma\rho' = \Sigma\rho + \Sigma\overline{AA'} - n\overline{MM'}$$

But, 35°, $\quad\quad \Sigma\rho' = 0 = \Sigma\rho$;

therefore, $\quad\quad n\overline{MM'} = \Sigma\overline{AA'} = \xi$, say.

Therefore $\overline{MM'}$ is parallel to ξ, that is, to the other ordinates.

Therefore M' is the projection of M, the mean point.

Since $\overline{MM'} = \dfrac{\Sigma AA'}{n} = \dfrac{\overline{A_1A'_1} \ldots \overline{A_nA'_n}}{n}$, the ordinate of the mean point is the mean of the ordinates of the system.

Section 2

Linear Equations connecting four Non-coplanar Vectors

37°. It has been shown, 27°, that if three vectors, a, β, γ, are coplanar, scalars can always be found, h, l, m, such that, $ha + l\beta + m\gamma = 0$. If, however, a, β, γ are not coplanar, the expression, $ha + l\beta + m\gamma$, cannot be equated to zero unless all three coefficients vanish. For $ha + l\beta = p\phi$, some vector in the plane OAB, fig. 7, and $p\phi + m\gamma = q\xi$, some vector in the plane containing ϕ and γ, *i.e.*, some plane different from OAB, OBC, and OCA. Hence the expression, $ha + l\beta + m\gamma$, represents some fourth vector, say $-n\delta$, whose coefficient, n, is $\gtreqless$ zero.

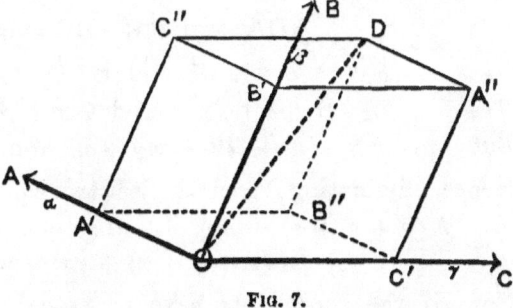

Fig. 7.

In symbols,
$$h\alpha + l\beta + m\gamma + n\delta = 0;$$
or,
$$\delta = \frac{-h}{n}\alpha + \frac{-l}{n}\beta + \frac{-m}{n}\gamma.$$

If we take $\overline{OA'} = \frac{-h}{n}\alpha$, $\overline{OB'} = \frac{-l}{n}\beta$, $\overline{OC'} = \frac{-m}{n}\gamma$, and complete the parallelopiped OA''B''C'', we determine a point D, such that,
$$\overline{OD} = \overline{OC''} + \overline{C''D} = \overline{OC''} + \overline{OC'} = \overline{OA'} + \overline{OB'} + \overline{OC'}$$
$$= \frac{-h}{n}\alpha + \frac{-l}{n}\beta + \frac{-m}{n}\gamma = \delta.$$

Hence, since α, β, γ may be any actual vectors, and since h, l, m may have any values whatever, the sum of the three coinitial edges of a parallelopiped is the internal coinitial diagonal.

38°. If $h\alpha + l\beta + m\gamma + n\delta = 0$, what must be the relation between the scalars in order that the point D may be situated in the fourth given plane ABC; or, in other words, what is the condition of coplanarity of the four points, A, B, C, D?

If D lies in the plane ABC, the vectors $\overline{DA}, \overline{DB}, \overline{DC}$ are coplanar, and are consequently, 27°, connected together by an equation of the form
$$p\overline{DA} + q\overline{DB} + r\overline{DC} = 0;$$
or, $\quad p(\alpha - \delta) + q(\beta - \delta) + r(\gamma - \delta) = 0;$
or, $\quad p\alpha + q\beta + r\gamma - (p + q + r)\delta = 0.$
But $\quad h\alpha + l\beta + m\gamma + n\delta = 0.$

Hence, eliminating δ from the last two equations,
$$\{h(p+q+r) + np\}\alpha + \{l(p+q+r) + nq\}\beta$$
$$+ \{m(p+q+r) + nr\}\gamma = 0.$$

Now, if the coefficients have an actual value, α, β, γ are coplanar. But, by hypothesis, α, β, γ are not coplanar. Therefore the coefficients have not an actual value, and must be equated to zero.

Therefore,
$$h = \frac{-np}{p+q+r};\ l = \frac{-nq}{p+q+r};\ m = \frac{-nr}{p+q+r};$$

LINEAR EQUATIONS CONNECTING FOUR VECTORS 29

and
$$h+l+m+n = -n\left(\frac{p}{p+q+r} + \frac{q}{p+q+r} + \frac{r}{p+q+r}\right) + n = 0;$$
the required condition of coplanarity of the four points, A, B, C, D.

39°. The equation just deduced may be written,
$$\frac{h}{-n} + \frac{l}{-n} + \frac{m}{-n} = 1.$$

But, by construction,

$$\overline{OA'} = \frac{h}{-n}\overline{OA}, \text{ or } \frac{h}{-n} = \frac{OA'}{OA}; \quad \frac{l}{-n} = \frac{OB'}{OB}; \quad \frac{m}{-n} = \frac{OC'}{OC}.$$

Therefore,
$$\frac{OA'}{OA} + \frac{OB'}{OB} + \frac{OC'}{OC} = 1;$$

the equation of a plane in terms of the intercepts it makes on the Cartesian axes of coordinates OA, OB, OC.

PART II

DIVISION AND MULTIPLICATION OF TWO VECTORS

CHAPTER I

FIRST PRINCIPLES OF QUATERNIONS

Section 1

Definitions

1°. (*a*). *A Quaternion is an operator which turns any one vector into another* (Clifford).

(*b*). *The Reciprocal of any vector, a, which is written, as in Algebra, $\frac{1}{a}$ or a^{-1}, is another vector whose unit-vector is the opposite of the unit-vector, and whose tensor is the reciprocal of the tensor of the vector a.*

$$Ta^{-1} = \frac{1}{Ta}; \; Ua^{-1} = \frac{1}{Ua} = -Ua; \; a^{-1} = \frac{1}{a} = \frac{1}{TaUa} = \frac{-Ua}{Ta}.$$

(*c*). $\quad \dfrac{\beta}{a} = \beta\dfrac{1}{a} = \beta a^{-1}; \; \beta a = \beta \dfrac{1}{a^{-1}} = \dfrac{\beta}{a^{-1}}.$

(*d*). If a and β be any two vectors, and if

$$q = \frac{\beta}{a};$$

then, whatever be the nature of q,

$$qa = \frac{\beta}{a}a = \beta \quad \ldots \ldots \ldots \quad (1)$$

If $\qquad q' = \beta a = \dfrac{\beta}{a^{-1}};$

then $\qquad q'a^{-1} = \beta a \cdot a^{-1} = \dfrac{\beta}{a^{-1}}a^{-1} = \beta \quad . \quad . \quad (2)$

DEFINITIONS

The two vectors will in all cases be supposed to be co-initial, and to be inclined to one another at a Euclidian angle, between zero and π, unless the contrary be stated.

β is the Multiplier and a the Multiplicand of the product βa. The multiplier is *always* written to the left, the multiplicand to the right; and the symbol βa is to be read—'a multiplied by β,' or, shortly, 'β into a.'

It follows from (1) and (2) that the quotient and product of two vectors are quaternions.

(e). *The Angle of a quaternion, in the form of a quotient, is the angle contained by its constituent vectors.*

The Angle of a quaternion, in the form of a product, is the supplement of the angle contained by its constituent vectors.

(f). *The Plane of a quaternion is the plane containing its constituent vectors.*

(g). *Coplanar Quaternions are those whose planes are coincident or parallel.*

(h). *Diplanar Quaternions are those whose planes are not parallel.*

(i). If a, β, γ, &c., be any three vectors,

$$\frac{\delta}{\beta} \pm \frac{a}{\beta} = \frac{\delta \pm a}{\beta}; \quad \frac{\delta}{\beta} : \frac{a}{\beta} = \frac{\delta}{a}; \quad \frac{\delta}{a} \cdot \frac{a}{\gamma} = \frac{\delta}{\gamma}; \quad \frac{a}{\beta} = 1 : \frac{\beta}{a}.$$

(j). If $qa = \beta$ and $q'a = \beta$, then $q' = q$.

,, $\dfrac{\delta'}{\gamma'} = \dfrac{\delta}{\gamma}$,, $\gamma' = \gamma$, ,, $\delta' = \delta$.

,, ,, ,, ,, $\delta' = \delta$, ,, $\gamma' = \gamma$.

,, $\delta'\gamma' = \delta\gamma$,, $\gamma' = \gamma$, ,, $\delta' = \delta$.

,, ,, ,, ,, $\delta' = \delta$, ,, $\gamma' = \gamma$.

Section 2

The Nature of a Quaternion

2°. (a). Let $\overline{OA} = a$, $\overline{OB} = \beta$, fig. 8, be any two vectors in the plane AOB, inclined to one another at an angle θ. By definition, 1° (d), if $\dfrac{\beta}{a} = q'$, then $q'a = \dfrac{\beta}{a}a = \beta$; or q', or $\dfrac{\beta}{a}$, is such a

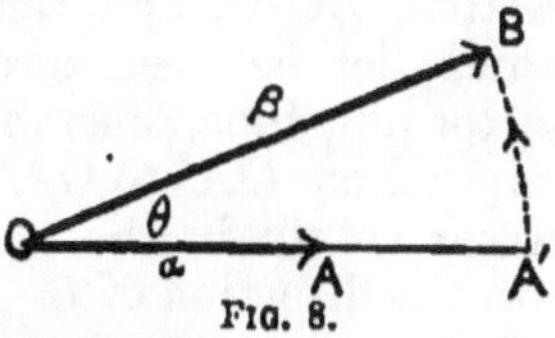

Fig. 8.

factor that when it operates upon the divisor, a, it transforms it into the dividend, β. Now, since a differs from

32   THE NATURE OF A QUATERNION

β, not only in *length*, but in *direction*, it is clear that two independent operations, of a totally different nature, are necessary in order to transform a into β. The one is an operation of tension, the other an operation of torsion, or version; and *the order in which the two operations take place is immaterial*. We may make a rotate round the point O until its direction coincides with that of β, and then alter its length until it is equal to that of β; or we may alter its length until it is equal to that of β, and then make it rotate round O until its direction coincides with that of β.

Now, a may acquire the direction of β either by a rotation round O in the plane AOB, or by conical rotation round a third coinitial vector bisecting the angle θ. To avoid ambiguity it is defined that the rotation from a to β takes place in the plane of the two vectors, AOB. Further, a may rotate in the plane AOB into the direction of β through either the angle θ or the amplitude, $2\pi - \theta$. For the same reason it is defined that rotation from a to β, in the plane OAB, takes place through the angle θ, which, 1° (*d*), lies between zero and π.

(*b*). Let $\overline{OA} = a$, $\overline{OB} = \beta$, fig. 9, still represent any two vectors in the plane AOB, inclined to one another at an angle θ; and let $\overline{OA'}$ be the reciprocal of $\overline{OA}$, 1° (*b*), or a^{-1}. Then, since Ua^{-1} is the opposite of Ua, the angle $BOA' = \pi - \theta$.

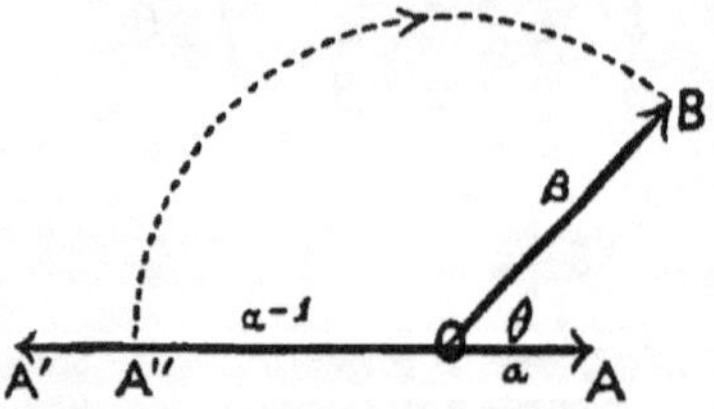

FIG. 9.

By definition, 1° (*d*), if $\beta a = q''$, then $q''a^{-1} = \beta a \cdot a^{-1} = \beta$; or q'', or βa, is such a factor that when it operates upon the reciprocal of the multiplicand, a^{-1}, it transforms it into the multiplier, β. As in the previous case, two operations are necessary in order to effect this transformation—one of tension and one of version, *the order of which is immaterial*. As before, also, it is defined that rotation from a^{-1} to β takes place in the plane of the vectors, BOA', and through the angle between them, $\pi - \theta$, which lies between zero and π when θ lies π and zero. The vector a^{-1}, then, may be transformed into β by altering its length from OA' to OA''= OB, and then making the altered vector rotate in the plane BOA', through the angle $(\pi - \theta)$ into the direction of β.

Such is the nature of the symbols q' or $\dfrac{\beta}{a}$, and q'' or βa.

THE NATURE OF A QUATERNION

Both, as factors, imply two operations—one of tension and one of version—which are heterogeneous and absolutely independent. No mere change of length can in any way affect the direction of a vector; no amount of rotation can alter its length.

3°. The operation of Tension is purely metric, and we need only *one* number to carry it out—namely, the number (whole or fractional) by which we must multiply the length of one line in order to make it equal to the length of another. Given this number, we can make the length of the one line equal to that of the other, without knowing the absolute length of either of them.

4°. The operation of Version is of a more complex nature, and will be found to involve a knowledge of *three* numbers. The first point to be explained is the means of giving rotation to a vector.

(*a*). Let
$\overline{OA} = U\alpha$, $\overline{OB} = U\beta$,
fig. 10, be any two unit-vectors in the plane of the paper, inclined to each other at any angle θ; and let
$OA' = -U\alpha$, $\overline{OB'} = -U\beta$,
be the opposites, or reciprocals, of $U\alpha$ and $U\beta$, 1° (*b*).

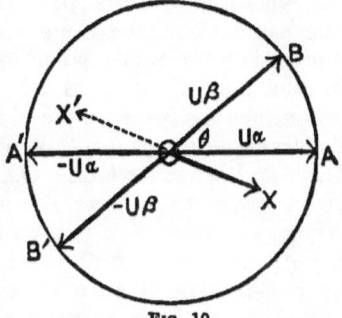

Fig. 10.

Let OX be a unit-vector perpendicular to the plane of the paper, drawn from the origin, O, *towards* the reader as he reads the book; and let $\overline{OX'}$ be the opposite unit-vector of $O\overline{X}$, drawn *from* the reader through the leaf of the book. Conceive OA and OA' to be two very fine wires so connected at O with two other very fine wires, OX and OX', that by twisting either OX or OX' about its longest axis, a motion of rotation is communicated at will to either OA or OA'. Motion of rotation would thus be communicated to OA or OA', as the case might be, in exactly the same way as if OA or OA' were the minute-hand, and OX or OX' the key of a clock which it was necessary to set; the key being applied in the case of OX to the face of the clock, and to the back of the clock in the case of OX'. Thus, if we conceive the unit-vectors to be gifted with the powers of the wires, by means of $\overline{OX}$ or $\overline{OX'}$, we can make $U\alpha$ or $-U\alpha$, or any

D

coinitial vector in the plane of the paper, rotate into the direction of $U\beta$, or any other direction in that plane.

Generally, rotation is given to any vector lying in any plane by operating on it with a coinitial unit-vector perpendicular to that plane.

When employed to give rotation to other vectors in planes perpendicular to themselves, unit-vectors are called Versors (*vertere*, to turn).

Versors can only operate upon—that is, give rotation to—vectors perpendicular to themselves.

(*b*). When twisting the wire OX about its longer axis, the reader is supposed to be in the position he occupies while reading the book—with his eye at X, looking towards O. When twisting OX' he is supposed to have moved to a position beyond X', facing his former position, with his eye at X', looking towards O. These two positions bear exactly the same relation to one another as the two positions one successively occupies when locking a door on the outside and on the inside. And as one sees different sides of the door when locking it on the outside and on the inside, so one sees different sides, or aspects, of the plane A'BA, when twisting OX' and when twisting OX. Furthermore, a right-handed twist given to OX at X appears to be a left-handed twist when seen from X'; just as locking the door on the inside by a right-handed turn of the key would appear to be locking it by a left-handed turn of the key to anyone viewing the operation through a glass door from the outside. In order, then, to estimate the direction of the twist, we must imagine ourselves to be in the position of the person giving the twist.

Right-handed rotation—the rotation of the hands of a clock when looked at to take the time—will be considered as positive; left-handed, or anti-clockwise rotation as negative, in this book.

(*c*). $U\alpha$ may be made to rotate through the angle θ into the direction of $U\beta$ by giving either a negative twist to $\overline{OX}$, or a positive twist to $\overline{OX'}$. To avoid ambiguity, it is defined that $\overline{OX'}$, which turns $U\alpha$ into the direction of $U\beta$ by positive rotation, is *the* versor by which this operation is to be carried out.

Similarly, $\overline{OX}$, which turns $-U\alpha$ into the direction of $U\beta$ by positive rotation, through the angle $\pi - \theta$, is defined to be *the* versor by which this operation is to be carried out.

THE NATURE OF A QUATERNION

Generally, rotation is communicated to any vector by that versor which turns it by positive rotation into the required direction.

We must now place a limitation to the turning powers of versors. Every versor possesses the power of turning any vector perpendicular to itself, by positive rotation, through a certain angle; but it cannot produce rotation through any other angle, greater or less. Thus, if $\overline{OX}$ possesses the power of turning $\overline{OB}$ through a definite angle θ, it can turn any other vectors, $\overline{OP}$, $\overline{OQ}$, &c., in the plane AOB, through the angle θ; but it can turn them through the angle θ only. In consequence of this limitation, we must modify our terminology. There are two different, although coincident, versors along OX : (a) the versor which turns $U\beta$ through the angle θ into the direction of Ua; (b) the versor which turns $-Ua$ through the angle $\pi - \theta$ into the direction of $U\beta$. There are also two different, although coincident, versors along OX': (c) the versor that turns Ua through the angle θ into the direction of $U\beta$; (d) the versor that turns $-U\beta$ through the angle $\pi - \theta$ into the direction of Ua.

For the moment we will designate these four different versors by the following symbols:

(a) by $\overline{OX}_\theta$;   (b) by $\overline{OX}_{\pi-\theta}$;
(c) by $\overline{OX'}_\theta$;   (d) by $\overline{OX'}_{\pi-\theta}$.

Since Ua and $U\beta$ are of equal length, when $U\beta$ is turned by OX_θ into the direction of Ua, it becomes equivalent to, or is transformed into, Ua. In symbols,

$$\overline{OX}_\theta \cdot U\beta = Ua.$$

Therefore, 1° (d),
$$\overline{OX}_\theta = \frac{Ua}{U\beta} \quad \dots \dots \quad (1)$$

Similarly, $\quad \overline{OX}_{\pi-\theta} \cdot Ua^{-1} = U\beta.$

Therefore, 1° (d),
$$\overline{OX}_{\pi-\theta} = \frac{U\beta}{Ua^{-1}} = U\beta Ua \quad \dots \quad (2)$$

In like manner,
$$\overline{OX'}_\theta = \frac{U\beta}{Ua} \quad \dots \dots \quad (3)$$

$$\overline{OX'}_{\pi-\theta} = Ua U\beta \quad \dots \dots \quad (4)$$

It follows that the quotient or product of any two unit-vectors is a third coinitial unit-vector perpendicular to their plane.

(*d*). Since an operation of version implies rotation in a certain plane, towards a certain hand, through a certain angle, at least *three* numbers are required for the complete determination of a versor; one to represent the magnitude of the angle of rotation, and two to fix the direction of the plane of rotation, or of the versor itself.

It will be observed that, as in the case of a vector, two numbers are required to determine its direction, and a third to define the amount of *motion of translation* communicated to a particle in that direction; so in the case of a versor, two numbers are required to determine its direction, and a third to define the amount of *motion of rotation* communicated to a vector at right angles to that direction.

5°. Since the operation of Tension depends upon *one* number, while the operation of Version depends upon *three* numbers, it is clear that for the complete determination of a quaternion a set of *four* numbers is required. Hence the name quaternion (*quaternio*, a set of four).

CHAPTER II

THE PROPERTIES OF A SYSTEM OF THREE MUTUALLY RECTANGULAR UNIT-VECTORS, i, j, k

Definitions

6°. (a). *The unit of versor measurement is one right angle.*

(b). *All unit-vectors which possess the property, as versors, of turning vectors perpendicular to themselves through a quadrant are designated by symbols whose index is unity, positive or negative according as the rotation is positive or negative.*

(c). *The function, or effect, as versors, of all unit-vectors designated by symbols whose index is unity, is to turn vectors perpendicular to themselves through a quadrant, positively or negatively according as the index is positive or negative.*

Such unit-vectors are called quadrantal, or right versors, and right-angled quaternions right quaternions.

7°. Let i $(\overline{OI})$, j $(\overline{OJ})$, k $(\overline{OK})$, fig. 11, be three given and mutually rectangular unit-vectors, with such relative directions that rotation from j to k (as seen from I), from k to i (as seen from J), and from i to j (as seen from K), is positive. Then the opposite unit-vectors,

$$\overline{OI'}, \overline{OJ'}, \overline{OK'}$$

will be $-i$, $-j$, $-k$, respectively. For the sake

FIG. 11.

of clearness, let the plane K'JK be the plane of the paper, i being drawn *towards* us, and $-i$ *from* us.

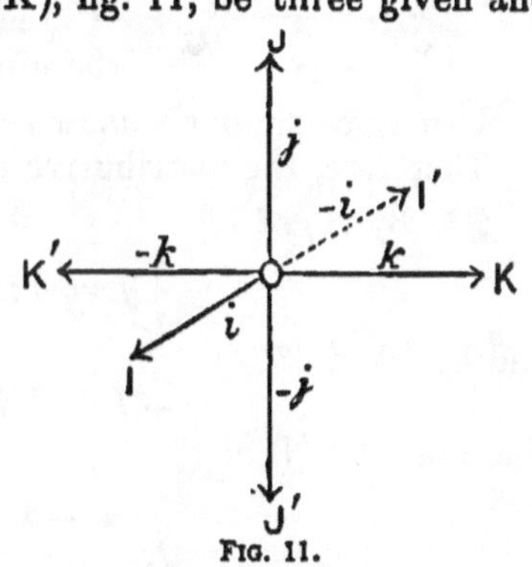

From the definitions, 6°, it follows that when i operates as a *versor* upon the *vector* j, the result of the operation is the vector k. Similarly, j operating upon k produces i, and k operating upon i produces j. In symbols,

$$ij = k \; ; \; jk = i \; ; \; ki = j \quad \ldots \ldots \quad (1)$$

similarly,

$$ji = -k \; ; \; kj = -i \; ; \; ik = -j \quad \ldots \quad (2)$$

From these two series of equations it is clear that the sign of the product changes when the order of the factors is changed. In other words, the Commutative Law of Multiplication—$ab = ba$—does not hold good for right versors. In algebra, $ab = ba$; in quaternions, $ij \neq ji$. But it will be observed that,

$$i(-j) = k = (-ij)$$

or, the product of two right versors is equal to the product of their opposites.

8°. The Distributive Law of Multiplication, however— $a(b + c) = ab + ac$—still holds true.

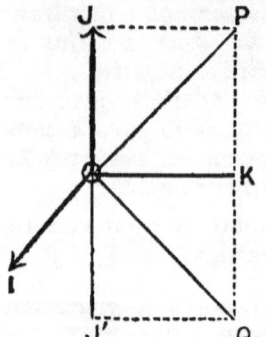

Fig. 12.

Let $\overline{OI}$, $\overline{OJ}$, $\overline{OK}$, fig 12, represent i, j, k. Complete the squares OJPK and OKQJ', and draw OP, OQ.

Then, since $T \cdot \overline{OP} = T \cdot \overline{OQ}$, and $\angle QOP = \frac{\pi}{2}$, we have by definition (c), 6°,

$$i \cdot \overline{OP} = \overline{OQ}.$$

But $\overline{OP} = j + k$; and
$\overline{OQ} = k - j = ij + ik$, 7° (1), (2);
therefore, $i(j + k) = ij + ik$.

It may be similarly shown that $i(j - k) = ij - ik$. Therefore, the distributive law applies to right versors.

9°. By (1) of 1°,

$$\frac{i}{j} j = i \; ;$$

and by (c) of 6°,

$$-kj = i \; ;$$

therefore, by (j) of 1°

$$\left. \begin{array}{l} \dfrac{i}{j} = -k. \\[4pt] \text{Similarly,} \quad \dfrac{j}{k} = -i \; ; \; \dfrac{k}{i} = -j \end{array} \right\} \quad \ldots \ldots \quad (3)$$

Further, $\quad \dfrac{j}{i} = k \; ; \; \dfrac{k}{j} = i \; ; \; \dfrac{i}{k} = j \quad \ldots \ldots \quad (4)$

THREE MUTUALLY RECTANGULAR VECTORS   39

Hence, by inverting a fraction, the sign of the quotient is changed.

In using a quotient as a factor, the same precautions as to multiplier and multiplicand must be observed as in the case of single vectors, 1° (d). For example,

$$\frac{i}{j} j = i \text{ ; but } j \cdot \frac{i}{j} \neq i. \quad \text{For } j \cdot \frac{i}{j} = j(-k) = -i.$$

Similarly, $\frac{i}{j} \frac{j}{k} = \frac{i}{k}$; while $\frac{j}{k} \cdot \frac{i}{j} = -i(-k) = -j = \frac{k}{i}$.

10°. (a). By the method of 9° we have $\frac{-j}{k} = i$; and also $\frac{k}{i} = i$. Therefore, writing i^2 for ii, we have

$$i^2 = \frac{-j}{k} \cdot \frac{k}{j} = \frac{-j}{j} = -1$$

for the square of any right versor.

Similarly, $\qquad j^2 = -1 \,;\, k^2 = -1.$

Again, we have $-j = \frac{-i}{k}$, and $-j = \frac{k}{i}$,

Therefore,

$$(-j)(-j) = (-j)^2 = \frac{-i}{k} \frac{k}{i} = \frac{-i}{i} = -1.$$

Similarly, $(-k)^2 = -1$; $(-i)^2 = -1$.

Therefore,

$$i^2 = j^2 = k^2 = -1 = (-i)^2 = (-j)^2 = (-k)^2 \quad . \quad . \quad (5)$$

In words, the square of any, and every, right versor is negative unity.

It must be observed that $(-j)^2 \neq -j^2$. For, as has just been shown, $(-j)^2 = -1$, while $-j^2 = -(j^2) = -(-1) = +1$.

(b). $i \cdot jk = i \cdot i = i^2$; $ij \cdot k = k \cdot k = k^2$;
 $j \cdot ki = j \cdot j = j^2$; $jk \cdot i = i \cdot i = i^2$;
 $k \cdot ij = k \cdot k = k^2$; $ki \cdot j = j \cdot j = j^2$;

Hence, $i \cdot jk = ij \cdot k = j \cdot ki = jk \cdot i = k \cdot ij = ki \cdot j. \ . \ . \ (6)$

The Associative Law of Multiplication, therefore, holds good for right versors. We may, consequently, suppress the points in (6), and write

$$ijk = jki = kij = i^2 = j^2 = k^2 = (-i)^2 = (-j)^2 = (-k)^2 = -1 \quad . . \quad (7)$$

(c). It may be similarly shown that

$$ikj = kji = jik = -i^2 = -j^2 = -k^2 = +1.$$

Hence a derangement in the cyclical order of the symbols changes the sign of the product.

11°. (a). It follows from 10° (7), that $i, j, k, -i, -j, -k$, denote six of the geometric square roots of negative unity, or,

$$i = j = k = \sqrt{-1} = -i = -j = -k \quad . . . \quad (8)$$

In the present Calculus, therefore, the imaginary of Algebra, $\sqrt{-1}$, admits of a geometrically real interpretation as an indeterminate right versor. It is indeterminate, because its direction is indeterminate. In other words, the equation, $i^2 + 1 = 0$, has indefinitely many roots, all of which are geometric reals.

We have now reached the point which Sir W. R. Hamilton pronounced ('Life, &c.,' III., 90) to be '*the* difficulty in the theory of the geometrical interpretation of Quaternions'; namely, the two meanings of i, as a *vector*, and as a *versor*.

In the equation, $ij = k$, j and k are vectors, while i is a versor. In fact we may regard k as the *vector* generated, when the *versor* i operates upon the *vector* j. Further, i is a perfectly definite versor, operating in the plane of j and k, to which it is perpendicular, so that rotation round it from j to k is positive.

In the equation, $i = \sqrt{-1}$, by analytically determining a value of i independent of j and k, we have abstracted from the conception of i the idea of a *plane* in which, and consequently of a *hand* towards which, it operates. Equation (8) is a corollary of definition (c), 6°. It asserts that all right versors are equivalent in respect to *angle*; and it asserts no more.

(b). It may be said that equation (8) violates the definition of equal vectors. This is not so. The definition asserts that unit-vectors with given directions are only equal, as *vectors*, when those directions are similar. Equation (8) asserts that all unit-vectors in the first power are equal, as *versors*, in respect to angle.

THREE MUTUALLY RECTANGULAR VECTORS 41

(c). Again, it may be said that since $i = jk$, and also $i = k = j = \sqrt{-1}$; we must have, $\sqrt{-1} = \sqrt{-1} \cdot \sqrt{-1} = -1$, which is absurd.

We cannot substitute $\sqrt{-1}$ for i and k in the equation, $i = jk$; because i and k are *vectors*, and the symbol, $\sqrt{-1}$, represents them *only* in their character of indeterminate right versors. It would be a contradiction to write, $i = \sqrt{-1} \cdot k$; for in this case k and i being given, the versor is not the indeterminate $\sqrt{-1}$, but the definite versor j.

12°. By 9° (3), (4),
$$\frac{k}{j} = i; \; \frac{j}{k} = -i.$$

But $\dfrac{j}{k} = 1 : \dfrac{k}{j}$; therefore, $-i = \dfrac{1}{i} = i^{-1}$; or, the reciprocal of a unit-vector is its opposite. Hence,
$$i^{-1}j = -ij = -k.$$

In words, j may be turned into the direction of $-k$, either by operating upon it with $-i$ and turning it through a *positive* quadrant, or by operating upon it with i and turning it through a *negative* quadrant; definition (c), 6°. But 4° (c), $-i$ (not i^{-1}) is *the* versor of the quaternion $\dfrac{-k}{j}$, because it operates positively.

13°. By 12° we obviously have,
$$a^{-1} = \frac{1}{a} = \frac{1}{Ta} \frac{1}{Ua} = \frac{1}{Ta}(-Ua) = \frac{-Ua}{Ta}.$$

To exhibit graphically a vector and its reciprocal: through any point C in the diameter A'A of a circle, fig. 13, draw ED perpendicular to A'A; draw any chord FG through C; and let CE, or CD, be the unit of length. Then,
CF . CG = CD . CE = CD² = CE² = 1;
and consequently, $CF = \dfrac{1}{CG}$.

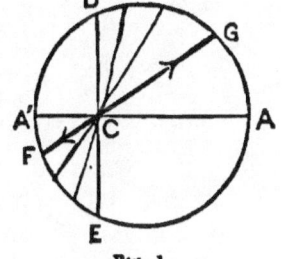

Fig. 1

Therefore, since $T \cdot \overline{CF} = \dfrac{1}{T \cdot CG}$, and $U \cdot \overline{CF} = -U \cdot \overline{CG}$; if $\overline{CF} = \rho$, then $\overline{CG} = \rho^{-1}$.

42 THREE MUTUALLY RECTANGULAR VECTORS

14°. Since $ii^{-1} = i(-i) = ikj = kji$,

and also, $i^{-1}i = (-i)i = kji$;

we have $ii^{-1} = i^{-1}i$;

or, a unit-vector and its reciprocal are commutative. But this only holds good for unit-vectors of the same name,

$$ii^{-1} = i^{-1}i\,;\text{ but } ki^{-1} \neq i^{-1}k.$$

CHAPTER III

THE VARIOUS FORMS OF A QUATERNION

SECTION 1

A Quaternion as the Product of a Tensor and a Versor

15°. A quaternion may be thrown into the form of the product of a tensor and a versor.

Let $q_1 = \dfrac{a}{\beta}$, fig. 10. Then, resolving a and β into their tensors and unit-vectors, we have,

$$q_1 = \frac{TaUa}{T\beta U\beta} = \frac{Ta}{T\beta}\frac{Ua}{U\beta} = \frac{Ta}{T\beta}\overline{OX}_\theta,\ 4°\ (c),\ (1).$$

$\dfrac{Ta}{T\beta}$ is called the tensor, and $\dfrac{Ua}{U\beta}$, or $\overline{OX}_\theta$, the versor, of the quaternion $\dfrac{a}{\beta}$. In symbols,

$$\left.\begin{array}{l} Tq_1 = T\dfrac{a}{\beta} = \dfrac{Ta}{T\beta}\ ;\ \ Uq_1 = U\dfrac{a}{\beta} = \dfrac{Ua}{U\beta} = \overline{OX}^\theta\ ; \\ q_1 = \dfrac{a}{\beta} = T\dfrac{a}{\beta}U\dfrac{a}{\beta} = Tq_1Uq_1. \end{array}\right\}\ \ .\ \ .\ (1)$$

Similarly, if $q_2 = \beta a$, we have

$$q_2 = \beta a = \frac{\beta}{a^{-1}} = \frac{T\beta}{Ta^{-1}}\frac{U\beta}{Ua^{-1}} = T\beta Ta\ .\ U\beta Ua$$

$$= T\beta Ta\ .\ \overline{OX}_{\pi-\theta},\ 4°\ (c),\ (2).$$

$T\beta Ta$ is called the tensor, and $U\beta Ua$, or $\overline{OX}_{\pi-\theta}$, the versor, of the quaternion βa. In symbols,

$$\left.\begin{array}{l} Tq_2 = T\beta a = T\beta Ta\ ;\ Uq_2 = U\beta a = \overline{OX}_{\pi-\theta}\ ; \\ q_2 = \beta a = T\beta a\ .\ U\beta a = Tq_2Uq_2 \end{array}\right\}\ .\ .\ (2)$$

In general, $\qquad\qquad q = TqUq$ . . . . (3)

44 A QUATERNION AS PRODUCT OF TENSOR AND VERSOR

In this equation, Tq *is the quotient or product of the two tensors, according as the quaternion is the quotient or product of the two vectors. In both cases* Uq *is a unit-vector drawn from the assumed origin,* O, *perpendicular to the plane of the quaternion, such that rotation round it, from the divisor to the dividend, or from the multiplier to the multiplicand, is positive.*

As a quaternion is the product of a tensor and a versor, so, conversely, every product of a tensor and a versor is a quaternion. For if (Tq . Uq) operate upon any vector *at right angles to itself*, it will obviously alter both its length and direction, that is, transform it into another vector, 1° (*a*).

16°. The versor of a versor is the versor itself:

$$U(U\beta) = U\beta\; ;\; U(Uq) = Uq.$$

It may be observed that the value of a composite vector expression is not altered by altering the order of the numerical quantities it may contain: $\beta b \gamma f d \delta = b \beta f \gamma \delta d = b d f \beta \gamma \delta$.

Section 2

A Quaternion as the sum of a Scalar and a Vector

17°. We are now in a position to investigate an expression for a quaternion explicitly involving its angle.

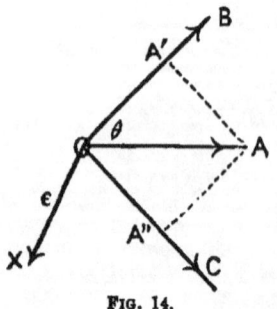

Fig. 14.

(*a*). Let $\overline{OA}$ (Ua) and $\overline{OB}$ (Uβ), fig. 14, be the unit-vectors of any two given vectors, a, β, inclined to one another at an angle θ, different from zero, $\tfrac{1}{2}\pi$, and π; and draw OC, of unit length, perpendicular to OB in the plane AOB. Let fall perpendiculars from A on OB, OC, cutting them in A', A" respectively; and draw from O, towards us, the unit-vector $\overline{OX}$, perpendicular to the plane AOB. Then, 4° (*c*), (1),

$$\overline{OX}_\theta = \frac{Ua}{U\beta} = \frac{OA}{OB} = \frac{OA'}{OB} + \frac{A'A}{OB} = \frac{OA'}{OB} + \frac{OA''}{OB}.$$

Now, $\dfrac{OA'}{OB}$ is a scalar—the ratio of the lengths of OA' and

A QUATERNION AS SUM OF A SCALAR AND A VECTOR

$\overline{OB}$. The length of $\overline{OA'} = OA \cos \theta = \cos \theta$, since $OA = 1$: the length of $\overline{OB}$ is unity.

Therefore, $\dfrac{OA'}{OB} = \cos \theta$. $\overline{OA''} = T\overline{OA''} \cdot U\overline{OA''}$.

But $T\overline{OA''} = OA \sin \theta = \sin \theta$, and $U\overline{OA''} = \overline{OC}$.

Therefore, $\overline{OA''} = \sin \theta \cdot \overline{OC}$, and $\dfrac{OA''}{OB} = \sin \theta \dfrac{OC}{OB}$.

But $\overline{OC}, \overline{OB}$ are rectangular unit-vectors. Their quotient, therefore, is a versor in the first power in the direction of $\overline{OX}$, which we will call ϵ. In symbols,

$$\dfrac{OC}{OB} = \epsilon, \text{ and } \dfrac{OA''}{OB} = \epsilon \sin \theta.$$

Therefore,

$$\overline{OX}_\theta = \dfrac{U\alpha}{U\beta} = \dfrac{OA'}{OB} + \dfrac{OA''}{OB} = \cos \theta + \epsilon \sin \theta \quad . \quad . \quad (1)$$

or, $\qquad U\dfrac{\alpha}{\beta} = \cos \theta + \epsilon \sin \theta. \quad . \quad . \quad . \quad . \quad (2)$

Equation (2) gives us an expression for the versor of the quaternion, $\dfrac{\alpha}{\beta}$, in terms of its angle, which will enable us for the future to discard the temporary symbol $\overline{OX}_\theta$.

If $\theta = 0$, we have $\dfrac{U\alpha}{U\beta} = 1$, or $U\beta = U\alpha$.

If $\theta = \pi, \dfrac{U\alpha}{U\beta} = -1$, or $U\beta = -U\alpha$.

If $\theta = \dfrac{\pi}{2}, \dfrac{U\alpha}{U\beta} = \epsilon$; which is merely the equation, $\dfrac{k}{j} = i$, with different symbols.

Multiplying equation (2) by $\dfrac{T\alpha}{T\beta}$, we get, 15°,

$$\dfrac{\alpha}{\beta} = \dfrac{T\alpha}{T\beta} (\cos \theta + \epsilon \sin \theta) \quad . \quad . \quad . \quad . \quad (3)$$

$$\dfrac{\alpha}{\beta} = \dfrac{T\alpha}{T\beta} \cos \theta + \dfrac{T\alpha}{T\beta} \sin \theta \cdot \epsilon. \quad . \quad . \quad . \quad (4)$$

46 A QUATERNION AS SUM OF A SCALAR AND A VECTOR

Equation (3) gives us an expression for the quaternion $\frac{a}{\beta}$ as the product of its tensor, $\frac{Ta}{T\beta}$, and its versor, $(\cos \theta + \epsilon \sin \theta)$, which turns β into the direction of a by positive rotation through the angle θ.

Equation (4) gives us the expression for the quaternion $\frac{a}{\beta}$ as the sum of a scalar and a vector quantity. $\frac{Ta}{T\beta} \cos \theta$ is called the Scalar; $\frac{Ta}{T\beta} \sin \theta \cdot \epsilon$, the Vector, of the quaternion $\frac{a}{\beta}$. In symbols,

$$S\frac{a}{\beta} = \frac{Ta}{T\beta} \cos \theta \; ; \; V\frac{a}{\beta} = \frac{Ta}{T\beta} \sin \theta \cdot \epsilon \quad \ldots \quad (5)$$

$$\frac{a}{\beta} = S\frac{a}{\beta} + V\frac{a}{\beta} \quad \ldots \quad \ldots \quad (6)$$

$\frac{Ta}{T\beta} \sin \theta$, (5), is called the Tensor of the Vector; ϵ, the Versor of the Vector, of the quaternion $\frac{a}{\beta}$. In symbols,

$$TV\frac{a}{\beta} = \frac{Ta}{T\beta} \sin \theta \; ; \; UV\frac{a}{\beta} = \epsilon \quad \ldots \quad (7)$$

For shortness' sake the versor of the vector is often called the Axis of a quaternion. It is a unit-vector coincident with the versor of the quaternion, Uq; but the two are generally unequal versors, because although they produce rotation in the same direction they operate in general through different angles. UVq, or $Ax \cdot q$, is *always* a *quadrantal* versor : Uq is a quadrantal versor only when $\angle q = \frac{\pi}{2}$.

The term, $\cos \theta$ (2), is called the Scalar of the Versor; $\sin \theta \cdot \epsilon$, the Vector of the Versor; $\sin \theta$, the Tensor of the Vector of the Versor of the quaternion $\frac{a}{\beta}$.

In symbols,

$$SU\frac{a}{\beta} = \cos \theta \; ; \; VU\frac{a}{\beta} = \epsilon \sin \theta \; ; \; TVU\frac{a}{\beta} = \sin \theta \quad \ldots \quad (8)$$

A QUATERNION AS SUM OF A SCALAR AND A VECTOR

(b). Let $\dots$ $(\cos\theta - \epsilon \sin\theta)$ . . . . (C)
same angle, as
until $OB' = O\dots$ $(-\cos\theta + \epsilon \sin\theta)$
unit length, pe $\{\cos(\pi - \theta) + \epsilon \sin(\pi - \theta)\}$ . . . (D)
in the plane Λ
pendiculars from ations of (B) and (D) express the versors of
cutting them in $\dots$s of θ, the angle of the quotients $\dfrac{a}{\beta}$ and $\dfrac{\beta}{a}$;
tively; and dra
us, the unit-ve us express them in terms of $(\pi - \theta)$, the
pendicular to the $\dots$'s themselves, 1° (e).
Then, 4° (c), (4), w reached the remarkable result that a
$$\overline{OX}'_{\pi - \theta} = U a U,$$ essed as the sum of a Number and a

that a number and a line are hetero-
" an no more be added together than
or, $U a \beta =$ culty exactly analogous is presented
Multiplying across by $Ta \dots$ differences by the symbol $1 + \Delta$;
$a\beta = TaT\beta(-\cos\theta - \dots$ to be added to the *characteristic*
" $= -TaT\beta \cos\theta - Ta\dots$ but the *sign of the operation*
In this case $(-\cos\theta - \epsilon \sin\theta)$, *function of x to the same*
the value of the versor $\overline{OX}'_{\pi - \theta}$, which $\dots$ Calculus, what the
the angle $(\pi - \theta)$ positively, into the direction $\dots$ (Hamilton's
Equations (10) are expressed in terms of θ, the $\dots \sin \theta)$
the quaternion $\dfrac{a}{\beta}$. To express them in terms of $(\pi - \theta)$, the
angle of $a\beta$, we have merely to write,

$$a\beta = TaT\beta \{\cos(\pi - \theta) - \epsilon \sin(\pi - \theta)\} \quad \dots \quad (11)$$
$$Sa\beta = -TaT\beta \cos\theta ; \quad Va\beta = -TaT\beta \sin\theta . \epsilon \quad \dots \quad (12)$$
$$a\beta = Sa\beta + Va\beta \quad \dots \quad \dots \quad \dots \quad (13)$$
$$TVa\beta = TaT\beta \sin\theta ; \quad UVa\beta = -\epsilon \quad \dots \quad \dots \quad (14)$$
$$SUa\beta = -\cos\theta ; \quad VUa\beta = -\epsilon \sin\theta ; \quad TVUa\beta = \sin\theta \quad \dots \quad (15)$$

(c). It may be similarly shown, by slight modifications of fig. 14 and 15, that

$$\dfrac{\beta}{a} = \dfrac{T\beta}{Ta}(\cos\theta - \epsilon \sin\theta) \quad \dots \quad \dots \quad (16)$$
$$\text{,,} = \dfrac{T\beta}{Ta}\cos\theta - \dfrac{T\beta}{Ta}\sin\theta ; \quad \dots \quad \dots \quad (17)$$
$$\beta a = T\beta Ta(-\cos\theta + \epsilon \sin\theta) \quad \dots \quad \dots \quad (18)$$
$$\text{,,} = -T\beta Ta \cos\theta + T\beta Ta \sin\theta . \epsilon \quad \dots \quad (19)$$

46 A QUATERNION AS SUM OF A SCALAR AND A VECTOR

Equation (3) gives us an expression for nion $\frac{a}{\beta}$ as the product of its tensor, $\frac{Ta}{T\beta}$, a (cos θ + ϵ sin θ), which turns β into the a by positive rotation through the angle θ.

Equation (4) gives us the expression for $\frac{a}{\beta}$ as the sum of a scalar and a vector quantity.

the Scalar; $\frac{Ta}{T\beta}$ sin θ . ϵ, the Vector, of the symbols,

$$S\frac{a}{\beta} = \frac{Ta}{T\beta} \cos \theta \; ; \; V\frac{a}{\beta} = \frac{Ta}{T\beta} \sin \theta \cdot \epsilon$$

$$\frac{a}{\beta} = S\frac{a}{\beta} + V\frac{a}{\beta}$$

$\frac{Ta}{T\beta}$ sin θ, (5), is called the Versor of the Vector, of ".

Marginal:
$\cos \theta - \epsilon \sin \theta.$
$- T a T\beta \cos \theta.$
$- T a T\beta \sin \theta . \epsilon.$
$= T a T\beta \sin \theta.$
$= - \epsilon.$
$= - \cos \theta.$
$VUq = - \epsilon \sin \theta.$
$TVUq = \sin \theta.$

$q = \beta a.$

$Tq = \dfrac{T\beta}{Ta}.$	$Tq = T\beta Ta.$
$Uq = \cos \theta - \epsilon \sin \theta.$	$Uq = -\cos \theta + \epsilon \sin \theta.$
$Sq = \dfrac{T\beta}{Ta} \cos \theta.$	$Sq = -T\beta Ta \cos \theta.$
$Vq = -\dfrac{T\beta}{Ta} \sin \theta . \epsilon.$	$Vq = T\beta Ta \sin \theta . \epsilon.$
$TVq = \dfrac{T\beta}{Ta} \sin \theta.$	$TVq = T\beta Ta \sin \theta.$
$UVq = -\epsilon.$	$UVq = \epsilon.$
$SUq = \cos \theta.$	$SUq = -\cos \theta.$
$VUq = -\epsilon \sin \theta.$	$VUq = \epsilon \sin \theta.$
$TVUq = \sin \theta.$	$TVUq = \sin \theta.$

$$\frac{a}{\beta} = \frac{Ta}{T\beta}(\cos \theta + \epsilon \sin \theta) \quad \ldots \ldots \ldots \quad (A)$$

$$\left.\begin{aligned} a\beta &= T a T\beta \, (-\cos \theta - \epsilon \sin \theta) \\ \text{„} &= T a T\beta \,\{\cos (\pi - \theta) - \epsilon \sin (\pi - \theta)\} \end{aligned}\right\} \quad \ldots \quad (B)$$

A QUATERNION AS SUM OF A SCALAR AND A VECTOR

$$\frac{\beta}{\alpha} = \frac{T\beta}{T\alpha}(\cos\theta - \epsilon \sin\theta) \quad \ldots \ldots \ldots \text{(C)}$$

$$\left. \begin{array}{l} \beta\alpha = T\beta T\alpha(-\cos\theta + \epsilon\sin\theta) \\ = T\beta T\alpha\{\cos(\pi-\theta) + \epsilon\sin(\pi-\theta)\} \end{array} \right\} \quad \ldots \text{(D)}$$

The first equations of (B) and (D) express the versors of $\alpha\beta$ and $\beta\alpha$ in terms of θ, the angle of the quotients $\frac{\alpha}{\beta}$ and $\frac{\beta}{\alpha}$; the second equations express them in terms of $(\pi - \theta)$, the angle of the products themselves, 1° (e).

19°. We have now reached the remarkable result that a versor may be expressed as the sum of a Number and a Vector.

It may be objected that a number and a line are heterogeneous quantities, and can no more be added together than a pint and a mile. A difficulty exactly analogous is presented in the Calculus of Finite Differences by the symbol $1 + \Delta$; 'where the *number* 1 appears to be added to the *characteristic* Δ, which is not a number at all, but the *sign of the operation of taking a finite difference.*' $1 + \Delta$ is, in fact, ' *the symbol of an operator which changes any given function of x to the same function of $x + 1$*'; and we learn, in that Calculus, what the proposed sum $1 + \Delta$ is by learning *what it does* (Hamilton's 'Lectures, &c.,' p. 388). In a similar way $(\cos\theta + \epsilon\sin\theta)$ is the symbol of an operator, a Versor, which has the power of turning any line upon which it operates in a plane perpendicular to itself, through an angle θ, positively.

This symbol represents a unit-vector, as may be proved by taking its tensor,

$$T(\cos\theta + \epsilon\sin\theta) = T\frac{\overline{OA'} + \overline{OA''}}{OB} = T\frac{OA}{OB} = \frac{TU\alpha}{TU\beta} = 1.$$

Its square is not negative unity, as are the squares of i, j, k, because it is not in general a right versor. In the special case when $\theta = \frac{1}{2}\pi$, however, its square is negative unity.

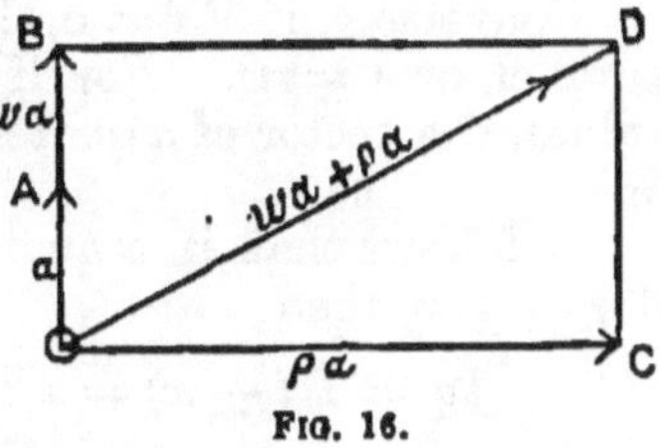

20°. It has been shown in 17° that a quaternion is the sum of a scalar and a vector. It remains to prove the converse : the sum of a scalar and a vector is a quaternion.

FIG. 16.

Let w and ρ be any scalar and any vector which

it is proposed to add together. Let $\overline{OA}$ (a), fig. 16, be any assumed vector in the plane of the paper, to which plane ρ is supposed to be perpendicular at O. Operating upon a with w, we obtain a vector, $\overline{OB}$, equal to wa. Operating upon a with ρ, we obtain a new vector, OC, equal to ρa at right angles to a. Completing the rectangle OBDC, and drawing the diagonal OD, we obtain $OD = wa + \rho a$; hence,

$$w + \rho = \frac{wa}{a} + \frac{\rho a}{a} = \frac{wa + \rho a}{a} = \frac{OD}{OA} = \text{a quaternion.}$$

21°. It is evident from equations (10), (18), and (19) of 17° that the commutative law of multiplication does not hold good for vectors: $\beta a \neq a\beta$.

22°. From equations B and D, 18°, we obtain, by adding and subtracting,

$$S a\beta = S\beta a = \tfrac{1}{2}(a\beta + \beta a) \quad \ldots \quad (1)$$
$$V a\beta = -V\beta a = \tfrac{1}{2}(a\beta - \beta a) \quad \ldots \quad (2)$$

23°. If $\theta = 0$ or π, the vector parts of (A), (B), (C), (D) vanish, and the quaternions degrade to scalars.

If q be a product, and $\theta = 0$, we have

$$\beta a = -T\beta Ta = -ba = \text{a negative scalar;}$$

and for $\theta = \pi$, $\beta a = T\beta Ta = ba = $ a positive scalar.

Hence the product of two parallel vectors is a scalar which is negative when the vectors have similar, and positive when they have contrary, directions.

If q be a quotient, and $\theta = 0$, we have $\dfrac{\beta}{a} = \dfrac{b}{a}$; and for $\theta = \pi$, $\dfrac{\beta}{a} = -\dfrac{b}{a}$; results which confirm those of 19°, Part I.

Conversely, if $Vq = 0$, the constituent vectors, a and β, are parallel, or $a = x\beta$. For if Ta and $T\beta$ have actual and real values, the vector of a quaternion can only vanish when $\theta = 0$ or π.

It follows that if a quaternion degrade into a scalar, or if $q = \pm x$, then

$$Tq = T(\pm x) = x\,; \quad Uq = U(\pm x) = \pm 1.$$

In words, the versor of a scalar, regarded as the limit of

a quaternion, is equal to positive or negative unity, according as the scalar itself is positive or negative (Hamilton).

24°. For the future $(T a)^2$ will generally be written $T^2 a$; $T(a^2)$ will be written $T a^2$; $(V q)^2$ will be written $V^2 q$; $V(q^2)$ will be written $V q^2$, &c., &c.

If $\theta = 0$ and $Ta = T\beta$, then $\beta = a$ and

$$\beta a = \beta^2 = (T\beta U \beta)^2 = T\beta U \beta T \beta U \beta = T^2 \beta U^2 \beta$$
$$\quad = T^2 \beta (-1) = -T^2 \beta = -b^2;$$

or, the square of a vector is a negative scalar, being the square of its tensor combined with the minus sign. It follows that the square of a vector must be considered as having *no direction in space.*

Since β^2 is a scalar,

$$V\beta^2 = 0 \,;\, S\beta^2 = \beta^2 = -b^2.$$

25°. If $\theta = \dfrac{\pi}{2}$, the scalar parts of (A), (B), (C), (D) vanish, and the quaternions degrade to vectors. For example, βa becomes $T\beta Ta \cdot \epsilon$, a vector which Sir W. R. Hamilton called the Index of the Right Quaternion βa, or $IV\beta a$. Conversely, if q be any quaternion, and if $Sq = 0$, then the constituent vectors are at right angles to each other. For, provided that Ta and $T\beta$ have real and actual values, the scalar of a quaternion can only vanish when $\theta = \dfrac{\pi}{2}$.

26°. $S\beta a$, or $-T\beta Ta \cos \theta$, is (neglecting signs) the area of a parallelogram whose sides are equal to OB and OA, and whose angle is the complement of $\angle$ BOA.

$TV\beta a$, or $T\beta Ta \sin \theta$, is the area of the parallelogram BOA.

$V\beta a$, or $T\beta Ta \sin \theta \cdot \epsilon$, is the Vector-Area of the same parallelogram, $T\beta a \sin \theta$ representing its numerical value, and ϵ indicating its sign, which is positive or negative according as the rotation of a particle round the periphery is positive or negative as seen from the term of ϵ. Thus,

$$V\beta a = ba \sin \theta \cdot \epsilon = \text{OABC};$$
$$V a\beta = ab \sin \theta (-\epsilon) = -ab \sin \theta \cdot \epsilon = \text{OCBA}.$$

Section 3
A Quaternion as the Power of a Vector

27°. Since i, or i^1, is a versor which turns any vector on which it operates, say j, through *one* right angle positively, it is natural to define i^2 to be a versor which turns the same vector through *two* right angles positively; i^3 through *three* right angles positively ... i^m through m right angles positively, m being a positive integer.

In the same way, since i^{-1} is a versor which turns the vector upon which it operates through *one* right angle negatively, we define i^{-2} to be a versor which turns the same vector through *two* right angles negatively, i^{-3} through *three* right angles negatively ... i^{-m} through m right angles negatively, m being still a positive integer.

In perfect consistency with the foregoing, we define $i^{\frac{1}{2}}$ to be a versor which turns the vector upon which it operates through *one-half* a right angle positively, $i^{\frac{1}{3}}$ through *one-third* of a right angle positively ... $i^{\frac{1}{m}}$ through *one* m^{th} of a right angle positively.

Similarly, $i^{-\frac{1}{m}}$ is a versor which turns the vector upon which it operates through *one* m^{th} of a right angle negatively.

Definition.—*If η is any unit-vector and t any scalar, whole or fractional, positive or negative, η^t is a versor which twists any vector at right angles to η through an angle $t \times \frac{\pi}{2}$, the direction of rotation depending upon the sign of t.*

Hence, every such power of a unit-vector is a versor; and, conversely, every versor may be represented by such a power (Professor Hardy).

Since the angle of a quaternion has been defined to lie between o and π, the value of t must lie between o and 2.

If the angle of the versor in degrees be θ, then $\theta = t\frac{\pi}{2}$, and $t = \frac{2}{\pi}\theta$, or (as it will for the future be written) $c\theta$. Hence $\eta^{\pm t} = \eta^{\pm c\theta}$.

28°. It was shown in 17° (*a*) that the value of the versor of $\frac{a}{\beta}$, which turns β positively through the angle θ, is

$$\cos \theta + \epsilon \sin \theta.$$

But the versor $\epsilon^{c\theta}$ would turn β positively through the same angle. Therefore,
$$\cos\theta + \epsilon \sin\theta = \epsilon^{c\theta}. \quad \ldots \ldots \quad (1)$$

Similarly, the value of the versor of $\dfrac{\beta}{\alpha}$, which turns α positively through the angle θ, is $\cos\theta - \epsilon \sin\theta$. But the versor $(-\epsilon)^{c\theta}$ would turn α positively through the same angle. Therefore,
$$\cos\theta - \epsilon \sin\theta = (-\epsilon)^{c\theta} \quad \ldots \ldots \quad (2)$$

If it be desired to give the value of this versor in terms of $+\epsilon$, we have only to bear in mind that the effect of turning any vector through any angle negatively by means of a versor OX, is equivalent to the effect of turning the same vector through the same angle positively by means of the versor $-OX$, and *vice versâ*. Hence, $(-\epsilon)^{c\theta} = \epsilon^{-c\theta}$, and consequently,
$$\cos\theta - \epsilon \sin\theta = (-\epsilon)^{c\theta} = \epsilon^{-c\theta}. \quad \ldots \quad (3)$$

But $(-\epsilon)^{c\theta}$, not $\epsilon^{-c\theta}$, is *the* versor of $\dfrac{\beta}{\alpha}$, because it operates through θ positively, 4° (c).

In precisely the same way, we have for the versor of $\beta\alpha$,
$$\cos(\pi - \theta) + \epsilon \sin(\pi - \theta) = \epsilon^{c(\pi - \theta)}; \quad \ldots \quad (4)$$
and for the versor of $\alpha\beta$,
$$\cos(\pi - \theta) - \epsilon \sin(\pi - \theta) = (-\epsilon)^{c(\pi - \theta)}. \quad \ldots \quad (5)$$

We may now discard the notion of two coincident versors, $\overline{OX}_\theta$ and $\overline{OX}_{\pi-\theta}$, in the direction of $\overline{OX}$, 4° (c), which was introduced merely for the purpose of explanation. The base $\overline{OX}$ may be considered as one and the same in both cases, being expressed by $\epsilon^{c\theta}$ when it operates through the angle θ, and by $\epsilon^{c(\pi-\theta)}$ when it operates through the angle $(\pi - \theta)$, &c., &c.

29°. As in the case of quadrantal versors, $i^{-1} = \dfrac{1}{i}$, so in the case of non-quadrantal versors, $\epsilon^{-c\theta} = \dfrac{1}{\epsilon^{c\theta}}$. For,
$$U\frac{\beta}{\alpha} = \frac{U\beta}{U\alpha} = \frac{U\beta}{U\alpha} \cdot \frac{U\beta}{U\alpha} = \frac{U\alpha}{U\alpha} : \frac{U\alpha}{U\beta} = 1 : \frac{U\alpha}{U\beta}.$$

But $U\dfrac{\beta}{\alpha} = \cos\theta - \epsilon \sin\theta = (-\epsilon)^{c\theta} = \epsilon^{-c\theta}$;

and $U\dfrac{\alpha}{\beta} = \cos\theta + \epsilon \sin\theta = \epsilon^{c\theta}.$

Therefore, $\qquad \epsilon^{-c\theta} = \dfrac{1}{\epsilon^{c\theta}}.$

But although

$i^{-1} = -i$, yet $\epsilon^{-c\theta} \neq -\epsilon^{c\theta}$, and $-\epsilon^{c\theta} \neq (-\epsilon)^{c\theta}$.

For, $\qquad \epsilon^{-c\theta} = (-\epsilon)^{c\theta} = \cos\theta - \epsilon \sin\theta,$

and $\qquad -\epsilon^{c\theta} = -(\epsilon^{c\theta}) = -\cos\theta - \epsilon\sin\theta;$

and the right-hand members of these two equations can only be equal in the particular case when $\theta = \dfrac{\pi}{2}$, that is, when $\iota = 1$. Therefore, in general,

$$\epsilon^{-c\theta} \neq -\epsilon^{c\theta}, \text{ and } -\epsilon^{c\theta} \neq (-\epsilon)^{c\theta}.$$

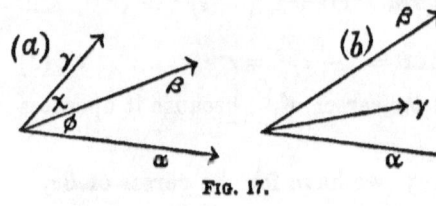

Fig. 17.

30°. Let α, β, γ, fig. 17 (a), be any three coinitial, coplanar vectors, the angle between α and β being ϕ, that between β and γ, χ. Then,

$$\mathrm{U}\dfrac{\alpha}{\beta} = \cos\phi + \epsilon\sin\phi = \epsilon^{c\phi},$$

$$\mathrm{U}\dfrac{\beta}{\gamma} = \cos\chi + \epsilon\sin\chi = \epsilon^{c\chi},$$

$$\mathrm{U}\dfrac{\alpha}{\beta}\mathrm{U}\dfrac{\beta}{\gamma} = \dfrac{\mathrm{U}\alpha}{\mathrm{U}\beta}\cdot\dfrac{\mathrm{U}\beta}{\mathrm{U}\gamma} = (\cos\phi + \epsilon\sin\phi)(\cos\chi + \epsilon\sin\chi) = \epsilon^{c\phi}\cdot\epsilon^{c\chi}.$$

Now,

$\dfrac{\mathrm{U}\alpha}{\mathrm{U}\beta}\cdot\dfrac{\mathrm{U}\beta}{\mathrm{U}\gamma} = \dfrac{\mathrm{U}\alpha}{\mathrm{U}\gamma};$ and $(\cos\phi + \epsilon\sin\phi)(\cos\chi + \epsilon\sin\chi)$

$$= \cos(\phi + \chi) + \epsilon\sin(\phi + \chi) = \epsilon^{c(\phi+\chi)}.$$

Therefore,

$$\epsilon^{c\phi}\cdot\epsilon^{c\chi} = \mathrm{U}\dfrac{\alpha}{\gamma} = \cos(\phi + \chi) + \epsilon\sin(\phi + \chi) = \epsilon^{c(\phi+\chi)} \ldots (1)$$

Suppose that γ lies between α and β, fig. 17 (b), and consequently that the angle between α and γ is $(\phi - \chi)$. Then,

A QUATERNION AS THE POWER OF A VECTOR   55

$\mathrm{UV}\frac{\beta}{\gamma} = -\mathrm{UV}\frac{\alpha}{\beta}$, since the rotations from β to α and from γ to β are contrary in direction.

Hence,

$$\mathrm{U}\frac{\alpha}{\beta} = \cos\phi + \epsilon \sin\phi = \epsilon^{c\phi},$$

$$\mathrm{U}\frac{\beta}{\gamma} = \cos\chi - \epsilon \sin\chi = \epsilon^{-c\chi} = \frac{1}{\epsilon^{c\chi}},$$

$$\mathrm{U}\frac{\alpha}{\beta} \cdot \mathrm{U}\frac{\beta}{\gamma} = (\cos\phi + \epsilon \sin\phi)(\cos\chi - \epsilon \sin\chi) = \frac{\epsilon^{c\phi}}{\epsilon^{c\chi}}.$$

Now, $\mathrm{U}\frac{\alpha}{\beta} \mathrm{U}\frac{\beta}{\gamma} = \mathrm{U}\frac{\alpha}{\gamma}$; and $(\cos\phi + \epsilon \sin\phi)(\cos\chi - \epsilon \sin\chi)$
$= \cos(\phi - \chi) + \epsilon \sin(\phi - \chi) = \epsilon^{c(\phi-\chi)}.$

Therefore, $\qquad \dfrac{\epsilon^{c\phi}}{\epsilon^{c\chi}} = \epsilon^{c(\phi-\chi)}. \qquad \ldots \ldots \ldots$ (2)

The meaning of $(\epsilon^{c\theta})^m$ may be investigated in the same way as that of η^t. $\epsilon^{c\theta}$, or $(\epsilon^{c\theta})^1$, is a versor which turns a vector at right angles to itself *once* through the angle θ, positively; $(\epsilon^{c\theta})^2$ turns the vector *twice* through the angle θ; ... $(\epsilon^{c\theta})^m$ turns it m *times* through the angle θ. And since the operation of turning a vector m *times* through the angle θ is equivalent to the operation of turning it *once* through the angle $m\theta$, we have,

$$(\epsilon^{c\theta})^m = \epsilon^{cm\theta} \ldots \ldots \ldots (3)$$

Hence, (1), (2), (3), the Algebraic Law of Indices holds good for versors:

$$\rho^m \times \rho^n = \rho^{m+n}; \quad \frac{\rho^m}{\rho^n} = \rho^{m-n}; \quad (\rho^m)^n = \rho^{mn}.$$

31°. Suppose that the plane of a quaternion is indeterminate, and consequently that the versor of its vector is $\sqrt{-1}$. Then the equation,

$(\epsilon^{c\theta})^m = \epsilon^{cm\theta}$, becomes $\{(\sqrt{-1})^{c\theta}\}^m = (\sqrt{-1})^{cm\theta}$;

or, $(\cos\theta + \sin\theta \cdot \sqrt{-1})^m = \cos m\theta + \sin m\theta \cdot \sqrt{-1}$,

which is Moivre's formula. This formula, then, admits of a real geometric interpretation when the symbol $\sqrt{-1}$ receives the interpretation assigned to it in this Calculus. According to that interpretation, Moivre's theorem asserts that the operation of turning a line m *times* successively through any angle θ, is equivalent to the operation of turning it *once* through an angle $m\theta$.

Those who wish to go further into this matter are referred to Professor A. S. Hardy's 'Elements of Quaternions,' pp. 50–55.

32°. If we assign any integer values to t, positive, negative, or null, it will be found that

if $\quad\quad \eta^t = \quad 1$, t is an even multiple of 2 ;
if $\quad\quad\quad ,, = -1,\quad ,,\quad$ odd $\quad ,,\quad\quad ,,\ $;
if $\quad\quad\quad ,, = \pm \eta, \quad ,,\quad$ odd number.

In symbols,
$$\eta^{2t} = \pm 1 \,;\, \eta^{2t+1} = \pm \eta\,;$$

the upper or lower signs being taken according as the number t (assumed to be a positive, negative, or null integer) is even or odd.

33°. From the preceding considerations we are justified in defining, that if ρ be any vector and t any scalar,
$$\rho^t = \mathrm{T}^t\rho \cdot \mathrm{U}^t\rho\,; \quad \ldots \ldots \ldots \quad (1)$$
$,, =$ product of a tensor and a versor ;
$,, =$ a quaternion, 15°.

From this equation we have at once

$$\left.\begin{aligned}
\mathrm{T}\rho^t &= \mathrm{T}^t\rho\,; \quad \mathrm{U}\rho^t = \mathrm{U}^t\rho\,; \\
\mathrm{U}\rho^t &= \mathrm{U}\rho^{c\theta} = \cos\theta + \sin\theta\,\mathrm{U}\rho\,; \\
\mathrm{S}\rho^t &= \mathrm{S}\rho^{c\theta} = \mathrm{T}\rho^{c\theta}\cos\theta\,; \\
\mathrm{V}\rho^t &= \mathrm{V}\rho^{c\theta} = \mathrm{T}\rho^{c\theta}\sin\theta\,\mathrm{U}\rho\,; \\
\mathrm{UV}\rho^t &= \mathrm{UV}\rho^{c\theta} = \pm\,\mathrm{U}\rho\,; \\
\angle\rho^t &= \angle\rho^{c\theta} = 2n\pi \pm \theta\,;
\end{aligned}\right\} \quad \cdots \quad (2)$$

the upper and lower signs accompanying each other, and n being an *integer*, positive, negative, or null.

With regard to the expression for $\angle \rho^{c\theta}$, it must be borne in mind that the amount of rotation from $\mathrm{U}\beta$ to $\mathrm{U}\alpha$, fig. 10, admits of being increased or diminished by any whole number of circumferences, or of entire revolutions, without altering the final direction of $\mathrm{U}\beta$. In symbols,

$$\eta^{c\theta} = \eta^{c(2n\pi+\theta)}\,;\, (-\eta)^{c\theta} = \eta^{c(2n\pi-\theta)} \quad \ldots \quad (3)$$

$2n\pi \pm \theta$ is the Amplitude, θ the Angle, of $\rho^{c\theta}$

A QUATERNION AS THE POWER OF A VECTOR

In the particular case when $t = 1$, ρ is the representative of a right quaternion; and since its angle is $\frac{\pi}{2}$, the general expression,

$$\rho^t = T\rho^t \left(\cos\frac{t\pi}{2} + U\rho \cdot \sin\frac{t\pi}{2}\right)$$

becomes $\quad \rho = T\rho U\rho$.

34°. It is now clear that *any* quaternion may be reduced to the form ρ^t by a suitable choice of the base, ρ, and of the scalar index, t. The conditions are,

$$\left. \begin{array}{c} t = \dfrac{2\theta}{\pi}; \ T\rho = Tq^{\frac{1}{t}}; \ U\rho = UVq; \\ t > 0; \ t < 2. \end{array} \right\} \quad \ldots \quad (4)$$

Section 4

A Quaternion in the form of a Quadrinomial

35°. Let XY, YZ, ZX, fig. 18, be three rectangular coordinate planes, and let i, j, k be unit-vectors along the three axes OX, OY, OZ respectively. Let $\overline{OP} = \rho$ be any vector; from its term let fall perpendiculars PL′, PM′, PN′, on the three planes; and complete the rectangular parallelopiped LL′.

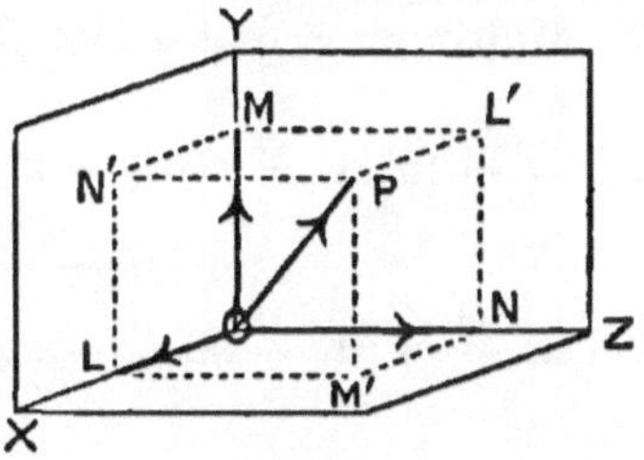

Then $T \cdot \overline{OL}, T \cdot \overline{OM}, T \cdot \overline{ON}$

Fig. 18.

are the Cartesian coordinates, x, y, z, of P, the term of ρ. Consequently, $\overline{OL} = xi$, $\overline{OM} = yj$, $\overline{ON} = zk$; and the equation of $\overline{OP}$ is, Part I., 37°,

$$\rho = xi + yj + zk \quad \ldots \quad \ldots \quad (1)$$

If the coordinate planes are not rectangular, and if a, β, γ are unit-vectors along OX, OY, OZ, the equation of OP becomes,

$$\rho = x\alpha + y\beta + z\gamma, \quad \ldots \quad \ldots \quad (2)$$

where x, y, z are the Cartesian coordinates of P, referred to oblique axes.

Since a quaternion is the sum of a scalar and a vector; if w be a scalar, *any* quaternion may be represented by an equation of the form,

$$q = w + xi + yj + zk; \quad \ldots \quad (3)$$

which, depending as it does upon the values of the *four* scalars, w, x, y, z, furnishes a new reason for calling the complex quantity, q, a quaternion.

From the last equation,

$$q^2 = (w^2 - x^2 - y^2 - z^2) + 2w(xi + yj + zk) \quad . \quad (4)$$

If $\angle q = \frac{\pi}{2}$, $w = 0$ in equation (3), and

$$q = xi + yj + zk, \quad \ldots \ldots \ldots (5)$$
$$q^2 = -(x^2 + y^2 + z^2) \quad \ldots \ldots \ldots (6)$$

36°. (*a*). Suppose we have any two vectors,

$$a = m_1 i + m_2 j + m_3 k,$$
$$\beta = n_1 i + n_2 j + n_3 k.$$

Multiplying, first a into β, and then β into a, we have

$$\left. \begin{array}{l} a\beta = -(m_1 n_1 + m_2 n_2 + m_3 n_3) + \begin{vmatrix} i, & j, & k \\ m_1, & m_2, & m_3 \\ n_1, & n_2, & n_3 \end{vmatrix} \\ \beta a = -(m_1 n_1 + m_2 n_2 + m_3 n_3) - \begin{vmatrix} i, & j, & k \\ m_1, & m_2, & m_3 \\ n_1, & n_2, & n_3 \end{vmatrix} \end{array} \right\} \quad . \quad . \quad (1)$$

Hence, we see again that the commutative law of multiplication does not hold good for vectors.[1]

(*b*). The multiplication of vectors, however, obeys the distributive law.

Let,
$$a = l_1 i + l_2 j + l_3 k,$$
$$\beta = m_1 i + m_2 j + m_3 k,$$
$$\gamma = n_1 i + n_2 j + n_3 k,$$

be any three vectors.

---

[1] This section was written a considerable time before I saw Herr Dillner's article on quaternions in the 'Mathematische Annalen,' vol. xi., for 1877.

A QUATERNION IN THE FORM OF A QUADRINOMIAL

Then,
$$\alpha + \beta = (l_1 + m_1)i + (l_2 + m_2)j + (l_3 + m_3)k ;$$
and (a),
$$(\alpha + \beta)\gamma = -\{(l_1 + m_1)n_1 + (l_2 + m_2)n_2 + (l_3 + m_3)n_3\}$$
$$+ \begin{vmatrix} i, & j, & k \\ l_1 + m_1, & l_2 + m_2, & l_3 + m_3 \\ n_1, & n_2, & n_3 \end{vmatrix} ;$$

$$\text{,,} \quad = -(l_1 n_1 + l_2 n_2 + l_3 n_3) + \begin{vmatrix} i, & j, & k \\ l_1, & l_2, & l_3 \\ n_1, & n_2, & n_3 \end{vmatrix}$$
$$- (m_1 n_1 + m_2 n_2 + m_3 n_3) + \begin{vmatrix} i, & j, & k \\ m_1, & m_2, & m_3 \\ n_1, & n_2, & n_3 \end{vmatrix} ;$$

,, $= \alpha\gamma + \beta\gamma.$

It can be proved in the same way that
$$\gamma(\alpha + \beta) = \gamma\alpha + \gamma\beta.$$

Therefore the multiplication of vectors is a doubly distributive operation in the case of three vectors.

(c). The associative law of multiplication also holds good for vectors.

Taking the vectors α, β, γ of (b), we have,

$$\alpha\beta \cdot \gamma = \left\{ -\Sigma lm + \begin{vmatrix} i, & j, & k \\ l_1, & l_2, & l_3 \\ m_1, & m_2, & m_3 \end{vmatrix} \right\} (n_1 i + n_2 j + n_3 k) ;$$

$$\text{,,} \quad = -n_1 i \Sigma lm - n_2 j \Sigma lm - n_3 k \Sigma lm$$
$$+ \begin{vmatrix} i, & j, & k \\ l_1, & l_2, & l_3 \\ m_1, & m_2, & m_3 \end{vmatrix} (n_1 i + n_2 j + n_3 k) ;$$

$$\text{,,} \quad = -n_1 i \Sigma lm - n_2 j \Sigma lm - n_3 k \Sigma lm$$
$$+ n_1 \begin{vmatrix} -1, & -k, & j \\ l_1, & l_2, & l_3 \\ m_1, & m_2, & m_3 \end{vmatrix} + n_2 \begin{vmatrix} k, & -1, & -i \\ l_1, & l_2, & l_3 \\ m_1, & m_2, & m_3 \end{vmatrix} + n_3 \begin{vmatrix} -j, & i, & -1 \\ l_1, & l_2, & l_3 \\ m_1, & m_2, & m_3 \end{vmatrix}.$$

Expanding the three determinants and rearranging the terms of the whole, we get

$$\alpha\beta \cdot \gamma = -l_1 i \Sigma mn - l_2 j \Sigma mn - l_3 k \Sigma mn$$
$$+ l_1 \begin{vmatrix} -1, & k, & -j \\ m_1, & m_2, & m_3 \\ n_1, & n_2, & n_3 \end{vmatrix} + l_2 \begin{vmatrix} -k, & -1, & i \\ m_1, & m_2, & m_3 \\ n_1, & n_2, & n_3 \end{vmatrix} + l_3 \begin{vmatrix} j, & -i, & -1 \\ m_1, & m_2, & m_3 \\ n_1, & n_2, & n_3 \end{vmatrix} ;$$

$$a\beta \cdot \gamma = -l_1 i \Sigma mn - l_2 j \Sigma mn - l_3 k \Sigma mn$$

$$+ l_1 i \begin{vmatrix} i, & j, & k \\ m_1, & m_2, & m_3 \\ n_1, & n_2, & n_3 \end{vmatrix} + l_2 j \begin{vmatrix} i, & j, & k \\ m_1, & m_2, & m_3 \\ n_1, & n_2, & n_3 \end{vmatrix} + l_3 k \begin{vmatrix} i, & j, & k \\ m_1, & m_2, & m_3 \\ n_1, & n_2, & n_3 \end{vmatrix};$$

$$\text{,,} \quad = (l_1 i + l_2 j + l_3 k) \left\{ -\Sigma mn + \begin{vmatrix} i, & j, & k \\ m_1, & m_2, & m_3 \\ n_1, & n_2, & n_3 \end{vmatrix} \right\};$$

,, $= a \cdot \beta\gamma$.

The multiplication of vectors, therefore, is an associative operation in the case of three vectors.

The method by which it has been proved that the distributive and associative laws apply to three vectors can obviously be extended to the multiplication of any number of vectors.

37°. By the aid of the distributive principle we can now find the values of

$$(a + \beta)^2, (a - \beta)^2, (a + \beta)(a - \beta), \text{ and } a\beta \cdot \beta a.$$

$$(a+\beta)^2 = (a+\beta)(a+\beta) = a^2 + a\beta + \beta a + \beta^2 = a^2 + 2Sa\beta + \beta^2 . \quad (2)$$

$$(a - \beta)^2 = a^2 - 2Sa\beta + \beta^2 \quad \ldots \quad \ldots \quad \ldots \quad (3)$$

$$(a + \beta)(a - \beta) = a^2 - a\beta + \beta a - \beta^2 = a^2 - (a\beta - \beta a) - \beta^2$$
$$= a^2 - 2Va\beta - \beta^2 . \quad \ldots \quad (4)$$

$$a\beta \cdot \beta a = (Sa\beta + Va\beta)(Sa\beta - Va\beta);$$

,, $= S^2 a\beta - Sa\beta V a\beta + Sa\beta V a\beta - V^2 a\beta;$

,, $= S^2 a\beta - V^2 a\beta \quad \ldots \quad \ldots \quad \ldots \quad (5)$

,, $= (-TaT\beta \cos \theta)^2 - (-TaT\beta \sin \theta \cdot \epsilon)^2;$

,, $= T^2 a\beta \quad \ldots \quad \ldots \quad \ldots \quad (6)$

By the associative law,

$a\beta \cdot \beta a = a \cdot \beta^2 a = a \cdot a\beta^2$ (since β^2 is a scalar, 24°);

,, $= a^2 \beta^2 \quad \ldots \quad \ldots \quad \ldots \quad (7)$

but this last expression is not to be confounded with $(a\beta)^2$.

38°. If a, β, γ be any three vectors, in general,

$$\frac{a}{\beta}\gamma \neq \frac{a\gamma}{\beta}.$$

For $\qquad \dfrac{a}{\beta}\gamma = a\beta^{-1}\gamma,$

and $\qquad \dfrac{a\gamma}{\beta} = a\gamma\beta^{-1}.$

But $\qquad \beta^{-1}\gamma \neq \gamma\beta^{-1};$

therefore, $\alpha\beta^{-1}\gamma \neq \alpha\gamma\beta^{-1}$;

or, $\dfrac{\alpha}{\beta}\gamma \neq \dfrac{\alpha\gamma}{\beta}$.

If, however, $\gamma = \beta$,

then, $\dfrac{\alpha}{\beta}\beta = \dfrac{\alpha\beta}{\beta}$;

for $\dfrac{\alpha}{\beta}\beta = \alpha\beta^{-1}\beta = (14°)\, \alpha\beta\beta^{-1} = \dfrac{\alpha\beta}{\beta}$.

Again, $\dfrac{\alpha}{\gamma}\cdot\dfrac{\gamma}{\beta} \neq \dfrac{\alpha\gamma}{\gamma\beta}$;

for

$\dfrac{\alpha}{\gamma}\cdot\dfrac{\gamma}{\beta} = \alpha\gamma^{-1}\cdot\gamma\beta^{-1} =, 36°, \alpha\cdot\gamma^{-1}\gamma\cdot\beta^{-1} = \alpha\beta^{-1} = \dfrac{\alpha}{\beta} = \dfrac{\alpha\gamma}{\beta\gamma}$.

But $\beta\gamma \neq \gamma\beta$;

therefore, $\dfrac{\alpha\gamma}{\beta\gamma} \neq \dfrac{\alpha\gamma}{\gamma\beta}$

and $\dfrac{\alpha}{\gamma}\cdot\dfrac{\gamma}{\beta} \neq \dfrac{\alpha\gamma}{\gamma\beta}$.

In such an expression as $\dfrac{\alpha\gamma}{\gamma\beta}$, the denominator must be treated as *one* quaternion; so that, if we equate the fraction to q, we have $\alpha\gamma = q\gamma\beta$,
and $q = \alpha\gamma\beta^{-1}\gamma^{-1}$ (Prof. Tait).

39°. From equations (1), 36° (*a*),

$S\alpha\beta = S\beta\alpha = -(m_1n_1 + m_2n_2 + m_3n_3)$;

$V\alpha\beta = -V\beta\alpha = \begin{vmatrix} i, & j, & k, \\ m_1, & m_2, & m_3 \\ n_1, & n_2, & n_3 \end{vmatrix}$;

,, $= (m_2n_3 - m_3n_2)i + (m_3n_1 - m_1n_3)j + (m_1n_2 - m_2n_1)k$.

Returning to the simpler form,

$$q = w + xi + yj + zk,$$

we have at once

$$Sq = w \quad \ldots \ldots \ldots \quad (1)$$
$$Vq = xi + yj + zk. \quad \ldots \ldots \quad (2)$$

62 A QUATERNION IN THE FORM OF A QUADRINOMIAL

Also, since $(\mathrm{T}\mathrm{V}q)^2 = -(\mathrm{V}q)^2 = x^2 + y^2 + z^2$,

$$\mathrm{T}\mathrm{V}q = \sqrt{x^2 + y^2 + z^2} \quad \ldots \quad \ldots \quad (3)$$

$$\mathrm{U}\mathrm{V}q = \frac{\mathrm{V}q}{\mathrm{T}\mathrm{V}q} = \frac{xi + yj + zk}{\sqrt{x^2 + y^2 + z^2}} \quad \ldots \quad (4)$$

Further, since $\mathrm{T}^2q = \mathrm{S}^2q - \mathrm{V}^2q$, 37° (5) and (6),

$$\mathrm{T}q = \sqrt{w^2 + x^2 + y^2 + z^2} \quad \ldots \quad (5)$$

$$\mathrm{U}q = \frac{q}{\mathrm{T}q} = \frac{w + xi + yj + zk}{\sqrt{w^2 + x^2 + y^2 + z^2}} \quad \ldots \quad (6)$$

$$\mathrm{S}\mathrm{U}q = \frac{\mathrm{S}q}{\mathrm{T}q} = \frac{w}{\sqrt{w^2 + x^2 + y^2 + z^2}} \quad \ldots \quad (7)$$

$$\mathrm{T}\mathrm{V}\mathrm{U}q = \frac{\mathrm{T}\mathrm{V}q}{\mathrm{T}q} = \sqrt{\frac{x^2 + y^2 + z^2}{w^2 + x^2 + y^2 + z^2}} \quad \ldots \quad (8)$$

CHAPTER IV

EQUALITY AND INEQUALITY OF QUATERNIONS

40°. (a). *Definition. If the tensors and versors, or the scalars and vectors, of two quaternions are respectively equal, the two quaternions are equal. And the converse.* In symbols,

$$\begin{aligned} q' = q, & \text{ if } & Tq' &= Tq, & \text{and } Uq' &= Uq\,; \\ \text{\,,\,} = \text{\,,\,} & \text{\,,\,} & Sq' &= Sq, & \text{\,,\,} \ Vq' &= Vq \end{aligned} \right\} \cdot \cdot (1)$$

$$\begin{aligned} Tq' &= Tq, \text{ and } Uq' = Uq, & \text{if } q' &= q,\,; \\ Sq' &= Sq, \text{\,,\,} \quad Vq' = Vq, & \text{\,,\,} \text{\,,\,} &= \text{\,,\,} \end{aligned} \right\} \cdot \cdot (2)$$

(b). On the equality of the tensors of two such quaternions as $\beta a = \delta \gamma$, $\dfrac{a}{\beta} = \dfrac{\sigma}{\tau}$, there is nothing to be said; the tensors are positive numbers obedient to the rules of Arithmetic.

(c). *Definition. Two versors are equal, and only equal, if the rotations they communicate to the vectors on which they operate, in planes perpendicular to themselves, are similar in direction and equal in amount.* And the converse.

As in the case of vectors, Part I., 7°, the phrase 'similar directions,' was defined to mean 'parallel directions with the same sense'; so in the case of versors the phrase is defined to mean 'in coincident, or parallel, planes towards the same hand, as seen from the same side of the two planes.' The phrase 'equal in amount' means 'through angles equal in magnitude.'

This definition may be expressed in symbols as follows:

if $\quad \begin{aligned} Uq &= Uq', \\ \angle q &= \angle q', \text{ and, } UVq = UVq' \end{aligned} \right\} \cdot \cdot \cdot \cdot (1)$

If $\angle q = \theta$, $UVq = \epsilon$; $\angle q' = \phi$, $UVq' = \eta$; (1) becomes,

if $\quad \begin{aligned} \epsilon^\circ &= \eta^\circ, \\ \theta &= \phi, \text{ and } \epsilon = \eta \end{aligned} \right\} \cdot \cdot \cdot \cdot \cdot \cdot (2)$

41°. If $\zeta\eta$ and $\nu\mu$ are coplanar quaternions, and if $\zeta\eta = \nu\mu$, then, obviously, $\eta\zeta = \mu\nu$, for their tensors and angles are equal, and the direction of rotation is the same for both quaternions.

For the same reasons, if $\dfrac{\beta}{\alpha} = \dfrac{\delta}{\gamma}$, then $\dfrac{\alpha}{\beta} = \dfrac{\gamma}{\delta}$.

Further, $\dfrac{\delta}{\beta} = \dfrac{\gamma}{\alpha}$. For, let $\dfrac{\beta}{\alpha}$ be made to slide and revolve in the common plane until its origin coincides with that of $\dfrac{\delta}{\gamma}$, and α and γ are collinear. Then, β and δ will be collinear, and since $\dfrac{d}{c} = \dfrac{b}{a}$, $\dfrac{d}{b} = \dfrac{c}{a}$; or, Part I., 20°, $\dfrac{\delta}{\beta} = \dfrac{\gamma}{\alpha}$.

42°. Any two quaternions, considered as geometric fractions, may be reduced to a common denominator. Let the two quaternions be $\dfrac{OB}{OA}$ in the plane LMQP, and $\dfrac{OD}{OC}$ in the plane PQSR, fig. 19. Whatever be the planes of the

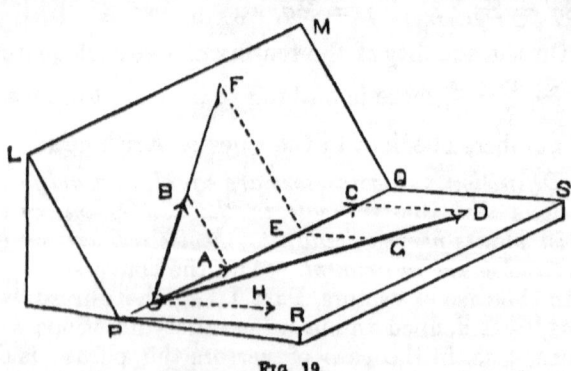

FIG. 19.

quaternions, or however they may be posited in these planes, by causing the quaternions to slide about and rotate *in their own planes* (without turning them over), they can be made to assume the positions shown in the figure, where their origins are coincident, and the divisor vectors are collinear, in the line of intersection of the two planes, PQ. Let E be any point in that line. Produce OB, and draw EF and EG parallel respectively to AB and CD. Then,

$$\frac{OF}{OE} = \frac{OB}{OA}; \quad \frac{OG}{OE} = \frac{OD}{OC}.$$

EQUALITY AND INEQUALITY OF QUATERNIONS

Let another vector, $\overline{OH}$, be drawn in the plane LMQP, making the angle $HOE = EOF$, and of such a length that $OF : OE :: OE : OH$. Then we have,
$$\frac{OE}{OH} = \frac{OF}{OE} = \frac{OB}{OA};$$
and, therefore,
$$\frac{OD}{OC} \pm \frac{OB}{OA} = \frac{OG}{OE} \pm \frac{OF}{OE} = \frac{OG \pm OF}{OE}; \quad \ldots \quad (1)$$
$$\frac{OD}{OC} \cdot \frac{OB}{OA} = \frac{OG}{OE} \cdot \frac{OE}{OF} = \frac{OG}{OF}; \quad \ldots \quad (2)$$
$$\frac{OD}{OC} \cdot \frac{OB}{OA} = \frac{OG}{OE} \cdot \frac{OF}{OE} = \frac{OG}{OE} \cdot \frac{OE}{OH} = \frac{OG}{OH}. \quad (3)$$

Any two quaternions, then, such as $\frac{OB}{OA}$ and $\frac{OD}{OC}$ may be reduced to the form $\frac{OF}{OE}$ and $\frac{OG}{OE}$, or to the form $\frac{OE}{OH}$ and $\frac{OG}{OE}$, without undergoing any change in value.

43°. It follows that no two diplanar quaternions can be equal. For suppose $\frac{OB}{OA} = \frac{OD}{OC}$. Then $\frac{OF}{OE} = \frac{OG}{OE}$, and consequently $\overline{OF} = \overline{OG}$, which is contrary to definition, since the two vectors have not similar directions.

Conversely, if two quaternions are equal, they are coplanar.

44°. If q and q' are equal quaternions, so that
$$Sq + Vq = Sq' + Vq';$$
then, by definition,
$$Sq = Sq', \text{ and } Vq = Vq'.$$

More generally, if an equation involves any number of scalar and vector quantities, the sums of the scalars and of the vectors on either side are respectively equal. For example, let
$$x + m\alpha + n\beta = y + z + t\gamma.$$
Then, $\quad\quad m\alpha + n\beta = (\text{say}) \, l\delta,$
and $\quad\quad x + l\delta = (y + z) + t\gamma.$

But $(x + l\delta)$ and $\{(y + z) + t\gamma\}$ are quaternions, 20°. Therefore, 40°,
$$S(x + l\delta), \text{ or } S(x + m\alpha + n\beta) = S\{(y + z) + t\gamma\},$$
$$V(x + m\alpha + n\beta) = V\{(y + z) + t\gamma\};$$
therefore, $\quad\quad x = y + z; \, m\alpha + n\beta = t\gamma.$

F

CHAPTER V

THE VARIOUS KINDS OF QUATERNIONS

45°. Collinear Quaternions.

Quaternions whose planes intersect in, or are parallel to, a common line are said to be Collinear. For example, the quaternions $\overline{OB} \cdot \overline{OA}$ and $\overline{OD} \cdot \overline{OC}$, fig. 19, 42°, are collinear; and $\overline{OL} \cdot \overline{ON}$, $\overline{OM} \cdot \overline{ON}$, fig. 18, 35°, are also collinear, whatever be the angles YZ, ZX, ZY.

Since the versors of collinears are each perpendicular to the common vector, it follows that if q, q', q'', &c., be collinear, Uq, Uq', Uq'', &c., are coplanar; and the converse.

Coplanar quaternions are always collinear (or can be made so by sliding and rotation *in the plane*), but the converse is not true. Collinears are not always coplanar.

46°. Reciprocal Quaternions.

The Reciprocal of a quaternion in the form of a fraction is obtained by interchanging its divisor and dividend vectors.

Thus, $\dfrac{\beta}{\alpha}$ is the reciprocal of $\dfrac{\alpha}{\beta}$.

Since $1 : \dfrac{\alpha}{\beta} = \dfrac{\beta}{\alpha}$, 1° (i), and $\dfrac{\alpha}{\beta} \dfrac{\beta}{\alpha} = \dfrac{\alpha}{\alpha} = 1$, it follows that either of two reciprocals is equal to unity divided by the other, and that the product of the two is positive unity. In symbols, if q and q' be reciprocal,

$$\left. \begin{array}{l} q = \dfrac{1}{q'} = q'^{-1}; \quad q' = \dfrac{1}{q} = q^{-1}; \\ qq' = q'q = 1 = q^{-1}q = qq^{-1}. \end{array} \right\} \quad \ldots \quad (1)$$

Reciprocal quaternions have, obviously, a common plane and angle, reciprocal tensors, and opposite axes—rotation from α to β being contrary to rotation from β to α; or,

$$\left. \begin{array}{l} \angle q^{-1} = \angle q; \quad Tq^{-1} = \dfrac{1}{Tq}; \\ UVq^{-1} = -UVq = \dfrac{1}{UVq}. \end{array} \right\} \quad \ldots \quad (2)$$

Hence, if
$$q = \frac{a}{\beta} = T\frac{a}{\beta}(\cos \theta + \epsilon \sin \theta) = T\frac{a}{\beta} \cdot \epsilon^{\epsilon\theta},$$
then,
$$q^{-1} = \frac{\beta}{a} = T\frac{\beta}{a}(\cos \theta - \epsilon \sin \theta) = T\frac{\beta}{a} \cdot (-\epsilon)^{\epsilon\theta} = T\frac{\beta}{a} \cdot \epsilon^{-\epsilon\theta} \quad \ldots (3)$$

The versors of reciprocals are reciprocal, $\epsilon^{\epsilon\theta}$ and $\epsilon^{-\epsilon\theta}$ being reciprocal,
$$U\frac{1}{q} = Uq^{-1} = \frac{1}{Uq}, \text{ and } Uq^{-1}Uq = UqUq^{-1} = 1; \ldots (4)$$
or, the versor of the reciprocal is equal to the reciprocal of the versor.

47°. Opposite Quaternions.

If any two opposite vectors, β and $-\beta$, be divided by any one common vector, a, the two unequal quotients thus formed, $\frac{\beta}{a}$ and $\frac{-\beta}{a}$, are called opposite quaternions. Accordingly, $-q$ is the opposite of q.

Since, 1° (*i*),
$$\frac{-\beta}{a} + \frac{\beta}{a} = \frac{-\beta + \beta}{a} = \frac{\text{o}}{a} = \text{o},$$
and
$$\frac{-\beta}{a} : \frac{\beta}{a} = \frac{-\beta}{a} \cdot \frac{a}{\beta} = \frac{-\beta}{\beta} = -1;$$

the sum of any two opposite quaternions is zero, and their quotient is negative unity,
$$-q + q = \text{o}; \quad \frac{q}{-q} = -1 \ . \ . \ (1)$$

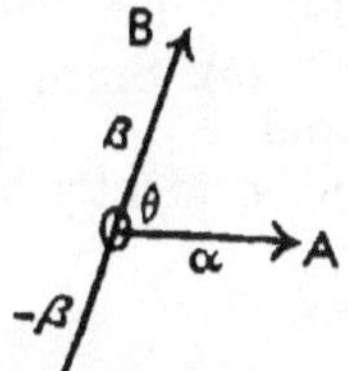

Opposite quaternions, fig. 20, have a common plane, equal tensors, supplementary angles, and opposite axes,
$$\left. \begin{array}{l} T(-q) = Tq; \ \angle(-q) = \pi - \angle q; \\ UV(-q) = -UVq = \frac{1}{UVq}. \end{array} \right\} \ldots (2)$$

Fig. 20.

Hence, if $q = \frac{a}{\beta} = T\frac{a}{\beta}(\cos \theta + \epsilon \sin \theta) = T\frac{a}{\beta} \cdot \epsilon^{\epsilon\theta},$
then,
$$-q = \frac{-a}{\beta} = T\frac{a}{\beta}\{\cos(\pi-\theta) - \epsilon \sin(\pi-\theta)\} = T\frac{a}{\beta} \cdot \epsilon^{-\epsilon(\pi-\theta)} \ldots (3)$$

48°. Let $\overline{OA}$, $\overline{OB}$, fig. 21, be any two vectors. From O draw $OB' = OB$ in the plane AOB, making $\angle AOB' = \angle AOB$; and draw BB', cutting OA produced in A'. Let $\overline{OB'} = \beta'$.

(a). *The unequal quotients*, $\dfrac{\beta}{a}$ *and* $\dfrac{\beta'}{a}$, *are called Conjugate Quaternions*, and if $\dfrac{\beta}{a} = q$, $\dfrac{\beta'}{a} = Kq$, read 'conjugate of q.'

Conjugate quaternions have a common plane, equal angles and tensors, and opposite axes:

$$\left. \begin{array}{l} \angle Kq = \angle q\,;\, TKq = Tq \\ UVKq = -UVq = \dfrac{1}{UVq} \end{array} \right\} \quad \ldots \quad (1)$$

Hence, if $q = \dfrac{a}{\beta} = T\dfrac{a}{\beta}(\cos\theta + \epsilon \sin\theta) = T\dfrac{a}{\beta} \cdot \epsilon^{\epsilon\theta}$,

then, $\quad Kq = K\dfrac{a}{\beta} = T\dfrac{a}{\beta}(\cos\theta - \epsilon \sin\theta) = T\dfrac{a}{\beta} \cdot \epsilon^{-\epsilon\theta} \ldots (2)$

The versors of conjugates are reciprocal, since $\epsilon^{\epsilon\theta}$ and $\epsilon^{-\epsilon\theta}$ are reciprocal, and the product of the versors is positive unity:

$$\left. \begin{array}{l} UKq = \dfrac{1}{Uq} = U\dfrac{1}{q}\,; \\ UKq \cdot Uq = Uq \cdot UKq = 1 \end{array} \right\} \quad \ldots \quad (3)$$

From the foregoing it is evident that $a\beta$ and βa are conjugate quaternions.

(b). Since $\quad a\beta = Ta\beta(-\cos\theta - \epsilon \sin\theta)$,
and $\quad Ka\beta = \beta a = T\beta a(-\cos\theta + \epsilon \sin\theta)$,
we evidently have

$$\left. \begin{array}{l} SKq = Sq \\ VKq = -Vq \end{array} \right\} \quad \ldots \ldots \quad (4)$$

Hence, we have as general expressions for a quaternion and its conjugate,

$$q = Sq + Vq, \ldots \ldots \ldots (5)$$
$$Kq = Sq - Vq\,; \ldots \ldots \ldots (6)$$

whence,

$$q + Kq = 2Sq, \ldots \ldots \ldots (7)$$
$$q - Kq = 2Vq \ldots \ldots \ldots (8)$$

(c). If $\angle q = 0$, Vq vanishes in (5), q degrades to a positive scalar, say x, and (6) becomes

$$Kx = x \quad \ldots \ldots \ldots (9)$$

Similarly, if $\angle q = \pi$, q in (5) degrades to a negative scalar, say $-x$, and (6) becomes

$$K(-x) = -x \quad \ldots \quad \ldots \quad (10)$$

If $\angle q = \frac{\pi}{2}$, $\underset{q}{S}$ vanishes in (5), q degrades to a positive vector, say γ, and (6) becomes

$$K\gamma = -\gamma \quad \ldots \quad \ldots \quad (11)$$

Since, 47° (3),

$$(-q) = -Sq - Vq, \quad \ldots \quad \ldots \quad (12)$$
$$K(-q) = -Sq + Vq \quad \ldots \quad \ldots \quad (13)$$

If, therefore, $\angle q = \frac{\pi}{2}$, $-Sq$ vanishes in (12), $-q$ degrades to a negative vector, say $-\gamma$, and (13) becomes

$$K(-\gamma) = \gamma \quad \ldots \quad \ldots \quad (14)$$

From (9), (10), (11), and (14), it is clear that,

(1) The conjugate of a scalar is the scalar itself;
(2) ,, ,, ,, vector is its opposite:

$$K(\pm x) = \pm x\,;\ K(\pm \delta) = \mp \delta \quad \ldots \quad (15)$$

(d). By adding and subtracting equations (5) and (6), it is seen that while the sum of a quaternion and its conjugate is a scalar, their difference is a vector.

(e). The most important formulæ of the last three sections are collected here for facility of reference:

$$Quaternion = q = \frac{a}{\beta} = \frac{Ta}{T\beta}(\cos\theta + \epsilon\sin\theta) . = T\frac{a}{\beta} \cdot \epsilon^{c\theta} \ldots \text{(J)}$$

$$Reciprocal = q^{-1} = \frac{\beta}{a} = \frac{T\beta}{Ta}(\cos\theta - \epsilon\sin\theta) = T\frac{\beta}{a} \cdot \epsilon^{-c\theta} \ldots \text{(L)}$$

$$Opposite = -q = \frac{-a}{\beta} = \frac{Ta}{T\beta}\left\{\cos(\pi-\theta) - \epsilon\sin(\pi-\theta)\right\} = \frac{Ta}{T\beta} \cdot \epsilon^{-c(\pi-\theta)} \ldots \text{(M)}$$

$$Conjugate = Kq = K\frac{a}{\beta} = \frac{Ta}{T\beta}(\cos\theta - \epsilon\sin\theta) = T\frac{a}{\beta} \cdot \epsilon^{-c\theta} \ldots \text{(N)}$$

49°. Miscellaneous Theorems.

(a). The reciprocal of the reciprocal, the opposite of the

opposite, or the conjugate of the conjugate, of a quaternion is the quaternion itself :

$$1 : \frac{1}{q} = q\,;\ -(-q) = q\,;\ \mathrm{KK}q = q.$$

(*b*). Let η be any versor. Then, since

$$\mathrm{K}(\eta) = -\eta,\ \mathrm{K}(\eta^{c\theta}) = (-\eta)^{c\theta} = \eta^{-c\theta};$$

or, the conjugate of the versor of any quaternion is equal to versor of the conjugate (N). Hence,

$$\mathrm{KU}q = \mathrm{UK}q = \mathrm{U}\frac{1}{q} = \frac{1}{\mathrm{U}q},\ 46^\circ\ (4)\quad \ldots\ (1)$$

Since $\mathrm{TK}q = \mathrm{T}q$, and $\mathrm{UK}q = 1 : \mathrm{U}q$, we have

$$q = \mathrm{T}q\,.\,\mathrm{U}q\,;\ \mathrm{K}q = \mathrm{T}q : \mathrm{U}q\,;\ \ldots\ (2)$$

whence, by multiplication and division,

$$q\mathrm{K}q = \mathrm{T}^2 q\,;\ q : \mathrm{K}q = \mathrm{U}^2 q. \quad \ldots\ (3)$$

(*c*). $\mathrm{K}\dfrac{\beta}{a} = \dfrac{\mathrm{T}\beta}{\mathrm{T}a}\cdot\dfrac{\mathrm{U}a}{\mathrm{U}\beta} = \dfrac{-\mathrm{U}a}{\mathrm{T}a}\cdot\dfrac{\mathrm{T}\beta}{-\mathrm{U}\beta} = \dfrac{-\mathrm{U}a}{\mathrm{T}a} : \dfrac{-\mathrm{U}\beta}{\mathrm{T}\beta} = \dfrac{a^{-1}}{\beta^{-1}}\ \ldots\ (4)$

Hence,

$$\mathrm{K}a\beta = \beta a = \frac{\beta}{a^{-1}} = \mathrm{K}\frac{a}{\beta^{-1}} \quad \ldots\ (5)$$

(*d*). The conjugates of opposite quaternions are themselves opposite ; or,

$$\mathrm{K}(-q) = -\mathrm{K}q\,;$$

an equation which is a particular case of a more general formula,

$$\mathrm{K}xq = x\mathrm{K}q,\ \ldots\ (6)$$

where x is any scalar.

This may be proved by supposing that the vectors $\overline{\mathrm{OB}}$, $\overline{\mathrm{OB}'}$, fig. 21, are multiplied by any common scalar ; or, that both are cut by any parallel to the line BB$'$.

(*e*). The conjugates of reciprocals are reciprocal ; or,

$$\mathrm{K}\frac{1}{q} = \frac{1}{\mathrm{K}q}.$$

For, suppose the two triangles AOB, AOB$'$, fig. 21, to revolve inwards round O in the plane B$'$OB until the points B, B$'$, coincide in D, a point in the line OA produced. Then FOD and EOD represent respectively the two triangles after the revolution. From B and B$'$ draw lines parallel to ED and FD, cutting OD produced in C ; circumscribe a circle to the triangle ABC ; and with O as centre and OB as radius describe the circle BDB'.

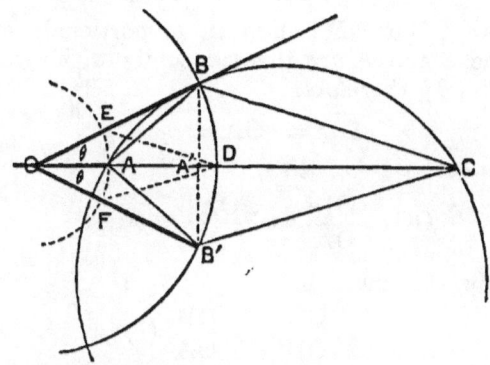

FIG. 21.

Let $q = \dfrac{OB}{OA}$. Then

$$K\dfrac{1}{q} = K\dfrac{OA}{OB} = K\dfrac{OF}{OD} = K\dfrac{OB'}{OC} = \dfrac{OB}{OC} \;(48°\;(a)) = \dfrac{OE}{OD}$$

$$= \dfrac{OA}{OB'} = 1 : \dfrac{OB'}{OA} = \dfrac{1}{Kq} \quad . \quad . \quad . \quad . \quad (7)$$

(*f*). If we are given such an equation as

$$\dfrac{\gamma}{a} = K\dfrac{\beta}{a}; \text{ or, } \dfrac{a}{\gamma} = K\dfrac{a}{\beta},$$

we can infer—first, that a, β, γ are coinitial and coplanar; secondly, that $T\gamma = T\beta$; and thirdly, that a bisects the angle between β and γ, or, that a (produced either way if necessary) bisects the join of the terms of β and γ at right angles ; or, again, since the angles of incidence and reflexion of a ray of light are equal, that the ray γ is the reflexion of the ray $-\beta$ (O being supposed to be a point on a plane mirror whose surface is perpendicular to a).

(*g*). Since $\angle$ OBA $=$ $\angle$ OB'A $=$ $\angle$ ODE $=$ $\angle$ OCB, fig. 21, it follows—first, that AB and BC are antiparallel, or that the triangles AOB and COB are *inversely* similar (the triangles DOE and COB are *directly* similar) ; and, secondly, that OB is a tangent to the circle ABC at the point B. Hence, the circles BDB' and ABC are orthogonal, because a tangent to BDB' at B would be perpendicular to OB, which is a tangent to ABC.

(*h*). Again,
$$OA : OB :: OB : OC.$$

Therefore, OB or OD is a mean proportional between OC and OA, and C and A are inverse points with respect to the circle BDB'. If, therefore,
$$\overline{OD} = v\overline{OA} = va,$$
where v is a scalar > 0; then,
$$OC = \frac{OD^2}{OA} = \frac{v^2 OA^2}{OA} = v^2 OA.$$

Consequently, the equation,
$$\frac{OC}{OB} = K\frac{OB}{OA}, \quad (7)$$
may be written,
$$\frac{v^2 a}{\beta} = K\frac{\beta}{a}; \quad \ldots \ldots \quad (8)$$

an equation which expresses that AB and BC are antiparallel, or that the triangles AOB and COB are inversely similar, but expresses nothing more. Now, in order that this relation should hold good, it is only necessary either that (1) $T . \overline{OB}$ should be a geometric mean between $T . \overline{OA}$ and $T . \overline{OC}$; or, that (2) $T . \overline{OB} = T . \overline{OD}$. If, then, O, A, D, C be fixed points, while B is a variable point and $\overline{OB} = \overline{OP} = \rho$, it is evident that the locus of P is the surface of a sphere with centre O and radius $T . OD = vTa$. Equation (8) then becomes
$$\frac{v^2 a}{\rho} = K\frac{\rho}{a}; \text{ or, } \frac{\rho}{a}K\frac{\rho}{a} = v^2. \quad \ldots \ldots \quad (9)$$

(*i*). If, then, we meet with an equation of this form, we can infer that the locus of P is the surface of a sphere with centre O and radius vTa. Further, if we take a point C such that $OC = v^2 a$, the sphere will be a common orthogonal to all the circles APC that pass through the fixed points A and C; because every radius of the sphere is a tangent, at the variable point P, to the circle APC, AP and PC being antiparallel.

(*j*). Since
$$qKq = T^2 q, \; v^2 = T^2 \frac{\rho}{a};$$

and the first equation of (9) becomes
$$T^2\frac{\rho}{a} \cdot \frac{a}{\rho} = K\frac{\rho}{a},$$

$$T^2\frac{\rho}{a} \cdot T\frac{a}{\rho} U\frac{a}{\rho} = TK\frac{\rho}{a} UK\frac{\rho}{a} = T\frac{\rho}{a} KU\frac{\rho}{a}, \ (b)\ (1);$$

or,
$$U\frac{a}{\rho} = KU\frac{\rho}{a}.$$

(*k*). Since, fig. 21,
$$\frac{BC}{AB} = \frac{BC}{ED} = \frac{OB}{OA} = \frac{OD}{OA} = \frac{v}{1},$$

we have
$$OB = OP = vOA \ ; \ BC = vAB. \quad \ldots \quad (10)$$

From the first equation we have at once,
$$T\rho = vTa \quad \ldots \ldots \ldots (11)$$

From the second,
$$T(\rho - v^2 a) = vT(\rho - a). \quad \ldots \ldots (12)$$

Since,
$\overline{AB} = \rho - a$, and $T(\overline{BC}) = T(-\overline{BC}) = T(\overline{CB}) = T(\overline{OB} - \overline{OC})$.

(*l*). Article (*h*) contains the solution of the problem of Apollonius of Perga : given any two points, C and A, in a plane, and a ratio of inequality, $1 : v$; to construct a circle BDB' in the plane such that the lengths of the two straight lines AB and CB, or AP and CP, which are inflected from the two given points to any common point, B or P, of its circumference, shall be to each other in the given ratio.

Cut AC externally at O in the duplicate of the given ratio of sides, so as to have $OC = v^2 OA$. Take OD, a geometric mean, to OA, OC ; and, with O as centre and OD as radius, describe a circle. This is the locus of all points for which
$$CP = vAP.$$

Paragraphs (*c*) to (*l*) are chiefly from Sir W. R. Hamilton's 'Elements.'

CHAPTER VI

THE POWERS OF QUATERNIONS

50°. Let $q = \rho^t$, $\angle q = \theta$, and $\mathrm{UV}q = \epsilon$. Then, by 33° (2), we have $\mathrm{U}^t\rho = \epsilon^t$, and

$$q^n = (\rho^t)^n = (\mathrm{T}^t\rho \cdot \mathrm{U}^t\rho)^n = (\mathrm{T}q \cdot \epsilon^t)^n = \mathrm{T}^nq \cdot \epsilon^{nt} = \mathrm{T}^nq \cdot \epsilon^{n\theta},$$
$$q^n = \mathrm{T}^nq\,(\cos n\theta + \epsilon \sin n\theta) \quad \ldots \ldots \ldots \quad (1)$$

From this equation we have at once,

$$\left.\begin{array}{l}\mathrm{T}q^n = \mathrm{T}^nq\,;\ \mathrm{U}q^n = \epsilon^{n\theta} = (\epsilon^{c\theta})^n = \mathrm{U}^nq\,;\ \angle q^n = n\angle q\,;\\ \mathrm{S}q^n = \mathrm{T}^nq \cdot \cos n\theta\,;\ \mathrm{V}q^n = \mathrm{T}^nq \cdot \sin n\theta \cdot \epsilon.\end{array}\right\} \cdot (2)$$

51°. If $n = 2$,

$$q^2 = \mathrm{T}^2q\,(\cos 2\theta + \epsilon \sin 2\theta) \quad \ldots \ldots \quad (3)$$

As this is the only power of a quaternion with which we will have to do in the following pages, it is desirable to inquire particularly into its nature.

The first question that arises is, has q^2 two square roots like an ordinary algebraic quantity?

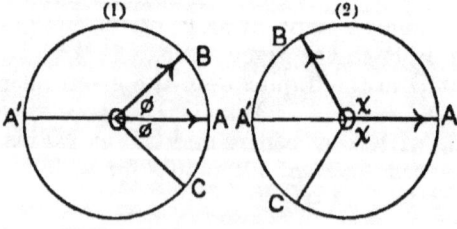

Fig. 22.

Let $\overline{\mathrm{OA}}$, $\overline{\mathrm{OB}}$, fig. 22 (1) and (2), be the unit-vectors of any two vectors α and β, inclined to each other at an acute angle ϕ in (1), and at an obtuse angle χ in (2). Draw OC making $\angle \mathrm{COA} = \phi$ in (1), and $= \chi$ in (2); and produce AO to meet the circle in A'. Then, if

$$\mathrm{U}q = \frac{\mathrm{OA}}{\mathrm{OB}},\ \mathrm{U}(-q) = \frac{-\mathrm{OA}}{\mathrm{OB}} = \frac{\mathrm{OA}'}{\mathrm{OB}}.$$

Since $q^2 = \mathrm{T}^2q \cdot \mathrm{U}^2q$, if q^2 has two square roots, either T^2q or U^2q must have two square roots. But as $\mathrm{T}q$ is always

THE POWERS OF QUATERNIONS

positive, T^2q can have only one square root, namely $+ Tq$. If, therefore, q^2 has two square roots, U^2q must have two square roots. What is U^2q?

Since

$$Uq = \frac{OC}{OA} = \frac{OA}{OB},$$

$$U^2q = \frac{OC}{OA} \cdot \frac{OA}{OB} = \frac{OC}{OB}.$$

Now, $\dfrac{OC}{OB}$ has two geometric square roots. For, first,

$$\frac{OC}{OB} = \frac{OC}{OA} \cdot \frac{OA}{OB} = \frac{OA}{OB} \cdot \frac{OA}{OB} = \left(\frac{OA}{OB}\right)^2.$$

Secondly,

$$\frac{OC}{OB} = \frac{OC}{OA'} \cdot \frac{OA'}{OB} = \frac{OA'}{OB} \cdot \frac{OA'}{OB} = \left(\frac{OA'}{OB}\right)^2 = \left(-\frac{OA}{OB}\right)^2.$$

Therefore,

$$\sqrt{U^2q} = \sqrt{\frac{OC}{OB}} = \pm \frac{OA}{OB} = \pm Uq.$$

Therefore, q^2 has two square roots; or,

$$\sqrt{q^2} = \pm q = Tq \cdot Uq \text{ or } Tq(-Uq),$$

whatever be the form of q.

Were the angle of a quaternion unlimited in magnitude, either of these real and unequal square roots might be used at will in calculation. But as the angle is defined to lie between the limits o and π, we must discriminate between them, and select as *the* square root (or the principal square root) of the quaternion, q^2, that one of the two which enables us to confine the angle of q^2 within the prescribed limits. If $\angle q$ is acute, fig. 22 (1), $\angle(-q)\left(= \pi - \angle q, 47°\right)$ is obtuse; $-q$, therefore, cannot be regarded as the square root of q^2; for, were it so, $\angle q^2 \left(= 2 \angle(-q)\right)$ would be $> \pi$. In this case, consequently, $\sqrt{q^2} = +q$. For a similar reason, if $\angle q$ is obtuse, fig. 22 (2), $\sqrt{q^2} = -q$.

That one, therefore, of the two opposite quaternions, q and $-q$, whose angle is acute is *the* square root of q^2.

In symbols,

$$\left.\begin{array}{l} \angle q^2 = 2\angle q;\ \mathrm{UV}q^2 = \mathrm{UV}q;\ q^2 = \mathrm{T}^2 q \cdot \epsilon^{2c\phi};\ \text{if } \angle q = \phi < \dfrac{\pi}{2}. \\ \angle q^2 = 2(\pi - \angle q);\ \mathrm{UV}q^2 = -\mathrm{UV}q;\ q^2 = \mathrm{T}^2 q \cdot (-\epsilon)^{2c(\pi-\chi)}; \\ \text{if} \qquad\qquad \angle q = \chi > \dfrac{\pi}{2}. \\ \angle \sqrt{q^2} = \tfrac{1}{2}\angle q^2;\ \mathrm{UV}\sqrt{q^2} = \mathrm{UV}q^2. \end{array}\right\} \ldots (4)$$

If $\angle q$ is 0 or π, $\mathrm{UV}q$ is indeterminate.

If $\angle q = \dfrac{\pi}{2}$, $\mathrm{U}q^2 = \epsilon^{\pm 2}$, and $q^2 = \mathrm{T}^2 q \cdot \epsilon^{\pm 2} = -(\mathrm{T}^2 q)$, a scalar.

If $q^2 = -1$, we have $\dfrac{\overline{OC}}{\overline{OA}} \cdot \dfrac{\overline{OA}}{\overline{OB}} = \dfrac{\overline{OC}}{\overline{OB}} = -1$;

or, $\qquad\qquad\qquad \overline{OC} = -\overline{OB}.$

Therefore, $\mathrm{T} \cdot \overline{OC} = \mathrm{T} \cdot \overline{OB}$, and $\mathrm{U} \cdot \overline{OC} = -\mathrm{U} \cdot \overline{OB}$, whatever be the length of the radii of the circles, fig. 22.

Consequently, $\angle q^2 = \pi$; $\angle q = \tfrac{1}{2}\angle q^2 = \dfrac{\pi}{2}$, (4);

or, q is a right quaternion whose constituent vectors are of equal length.

By (3),

$$\mathrm{SU}q^2 = \cos 2\angle q = 2\cos^2 \angle q - 1 = 2\,\mathrm{SU}^2 q - 1, \ldots (5)$$

where $\mathrm{SU}^2 q$ represents $(\mathrm{SU}q)^2$.

$$\mathrm{S}q^2 = \mathrm{T}^2 q\,\mathrm{SU}q^2 = \mathrm{T}^2 q\,(2\,\mathrm{SU}^2 q - 1) = 2\,\mathrm{T}^2 q\,\mathrm{SU}^2 q - \mathrm{T}^2 q$$
$$= 2\,\mathrm{S}^2 q - \mathrm{T}^2 q \quad \ldots \ldots (6)$$

Again,

$$\mathrm{S}q^2 + \mathrm{V}q^2 = q^2 = (\mathrm{S}q + \mathrm{V}q)^2 = \mathrm{S}^2 q + 2\,\mathrm{S}q\mathrm{V}q + \mathrm{V}^2 q.$$

Therefore, equating the scalar and vector parts, 44°,

$$\left.\begin{array}{l} \mathrm{S}q^2 = \mathrm{S}^2 q + \mathrm{V}^2 q;\\ \mathrm{V}q^2 = 2\,\mathrm{S}q\mathrm{V}q. \end{array}\right\} \ldots \ldots (7)$$

$$\mathrm{T}q^2 = \mathrm{T}^2 q = q\mathrm{K}q = (\mathrm{S}q + \mathrm{V}q)(\mathrm{S}q - \mathrm{V}q) = \mathrm{S}^2 q - \mathrm{V}^2 q. \ldots (8)$$

Finally, if we meet with an equation of the form

$$\frac{\delta}{\beta} = \sqrt{\frac{\gamma}{\beta}},$$

we know that δ bisects the angle between β and γ.

This equation may be written,

$$\delta^2 = \gamma\beta, \ldots \ldots \ldots (9)$$

where δ is called the Mean Proportional between β and γ.

CHAPTER VII

ADDITION AND SUBTRACTION OF QUATERNIONS

52°. The sum or difference of any two quaternions is a quaternion. For $q \pm q' = (Sq \pm Sq') + (Vq \pm Vq') =$ the sum of a Scalar and Vector = a quaternion. Since this process can be carried on to any extent with the same result, we may conclude that the sum, or difference, of any number of quaternions is a quaternion.

In symbols, if $\Sigma q = (q_1 + q_2 + \ldots q_n)$,
and $\Delta q = (q_1 - q_2 - \ldots q_n)$;

$$\left. \begin{array}{l} \Sigma q = \text{a quaternion,} \\ \Delta q = \text{„} \quad\quad \text{„} \end{array} \right\} \quad \ldots \ldots \quad (1)$$

The commutative and associative laws of addition and subtraction apply to quaternions.

For the sum or difference of n quaternions is the sum or difference of n scalars and n vectors; and it has been already shown, Part I., 20°, that the subtraction and addition of vectors are associative and commutative operations. Therefore &c.

53°. Let the quaternion Q be the sum of n quaternions,

$$q_1 = Sq_1 + Vq_1,$$
$$q_2 = Sq_2 + Vq_2,$$
$$\ldots \ldots$$
$$q_n = Sq_n + Vq_n.$$

Then,
$Q = (Sq_1 + Sq_2 + \ldots Sq_n) + (Vq_1 + Vq_2 + \ldots Vq_n) = \Sigma Sq + \Sigma Vq;$
But
$Q = SQ + VQ = S(q_1 + q_2 + \ldots q_n) + V(q_1 + q_2 + \ldots q_n);$
„ „ $= S\Sigma q + V\Sigma q.$

78 ADDITION AND SUBTRACTION OF QUATERNIONS

Therefore, 44°,
$$(Sq_1 + Sq_2 + \ldots Sq_n) = S(q_1 + q_2 + \ldots q_n);$$
$$(Vq_1 + Vq_2 + \ldots Vq_n) = V(q_1 + q_2 + \ldots q_n);$$
or, $\quad\quad\quad \Sigma Sq = S\Sigma q\,;\ \Sigma Vq = V\Sigma q$ . . . . . (1)
Similarly, $\quad\quad \Delta Sq = S\Delta q\,;\ \Delta Vq = V\Delta q.$ . . . . (2)

In words, S and V are distributive symbols.

Taking the conjugates of the constituent quaternions above,
$$Kq_1 = Sq_1 - Vq_1,$$
$$Kq_2 = Sq_2 - Vq_2,$$
$$\ldots\ldots\ldots$$
$$\overline{Kq_n = Sq_n - Vq_n,}$$
we have
$$\Sigma Kq = \Sigma Sq - \Sigma Vq = S\Sigma q - V\Sigma q = SQ - VQ = KQ = K\Sigma q. \ . \ (3)$$
Similarly, $\quad\quad\quad \Delta Kq = K\Delta q$ . . . . (4)

Therefore, K is a distributive symbol.

Also, since
$$KSq = Sq = SKq, \ldots\ldots\ldots (5)$$
and $\quad\quad\quad KVq = -Vq = VKq, \ldots\ldots (6)$

it follows that K is commutative with S and V.

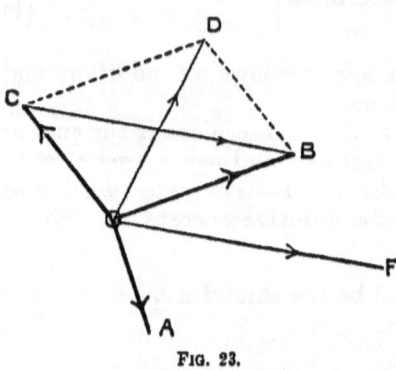

Fig. 23.

54°. Let any two quaternions, $q_1 = \dfrac{\zeta}{\mu}$, $q_2 = \dfrac{\eta}{\nu}$, be reduced to a common denominator, $\overline{OA}$, fig. 23, $\overline{OA}$ not lying in the plane OBC, but being drawn *towards us* from O. Let the reduced quaternions be $\dfrac{\overline{OB}}{\overline{OA}}$ and $\dfrac{\overline{OC}}{\overline{OA}}$ or $\dfrac{\beta}{\alpha}$ and $\dfrac{\gamma}{\alpha}$. Complete the parallelogram $OCDB$; draw the diagonals $\overline{CB}$ and $\overline{OD} = \delta$; and draw,
$$\overline{OF} = \overline{CB} = \overline{CO} + \overline{OB} = \beta - \gamma.$$

Then,
$$T(q_1 + q_2) = T\left(\frac{\beta}{\alpha} + \frac{\gamma}{\alpha}\right) = T\frac{\beta + \gamma}{\alpha} = T\frac{\delta}{\alpha} = \frac{T.OD}{T.OA},$$
$$Tq_1 + Tq_2 = T\frac{\beta}{\alpha} + T\frac{\gamma}{\alpha} = \frac{T\beta + T\gamma}{T\alpha} = \frac{T.OB + T.OC}{T.OA} = \frac{T.OB + T.BI}{T.OA}$$

ADDITION AND SUBTRACTION OF QUATERNIONS 79

Consequently,
$$Tq_1 + Tq_2 = T(q_1 + q_2), \text{ if, } T.\overline{OB} + T.\overline{BD} = T.\overline{OD}.$$
But $\quad T.\overline{OB} + T.\overline{BD} > T.\overline{OD}$, Euclid I., 20.
Therefore, $\qquad Tq_1 + Tq_2 > T(q_1 + q_2)$.

Let $q_1 + q_2 = w$, and let q_3 be any third quaternion. Then, similarly,
$$Tw + Tq_3 > T(w + q_3) = T(q_1 + q_2 + q_3).$$
But $\quad Tq_1 + Tq_2 > Tw$.
Therefore, *a fortiori*,
$$Tq_1 + Tq_2 + Tq_3 > T(q_1 + q_2 + q_3).$$

As this process may be carried on to any extent with similar results, we may infer that, generally,
$$T\Sigma q \neq \Sigma Tq \quad \ldots \ldots \ldots \quad (1)$$
It may be similarly proved that
$$T\Delta q \neq \Delta Tq \quad \ldots \ldots \ldots \quad (2)$$

If $\angle BOC = 0$, that is, if $U\gamma = U\beta$; then $T\left(\dfrac{\gamma}{a} + \dfrac{\beta}{a}\right) = T\dfrac{\gamma}{a} + T\dfrac{\beta}{a}$.

If $\angle BOC = \pi$,, ,, $U\gamma = -U\beta$; ,, $T\left(\dfrac{\gamma}{a} + \dfrac{\beta}{a}\right) = T\dfrac{\gamma}{a} \sim T\dfrac{\beta}{a}$.

In general, if the quaternions, $q_1, q_2 \ldots q_n$, bear scalar and positive ratios to each other, *i.e.*, if they are coplanar, with versors similarly directed ; then, $T\Sigma q = \Sigma Tq$.

55°. In fig. 23, let the angles
$AOB = \phi$, $AOC = \chi$, $AOD = \theta$, $BOD = \sigma_1$, $DOC = \sigma_2$, $BOC = \sigma$.
Then, for the three trihedral angles,
$$O - BAD, \; O - CDA, \; O - CBA,$$
$$\phi + \sigma_1 > \theta,$$
$$\chi + \sigma_2 > \theta,$$
or, $\qquad (\phi + \chi) + \sigma > 2\theta\,;$
and $\qquad \phi + \chi >.\sigma.$
Therefore, $\quad 2(\phi + \chi) + \sigma > 2\theta + \sigma,$
and $\qquad \phi + \chi > \theta\,;$
or, $\qquad \angle q_1 + \angle q_2 > \angle(q_1 + q_2).$

If q_3 be any other quaternion, it may be proved in a similar way that
$$\angle (q_1 + q_2) + \angle q_3 > \angle (q_1 + q_2 + q_3).$$
But $\angle q_1 + \angle q_2 > \angle (q_1 + q_2)$;
therefore, *a fortiori,*
$$\angle q_1 + \angle q_2 + \angle q_3 > \angle (q_1 + q_2 + q_3).$$

As this process may be carried on to any extent with similar results, we may infer that
$$\Sigma \angle q \neq \angle \Sigma q \quad \ldots \ldots \quad (1)$$
It may be similarly proved that
$$\Delta \angle q \neq \angle \Delta q \quad \ldots \ldots \quad (2)$$

56°. Let $\angle \text{BOC} = \theta$, fig. 23. Then,
$$\frac{\text{OD}}{\text{OA}} = \frac{\text{OB}}{\text{OA}} + \frac{\text{OC}}{\text{OA}} = q + q',$$
and $\quad T(q + q') U(q + q') = TqUq + Tq'Uq'$.

If, therefore, $U(q + q') = Uq + Uq'$, we must have
$$T(q + q') = Tq = Tq';$$
or, $\quad \text{OD} = \text{OB} = \text{OC}$.

Let $\text{OB} = \text{OC}$, and we have
$$\text{OD}^2 = 2\text{OB}^2 (1 + \cos \theta),$$
and $\quad \text{OD} = 2\text{OB} \cdot \cos \dfrac{\theta}{2}$.

In order, therefore, that $\text{OD} = \text{OB}$, we must have
$$\cos \frac{\theta}{2} = \tfrac{1}{2}; \text{ or, } \theta = 120°.$$

Evidently, then,
$$U(q + q') = Uq + Uq',$$
only when $Tq = Tq'$, and $\angle \theta = \text{BOC} = \dfrac{2\pi}{3}$, *i.e.*, in a special case. In general, therefore,
$$U(q + q') \neq Uq + Uq'.$$
More generally still,
$$U\Sigma q \neq \Sigma Uq \quad \ldots \ldots \quad (1)$$
Similarly,
$$\Delta Uq \neq U\Delta q. \quad \ldots \ldots \quad (2)$$

The result of 53° to 56° is, that the symbols S, V, and K are, while T, $\angle$, and U are not, distributive in the addition and subtraction of quaternions.

CHAPTER VIII

MULTIPLICATION AND DIVISION OF TWO QUATERNIONS

SECTION 1

Diplanar Quaternions

57°. Before proceeding further it is necessary to explain the meaning of certain forms of expression that will be met with in the present and succeeding chapters. Sq_1q_2 means the scalar of the product q_1q_2. Similarly, Kq_1q_2 means the conjugate of the product q_1q_2. It does not mean the conjugate of q_1 multiplied into q_2, which will be written $Kq_1 \cdot q_2$, or, $Kq_1(q_2)$, or $(Kq_1)q_2$. And so on for the other symbols.

Points and brackets should *never* be omitted if their omission is likely to lead to any misapprehension.

The product of any two quaternions is a quaternion.
For, let the quaternions be thrown into the form,

$$q_1 = \frac{\alpha}{\beta},\ q_2 = \frac{\beta}{\gamma}.$$

Then, $\qquad q_1q_2 = \frac{\alpha}{\beta} \cdot \frac{\beta}{\gamma} = \frac{\alpha}{\gamma} =$ a quaternion $\quad . \quad . \quad (1)$

The quotient of any two quaternions is a quaternion.
For, let the two quaternions be reduced to the form,

$$q_1 = \frac{\sigma}{\lambda},\ q_2 = \frac{\tau}{\lambda}.$$

Then, $\quad \dfrac{q_1}{q_2} = \dfrac{\sigma}{\lambda} : \dfrac{\tau}{\lambda} = \dfrac{\sigma}{\lambda} \cdot \dfrac{\lambda}{\tau} = \dfrac{\sigma}{\tau} =$ a quaternion $\ . \ . \ (2)$

58°. The tensor of the quotient (or product) of any two quaternions is equal to the quotient (or product) of the tensors of the two quaternions.

82 MULTIPLICATION AND DIVISION OF QUATERNIONS

For, let the two quaternions, reduced to a common denominator, be

$$q_1 = \frac{\gamma}{\alpha},\ q_2 = \frac{\beta}{\alpha}.$$

Then,

$$\mathrm{T}\frac{q_1}{q_2} = \mathrm{T}\frac{\gamma}{\beta} = \frac{\mathrm{T}\gamma}{\mathrm{T}\beta} = \frac{\mathrm{T}\gamma}{\mathrm{T}\alpha}\cdot\frac{\mathrm{T}\alpha}{\mathrm{T}\beta} = \frac{\mathrm{T}\gamma}{\mathrm{T}\alpha} : \frac{\mathrm{T}\beta}{\mathrm{T}\alpha} = \frac{\mathrm{T}q_1}{\mathrm{T}q_2}. \quad (1)$$

Again, if the two quaternions be reduced to the forms

$$q_1 = \frac{\gamma}{\alpha},\ q_2 = \frac{\alpha}{\delta}.$$

Then,

$$\mathrm{T}q_1 q_2 = \mathrm{T}\left(\frac{\gamma}{\alpha}\cdot\frac{\alpha}{\delta}\right) = \mathrm{T}\frac{\gamma}{\delta} = \frac{\mathrm{T}\gamma}{\mathrm{T}\delta} = \frac{\mathrm{T}\gamma}{\mathrm{T}\alpha}\cdot\frac{\mathrm{T}\alpha}{\mathrm{T}\delta} = \mathrm{T}q_1 \mathrm{T}q_2 = \mathrm{T}q_2 \mathrm{T}q_1 .. (2)$$

Equation (2) embodies Euler's theorem, that the sum of four squares may be resolved into two factors, each of which is the sum of four squares.

For the tensors of the quaternions q_1, q_2, may, 39° (5), be thrown into the form,

$$\sqrt{w_1^2 + x_1^2 + y_1^2 + z_1^2}$$

and

$$\sqrt{w_2^2 + x_2^2 + y_2^2 + z_2^2}$$

respectively; and the product, $q_1 q_2$, is some quaternion, say.

$$W + Xi + Yj + Zk,$$

whose tensor is $\sqrt{W^2 + X^2 + Y^2 + Z^2}$.

Hence, by squaring the equation,

$$\mathrm{T}q_1 q_2 = \mathrm{T}q_1 \cdot \mathrm{T}q_2,$$

we have at once

$$(W^2 + X^2 + Y^2 + Z^2) = (w_1^2 + x_1^2 + y_1^2 + z_1^2)(w_2^2 + x_2^2 + y_2^2 + z_2^2).$$

59°. The versor of the product (or quotient) of any two quaternions is equal to the product (or quotient) of the versors of the two quaternions.

For, let $\quad q = q_1 q_2.$

Then $\quad \mathrm{T}q\mathrm{U}q = \mathrm{T}q_1 \mathrm{T}q_2 \mathrm{U}q_1 \mathrm{U}q_2.$

But $\quad \mathrm{T}q = \mathrm{T}q_1 q_2 = \mathrm{T}q_1 \mathrm{T}q_2,$

and $\quad \mathrm{U}q = \mathrm{U}q_1 q_2;$

therefore, $\quad \mathrm{T}q_1 \mathrm{T}q_2 \mathrm{U}q_1 q_2 = \mathrm{T}q_1 \mathrm{T}q_2 \mathrm{U}q_1 \mathrm{U}q_2;$

or, $\quad \mathrm{U}q_1 q_2 = \mathrm{U}q_1 \mathrm{U}q_2.$

Similarly, $\quad \mathrm{U}\dfrac{q_1}{q_2} = \dfrac{\mathrm{U}q_1}{\mathrm{U}q_2}.\quad\Bigg\}\quad \cdots \cdots (1)$

MULTIPLICATION AND DIVISION OF QUATERNIONS. 83

60°. Let $q\,(= Sq + Vq)$ and $r\,(= Sr + Vr)$ be any two quaternions.

Then, $\quad qr = SqSr + SrVq + SqVr + VqVr,$
$\qquad\qquad rq = SrSq + SrVq + SqVr + VrVq\,;$

or, resolving the quaternions $VqVr$ and $VrVq$,

$qr = (SqSr + S\,.\,VqVr) + (SrVq + SqVr + V\,.\,VqVr)\,..\,(1)$
$rq = (SrSq + S\,.\,VrVq) + (SrVq + SqVr + V\,.\,VrVq)\,..\,(2)$

Since the right hand member of both of these two equations is the sum of a scalar and a vector, we have a fresh proof that the product of any two quaternions is a quaternion.

(a). From (1) and (2) we have

$$Sqr = SqSr + S\,.\,VqVr,$$
$$Srq = SrSq + S\,.\,VrVq.$$

Now, obviously,
$$SrSq = SqSr\,;$$
and, 22° (1), $\quad S\,.\,VrVq = S\,.\,VqVr\,;$
therefore, $\qquad Srq = Sqr \quad \ldots\ldots\ldots\,(3)$
$\qquad\qquad Sqr \neq SqSr$
unless $\qquad S\,.\,VqVr = 0,$

i.e. unless the planes of the two quaternions are at right angles.

(b). From (1) and (2) we also have

$$Vqr = SrVq + SqVr + V\,.\,VqVr,$$
$$Vrq = SrVq + SqVr + V\,.\,VrVq.$$

But, 22° (2), $\qquad V\,.\,VrVq = -\,V\,.\,VqVr.$

Therefore,
$$\left.\begin{array}{l}Vqr = SrVq + SqVr + V\,.\,VqVr,\\ Vrq = SrVq + SqVr - V\,.\,VqVr.\end{array}\right\} \quad \ldots\,(4)$$

Therefore, $\qquad Vqr \neq Vrq, \ldots\ldots\ldots\,(5)$
unless, $\qquad V\,.\,VqVr = 0,$

i.e. unless the quaternions are coplanar.

Hence, in general,
$$qr \neq rq\,.\,\ldots\ldots\ldots\,(6)$$

Adding and subtracting the equations of (4),
$$\left.\begin{array}{l}Vqr + Vrq = 2\,(SrVq + SqVr)\\ Vqr - Vrq = 2\,V\,.\,VqVr\end{array}\right\} \quad \ldots\,(7)$$

G 2

61°. (a).
$$Sqr = Tqr \cdot SUqr,$$
$$Srq = Trq \cdot SUrq.$$
But $Sqr = Srq$; $Tqr = Trq$;
therefore, $SUqr = SUrq,$
and
$$\angle qr = \angle rq \quad \cdots \cdots \quad (1)$$

(b). Further, since $Sqr \neq SqSr$;
$$Tqr \cdot SUqr \neq TqTrSUqSUr,$$
and
$$SUqr \neq SUqSUr \quad \cdots \cdots \quad (2)$$

62°. (a). From (1) of 60°,
$$Kqr = (SqSr + S \cdot VqVr) - (SrVq + SqVr + V \cdot VqVr)$$
$$\text{„} \quad = SqSr - SrVq - SqVr + (S \cdot VrVq + V \cdot VrVq)$$
$$\text{„} \quad = SqSr - SrVq - SqVr + VrVq$$
$$\text{„} \quad = (Sr - Vr)(Sq - Vq)$$
$$\text{„} \quad = KrKq \quad \cdots \cdots \quad (1)$$

(b). Let $qr = s$. Then, 48° (b), (7),
$$s + Ks = 2 Ss;$$
$$qr + Kqr = 2 Sqr = 2 (SqSr + S \cdot VqVr) \ldots (2)$$

(c). $S \cdot qKr = S \cdot (Sq + Vq)(Sr - Vr) = SqSr - S \cdot VqVr$;
$$S(Kq \cdot r) = S \cdot (Sq - Vq)(Sr + Vr) = SqSr - S \cdot VqVr;$$
therefore, $S \cdot qKr = S(Kq \cdot r) \quad \cdots \cdots \quad (3)$

63°. (a). Since $qr \neq rq$, 60° (6), it follows that the multiplication of diplanar quaternions does not obey the commutative law.

(b). The distributive law applies to the multiplication of quaternions. For, if we take four quaternions, p, q, r, s, in the quadrinomial form, 35°, it will be found by actual multiplication that
$$(p+q)(r+s) = pr+qr+ps+qs = pr+ps+qr+qs = \&c.$$
The distributive law, therefore, applies to four quaternions.

(c). If we actually multiply the product pq into r, the result will be found to be equal to the result of multiplying p into the product qr. The associative law, therefore, applies to three quaternions.

It may be similarly shown that the multiplication of any number of quaternions is distributive and associative.

Section 2
Coplanar Quaternions

64°. The multiplication of diplanar quaternions is not commutative: the multiplication of coplanar quaternions is commutative.

For, if two quaternions, q and r, are coplanar, Vq and Vr are parallel; and, consequently, $V \cdot VqVr = o = V \cdot VrVq$, 23°. Therefore the two equations of 60° (4) are equal, and
$$qr = rq.$$

65°. Hence, any quaternion, its reciprocal, its opposite, its conjugate, and any power of the quaternion, all of which are coplanar, are commutative; or,

$$qKq = Kq \cdot q \,;\, q^{-1}(-q) = -q \cdot q^{-1} \,;\, Kq \cdot q^n = q^n Kq, \text{ &c., &c.}$$

Section 3
Right Quaternions

66°. Let v_1, v_2 be any two right quaternions, with axes ϵ and η respectively. Then,
$$Sv_1 = o \,;\, Vv_1 = v_1 \,;\, Uv_1 = A x \cdot v_1 = \epsilon \,;$$
$$Kv_1 = KVv_1 = -Vv_1 = -v_1 \,;$$
with corresponding values for v_2.

Consequently, equations (1) and (2) of 60° become,
$$\left. \begin{array}{l} v_1 v_2 = S \cdot Vv_1 Vv_2 + V \cdot Vv_1 Vv_2 = Sv_1 v_2 + Vv_1 v_2 \,; \\ v_2 v_1 = S \cdot Vv_1 Vv_2 + V \cdot Vv_2 Vv_1 = Sv_1 v_2 - Vv_1 v_2. \end{array} \right\} \quad \ldots \quad (1)$$

Adding and subtracting,
$$\left. \begin{array}{l} Sv_1 v_2 = \tfrac{1}{2}(v_1 v_2 + v_2 v_1), \\ Vv_1 v_2 = \tfrac{1}{2}(v_1 v_2 - v_2 v_1). \end{array} \right\} \quad \ldots \ldots \quad (2)$$

Again, 62° (a),
$$Kv_1 v_2 = Kv_2 Kv_1 = (-v_2)(-v_1) = v_2 v_1 \quad \ldots \quad (3)$$

67°. Suppose the plane of v_1 to be at right angles to the plane of v_2, and the direction of rotation to be such that
$$v_1 = Tv_1 \cdot i \,;\, v_2 = Tv_2 \cdot j.$$
Then, $\qquad v_1 v_2 = Tv_1 Tv_2 \cdot ij = Tv_1 Tv_2 \cdot k, \quad \ldots \quad (1)$
$\qquad\qquad v_2 v_1 = Tv_2 Tv_1 \cdot ji = -Tv_1 Tv_2 \cdot k \quad \ldots \quad (2)$
Therefore, $\qquad v_2 v_1 = -v_1 v_2 \,; \quad \ldots \ldots \ldots \quad (3)$
and $\qquad\qquad \angle v_2 v_1 = \angle v_1 v_2 = \dfrac{\pi}{2}$, 25°, and (1) and (2).

Further, the versors of v_1v_2 and v_2v_1 (k and $-k$) are perpendicular to the versors of both v_1 and v_2 (i and j); or, the plane of v_1v_2 (and consequently the plane of its opposite, v_2v_1, or $-v_1v_2$) is perpendicular to the plane of v_1 and to the plane of v_2.

Hence, the product of any two right quaternions in rectangular planes is a third right quaternion (v_1v_2) in a plane rectangular to both, which is changed to its own opposite ($-v_1v_2$) by reversing the order of the factors (Hamilton). In symbols,

$$Vv_1v_2 = Vv_1Vv_2.$$

Section 4
On Circular Vector-Arcs

68°. Let O be the centre of a sphere of unit-radius. Then any arc AB of any great circle of the sphere may be regarded as the representative of the versor $\dfrac{OB}{OA}$. For the plane of the versor is the plane of the arc; the angle of the versor is measured by the length of the arc; and the direction of rotation is indicated by the direction in which the arc AB is drawn—from A to B, fig. 24.

Definition.—Two vector-arcs are equal, and only equal, when the origin and term of the first can be brought to coincide simultaneously with the origin and term of the second, by sliding the first backwards or forwards on its own great circle.

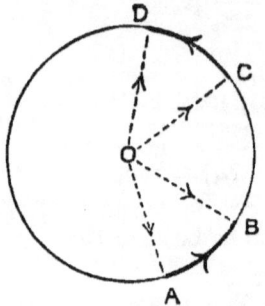

Fig. 24.

Thus, if on sliding (either way) the arc AB round the great circle of a unit-sphere, shown in fig. 24, the point B coincides with D when A coincides with C; then,

$$\widehat{AB} = \widehat{CD}.$$

Two consequences follow from this definition. First, no two vector-arcs of the same great circle are equal, unless the direction of both, as seen from either pole of the common great circle, is towards the same hand. Secondly, whatever their length, no two vector-arcs of different great circles can be equal, except in one particular case. This case occurs when both the arcs are great semicircles. All great semicircles are equal vector-arcs, since they all represent versors of the form $\frac{OA}{-OA} = -1$, and the plane of -1 is indeterminate.

69°. Let any two arcs, $C'C$ and AA', of different great circles bisect each other in B, fig. 25. Join A and C, C' and A', by arcs of great circles, and let the versors of any two quaternions, reduced to the form

$$q = \frac{\beta}{a}, \quad q' = \frac{\gamma}{\beta}, \text{ be}$$

$$Uq = \frac{OB}{OA} = \widehat{AB}; \quad Uq' = \frac{OC}{OB} = \widehat{BC}.$$

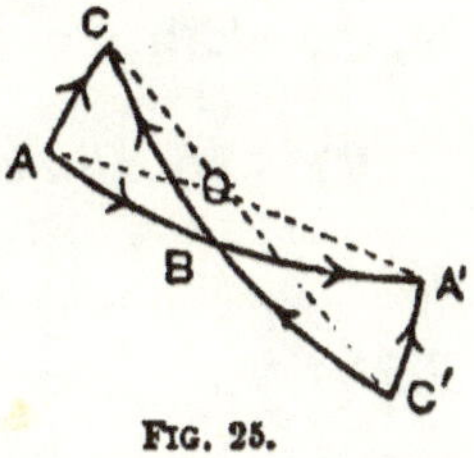

Fig. 25.

Then,

$$Uq'Uq = \frac{OC}{OB} \cdot \frac{OB}{OA} = \frac{OC}{OA} = \widehat{AC} = \widehat{BC} + \widehat{AB} \quad .. \quad (1)$$

where $\widehat{BC}$ is said to be added to $\widehat{AB}$.

Similarly,

$$UqUq' = \frac{OB}{OA} \cdot \frac{OC}{OB} = \frac{OA'}{OB} \cdot \frac{OB}{OC'} = \frac{OA'}{OC'} = \widehat{C'A'} = \widehat{BA'} + \widehat{C'B} .. (2)$$

The multiplication of versors is thus reduced to the addition of circular vector-arcs.

70°. Unlike the addition of rectilinear vectors, and of quaternions, the addition of diplanar vector-arcs is not commutative;

$$\widehat{BC} + \widehat{AB} \neq \widehat{AB} + \widehat{BC}.$$

For $\widehat{BC} + \widehat{AB} = \widehat{AC}$; and $\widehat{AB} + \widehat{BC} = \widehat{BA'} + \widehat{C'B} = \widehat{C'A'}$.

But $\widehat{AC} \neq \widehat{C'A'}$, although the two arcs are of equal length. For, if $C'C$ and AA' are both less than great semicircles (as shown in fig. 25), or if one of the two is a semicircle and the other less than a semicircle, in both cases $\widehat{AC}$ and $\widehat{C'A'}$ belong to two distinct great circles, and are therefore unequal by definition. Were $C'C$ and AA' both semicircles, $\widehat{AC}$ and

$\widehat{C'A'}$ would both belong to the same great circle, of which I would be a pole; but they would have contrary directions and would therefore be unequal by definition. In every case therefore, $\widehat{AC} \neq \widehat{C'A'}$, and, consequently,

$$\widehat{AB} + \widehat{BC} \neq \widehat{BC} + \widehat{AB};$$

or, the addition of diplanar vector-arcs is not commutative.

71°. We now see why (in general)

$$q'q \neq qq', 60° (6).$$

For $\widehat{C'A'} \neq \widehat{AC}$;

therefore, $UqUq' \neq Uq'Uq$; therefore, $qq' \neq q'q$.

We also see why $\angle qq' = \angle q'q$, 61° (1).

For $\angle Uqq' = \angle (UqUq') = \angle \dfrac{OA'}{OC'} = \angle C\,OA'$;

$\angle Uq'q = \angle (Uq'Uq) = \angle \dfrac{OC}{OA} = \angle AOC.$

But $\angle C'OA' = \angle AOC$, because $\widehat{C'A'}$ and $\widehat{AC}$ are equally long. Therefore, $\angle Uqq' = \angle Uq'q$; or,

$$\angle qq' = \angle q'q.$$

72°. The addition of coplanar vector-arcs, however, is commutative; for, evidently, fig. 25,

$$\widehat{BC} + \widehat{C'B} = \widehat{C'C} = \widehat{C'B} + \widehat{BC}. \quad . \quad . \quad (1)$$

These equations show that the multiplication of coplanar quaternions is commutative, since they are equivalent to

$$\dfrac{OC}{OB} \cdot \dfrac{OB}{OC'} = \dfrac{OB}{OC'} \cdot \dfrac{OC}{OB}; \quad . \quad . \quad . \quad . \quad (2)$$

or, $Uq' \cdot Uq = Uq \cdot Uq'.$

Hence, $qq' = q'q,$

a confirmation of 64°.

73°. For the same reason that $\widehat{AB}$ represents the versor $\frac{OB}{OA}$, $\widehat{BA}$ represents the versor $\frac{OA}{OB}$. But, if

$$\frac{OB}{OA} = Uq, \quad \frac{OA}{OB} = \frac{1}{Uq} = U\frac{1}{q} = UKq, \quad 48° \quad (3).$$

Hence, if a vector-arc represents the versor of any quaternion, the revector-arc (or the arc reversed) represents the versor of the reciprocal, or of the conjugate, of the quaternion. Consequently, fig. 25,

$$\widehat{CA} \text{ represents } U\frac{1}{q'q} = UKq'q ;$$

$$\widehat{BA} \quad „ \quad U\frac{1}{q} = UKq ;$$

$$\widehat{CB} \quad „ \quad U\frac{1}{q'} = UKq'.$$

But $\widehat{CA} = \widehat{BA} + \widehat{CB}$;

therefore, $$\frac{1}{q'q} = \frac{1}{q} \cdot \frac{1}{q'},$$

$$Kq'q = KqKq',$$

a confirmation of 62°.

74°. If $\widehat{C'C}$ and $\widehat{AA'}$, fig. 25, are both great semicircles, $\widehat{AB}$ ($= Uq$) and $\widehat{BC}$ ($= Uq'$) will be quadrants, *i.e.* q and q' will be right quaternions; and $\widehat{C'A'}$ and $\widehat{AC}$ will belong to the same great circle, but will have contrary directions. Therefore, since $\widehat{C'A'}$ and $\widehat{AC}$ are equally long, $\widehat{C'A'}$ is the revector of $\widehat{AC}$; and since $\widehat{AC} = Uq'q$,

$$Uqq' = \widehat{C'A'} = U\frac{1}{q'q} = UKq'q ;$$

or, $$qq' = Kq'q ; \quad \ldots \ldots \quad (1)$$

$$„ = \frac{1}{q'q}.$$

Equation (1) is simply equation (3) of 66°, in different symbols,
$$v_2 v_1 = K v_1 v_2.$$

If the semicircles $\overparen{CC'}$ and $\overparen{AA'}$ cut each other at right angles, $\overparen{C'A'}$ and $\overparen{AC}$ will be quadrants of the same great circle with contrary directions, *i.e.* qq' and $q'q$ will be right quaternions, and, consequently,

$$U qq' = UK q'q = KU q'q = - VU\, q'q,\ 66°\,;$$
or, $\qquad qq' = -q\,q,$

which is a confirmation of (3) of 67°, $v_2 v_1 = -v_1 v_2$.

75°. It remains to show how either of the two unequal quaternions, $q'q$ and qq', may be geometrically transformed into the other.

Let ABC be any spherical triangle, O being the centre of the unit-sphere; and let the versors of any two quaternions, reduced to the form $\dfrac{\beta}{a}$ and $\dfrac{\gamma}{\beta}$, be $Uq = \dfrac{OB}{OA}$, $Uq' = \dfrac{OC}{OB}$. Let P be the Positive Pole of $\overparen{AB}$, *i.e.* that one of its two poles round which rotation from A to B, or OA to OB, would appear to be right-handed to an observer standing upon the surface of the sphere at P. Let Q be the positive pole of $\overparen{BC}$, and S the positive pole of $\overparen{CA}$; S being, consequently, the negative pole of $\overparen{AC}$. Then, joining the points P, Q, and S by arcs of great circles, we have

$$\overline{OP}=\frac{OB}{OA}=Uq\,;\ \ \overline{OQ}=\frac{OC}{OB}=Uq'\,;\ \ \overline{OS}=\frac{OA}{OC}=UK q'q,\ 73°;\ \ldots (1)$$

and, from the known properties of the polar triangle,

$$\angle\, q = AOB = APB = \pi - QPS\,;\ \text{or},\ \angle\, QPS = \pi - \angle\, q,\ \ldots (2)$$
$$\angle\, q' = BOC = BQC = \pi - SQP\,;\ \text{or},\ \angle\, SQP = \pi - \angle\, q'.\ \ldots (3)$$

Further, since the angle of a quaternion is equal to the angle of its conjugate, or, $\angle\, \dfrac{OA}{OC} = \angle\, \dfrac{OC}{OA} = \angle\, q'q$,

$$\angle\, q'q = COA = CSA = \pi - PSQ\,;\ \text{or},\ \angle\, PSQ = \pi - \angle\, q'q\ \ldots (4)$$

Let us now pass from the triangle PQS to a third triangle, PQR, where R is the point upon the sphere diametrically opposite to S, and is consequently the positive pole of $\overparen{AC}$. Then, since the versors of conjugate quaternions are opposite unit-vectors, and since $\overline{OS} = UK q'q$, (1),

$$\overline{OR} = U q'q\ \ \ldots\ \ldots\ \ldots\ \ldots (5)$$

Calling the angles of the triangle PQR, P, Q, R, we have
$$\angle P = \pi - QPS = \angle q, (2); \angle Q = \pi - SQP = \angle q', (3); \\ \angle R = PSQ = \pi - \angle q'q, (4) \quad \Big\} \ldots (6)$$

In fig. 26 the arcs $C'C$ and AA' bisect each other in B, as in fig. 25, and the triangle PQR is derived from the original triangle ABC in the manner just described. Let R' be the positive pole of $C'A'$; join R' with P and Q by arcs of great circles; and draw OR'. Then,

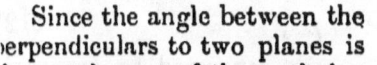

Fig. 26.

$$OR' = \frac{OA'}{OC'} = Uqq', 69° (2) \ldots (7)$$

Since the angle between the perpendiculars to two planes is the supplement of the angle between the planes,

$$\angle QOR = \pi - \angle C = \pi - \angle C' = \angle QOR',$$
$$\angle POR = \pi - \angle A = \pi - \angle A' = \angle POR'.$$

Therefore, $QR = QR'$, and $PR = PR'$ (in length); and from the equality of the triangles PQR, PQR', it follows that
$$\angle QPR = \angle QPR'.$$
But, (6), $\qquad\qquad = \angle P = \angle q;$
therefore, $\qquad \angle RPR' = 2\angle q \ \ldots \ldots \ldots$ (8)

Since $PR = PR'$, a small circle, described with P as its positive pole, which passes through R, will also pass through R'. Therefore, $\overline{OR}$ $(= Uq'q)$ may be transformed into OR' $(=Uqq')$ by the Conical Rotation of OR round OP through the angle $RPR' = 2\angle q$.

In symbols,
$$Uqq' = \frac{OB}{OA}\frac{OC}{OB} = \frac{OB}{OA}\frac{OC}{OA}\frac{OA}{OB} = Uq\,(Uq'q)\,Uq^{-1};$$
or, $\qquad\qquad q\,(q'q)\,q^{-1} = qq' \ \ldots \ldots \ldots$ (9)

It is evident that the symbol $q\,(\quad)\,q^{-1}$ is an operator which produces a positive conical rotation of the versor, or axis, of the operand quaternion (which is written within the parentheses) round the versor, or axis, of the operating quaternion, q, through an angle $= 2\angle q$, without altering the angle or tensor of the operand $q'q$ (since $Tqq' = Tq'q$, and

$\angle qq' = \angle q'q$). This rotation is positive, because it is right-handed as seen from P, the term of Uq. Were it negative, the operator would be written q^{-1} (   ) q. Thus,

$$\mathrm{U}q'q = \frac{\mathrm{OC}}{\mathrm{OB}}\frac{\mathrm{OB}}{\mathrm{OA}} = \frac{\mathrm{OA}}{\mathrm{OB}}\frac{\mathrm{OB}}{\mathrm{OA}}\frac{\mathrm{OC}}{\mathrm{OB}}\frac{\mathrm{OB}}{\mathrm{OA}} = \mathrm{U}q^{-1}\,(\mathrm{U}qq')\,\mathrm{U}q\,;$$

or, $\qquad\qquad q^{-1}\,(qq')\,q = q'q\,.\,\ldots\ldots$ (10)

Regarding vectors as right quaternions, it follows from the preceding argument that, if

$$q\beta q^{-1} = \beta'\,;\ \ldots\ldots\ (11)$$

then β' is the vector generated by the positive conical rotation of β round the axis of q through $2\angle q$. Evidently Tβ' = Tβ.

Finally, if

$$a\beta a^{-1} = \beta'\,;\ \ldots\ldots\ (12)$$

then β' or $\overline{\mathrm{OB}'}$, fig. 21, is the vector generated by the positive conical rotation of β round Ua through twice the angle of a considered as a right quaternion, that is, through π.

CHAPTER IX

FORMULÆ

76°. Let $a_1, a_2 \ldots a_n$ be any coinitial vectors.

$V\gamma\beta a = V(S\gamma\beta + V\gamma\beta)a = V \cdot aS\beta\gamma - V \cdot aV\gamma\beta = V \cdot aS\beta\gamma + V \cdot aV\beta\gamma$

,, $= V \cdot a(S\beta\gamma + V\beta\gamma) = Va\beta\gamma$.

By extending this process we obtain

$$V(a_1 a_2 \ldots a_n) = \mp V(a_n a_{n-1} \ldots a_1), \quad \ldots (1)$$

according as n is even or odd. For example,

$$Va\beta = -V\beta a.$$

$Sa\beta\gamma = S \cdot a(S\beta\gamma + V\beta\gamma) = S \cdot aV\beta\gamma = S \cdot V\beta\gamma(a)$
$ = S(S\beta\gamma + V\beta\gamma)a = S\beta\gamma a.$

By extending this process we obtain

$S(a_1 a_2 \ldots a_n) = S(a_2 a_3 \ldots a_n a_1) = S(a_3 a_4 \ldots a_n a_1 a_2) = \&c. \ldots (2)$

$Sa\beta\gamma = S\gamma a\beta = S\gamma(Sa\beta + Va\beta) = S \cdot \gamma Sa\beta + S\gamma Va\beta$;

therefore, $\qquad Sa\beta\gamma = S\gamma Va\beta.$

And $\qquad S\gamma\beta a = S\gamma V\beta a = -S\gamma Va\beta$;

therefore, $\qquad S\gamma\beta a = -Sa\beta\gamma.$

By extending this process we obtain

$$S(a_1 a_2 \ldots a_n) = \pm S(a_n a_{n-1} \ldots a_1), \quad \ldots (3)$$

according as n is even or odd. For example,

$$S\beta a = Sa\beta.$$

It is unnecessary to write $S \cdot \gamma Va\beta$ above, instead of $S\gamma Va\beta$; for, if the expression has a value different from zero, it cannot mean $S\gamma \cdot Va\beta$, because $S\gamma = 0$.

The product of any number of vectors in space is generally a quaternion; for $a\beta\gamma\delta = a\beta \cdot \gamma\delta = q_1 q_2 = q_3$. If the number of vectors be odd, one of them may be treated as the representative of a right quaternion.

The product of any even number of coplanar vectors is generally a quaternion whose axis is perpendicular to their plane.

The product of any odd number of coplanar vectors is always a vector in the same plane.

Since cyclical permutation is permitted under the signs S and T, it is obviously permitted under the signs SU and $\angle$;

or, $\quad$ SU $(a_1 a_2 \ldots a_n) =$ SU $(a_2 a_3 \ldots a_n a_1) = $ &c. $\ldots$ (4)

$\quad\quad\quad \angle (a_1 a_2 \ldots a_n) = \angle (a_2 a_3 \ldots a_n a_1) = $ &c. $\ldots$ (5)

77°. By 22°, $\quad 2V\beta\gamma = \beta\gamma - \gamma\beta$.

Multiplying both sides by a and taking the vectors,

$$2V . aV\beta\gamma = V . a (\beta\gamma - \gamma\beta) = V (a\beta\gamma - a\gamma\beta),$$
$$ = V (a\beta\gamma - a\gamma\beta + \beta a\gamma - \beta a\gamma),$$
$$ = V . (a\beta + \beta a) \gamma - V . (a\gamma + \gamma a) \beta,$$
$$ = 2\gamma Sa\beta - 2\beta S\gamma a$$

or, $\quad V . aV\beta\gamma = \gamma Sa\beta - \beta S\gamma a \ldots \ldots \ldots$ (1)

From a mere inspection of (1) it is evident that $V . aV\beta\gamma$ is perpendicular to a and coplanar with β and γ. If equation (1) be given in the form

$$\delta = \gamma Sa\beta - \beta S\gamma a,$$

it is easy to show that a is at right angles to δ. For, multiplying both sides of the equation by a, and taking scalars, we get, $\quad Sa\delta = Sa\gamma Sa\beta - Sa\beta Sa\gamma = 0$.

Therefore, a and δ are at right angles.

78°. $\quad\quad\quad \beta\gamma = S\beta\gamma + V\beta\gamma$.

Multiplying a into this equation, and taking the vectors,

$$Va\beta\gamma = aS\beta\gamma + V . aV\beta\gamma$$
$$ = aS\beta\gamma - \beta S\gamma a + \gamma Sa\beta \ldots \ldots (1)$$

This equation is of the form,

$$\delta = la + m\beta + n\gamma.$$

$Va\beta\gamma$, therefore, is the intermediate diagonal of the parallelopiped of which the three coinitial edges are $aS\beta\gamma$, $-\beta S\gamma a$; and $\gamma Sa\beta$, Pt. I., 37°.

79°. $\quad\quad V . \sigma V\gamma\delta = \delta S\sigma\gamma - \gamma S\delta\sigma$.

Let $\sigma = Va\beta$, and

$$V . Va\beta V\gamma\delta = \delta S (Va\beta) \gamma - \gamma S\delta Va\beta.$$

FORMULÆ

Introducing the null terms $S\gamma S\alpha\beta$ and $S\delta S\alpha\beta$,

$V . V\alpha\beta V\gamma\delta = \delta S \{(S\alpha\beta)\gamma + (V\alpha\beta)\gamma\} - \gamma S (\delta S\alpha\beta + \delta V\alpha\beta)$
" $= \delta S . (S\alpha\beta + V\alpha\beta)\gamma - \gamma S . \delta (S\alpha\beta + V\alpha\beta)$
" $= \delta S\alpha\beta\gamma - \gamma S\delta\alpha\beta$ . . . . (1)

It is evident from inspection that $V . V\alpha\beta V\gamma\delta$ is coplanar with γ and δ. Further,

$$V . V\alpha\beta V\gamma\delta = V . V\delta\gamma V\alpha\beta = \beta S\delta\gamma\alpha - \alpha S\beta\delta\gamma.$$

Therefore, $V . V\alpha\beta V\gamma\delta$ is also coplanar with α and β. Therefore, $V . V\alpha\beta V\gamma\delta$ must lie along the only line which the plane containing α and β and the plane containing γ and δ have in common—their line of intersection.

80°. $\qquad V . \sigma V\beta\gamma = \gamma S\sigma\beta - \beta S\gamma\sigma.$

Let $\sigma = V\alpha\beta$, and

$V . V\alpha\beta V\beta\gamma = \gamma S . (V\alpha\beta) \beta - \beta S . \gamma V\alpha\beta$
" $= \gamma S\beta V\alpha\beta - \beta S\gamma\alpha\beta.$

But $S\beta V\alpha\beta = 0$, because β and $V\alpha\beta$ are at right angles.
Therefore, $\qquad V . V\alpha\beta V\beta\gamma = - \beta S\gamma\alpha\beta$ . . . . (1)

We have, therefore,

$\alpha S\alpha\beta\gamma = V . V\beta\alpha V\alpha\gamma ; \quad \beta S\alpha\beta\gamma = V . V\gamma\beta V\beta\alpha ;$
$\gamma S\alpha\beta\gamma = V . V\alpha\gamma V\gamma\beta$ . . . . . (2)

81°. $\qquad V . V\alpha\beta V\gamma\rho = \rho S\alpha\beta\gamma - \gamma S\rho\alpha\beta,$
$- V . V\alpha\beta V\gamma\rho = V . V\gamma\rho V\alpha\beta = \beta S\gamma\rho\alpha - \alpha S\beta\gamma\rho.$

Adding $\qquad \rho S\alpha\beta\gamma = \alpha S\beta\gamma\rho + \beta S\gamma\alpha\rho + \gamma S\alpha\beta\rho,$ . . . (1)

a formula expressing a vector, ρ, in terms of three given diplanar vectors, α, β, γ.

$\rho S\alpha\beta\gamma$ is the intermediate diagonal of the parallelopiped of which the three coinitial edges are $\alpha S\beta\gamma\rho$, $\beta S\gamma\alpha\rho$, and $\gamma S\alpha\beta\rho$.

82°. Assume,

$$\rho S\alpha\beta\gamma = xV\beta\gamma + yV\gamma\alpha + zV\alpha\beta ;$$

it is required to determine the values of x, y, z.

Multiplying α into the equation, and taking scalars,

$S\alpha\rho S\alpha\beta\gamma = xS\alpha V\beta\gamma + yS\alpha V\gamma\alpha + zS\alpha V\alpha\beta$
" $= xS\alpha\beta\gamma + yS\gamma\alpha^2 + zS\alpha^2\beta$
" $= xS\alpha\beta\gamma.$

Therefore, $\qquad x = S\rho\alpha.$

Similarly, $\qquad y = S\rho\beta ; z = S\rho\gamma.$

Therefore, $\rho S\alpha\beta\gamma = S\rho\alpha V\beta\gamma + S\rho\beta V\gamma\alpha + S\rho\gamma V\alpha\beta.$. (1)

83°. $\quad S\alpha\beta\gamma\delta = S . (S\alpha\beta\gamma + V\alpha\beta\gamma) \delta$
,, $\quad = S . (V\alpha\beta\gamma) \delta$
,, $\quad = S . (\alpha S\beta\gamma - \beta S\gamma\alpha + \gamma S\alpha\beta) \delta$
$\quad = S\alpha\delta S\beta\gamma - S\alpha\gamma S\beta\delta + S\alpha\beta S\gamma\delta \ldots$ (1)

84°. $S . V\alpha\beta V\gamma\delta = S . (\alpha\beta - S\alpha\beta)(\gamma\delta - S\gamma\delta)$
,, $\quad = S\alpha\beta\gamma\delta - S\alpha\beta S\gamma\delta$
$\quad = S\alpha\delta S\beta\gamma - S\alpha\gamma S\beta\delta \ldots \ldots$ (1)

85°. $S (V\alpha\beta V\beta\gamma V\gamma\alpha) = S \{V\alpha\beta . V (V\beta\gamma V\gamma\alpha)\}$
,, $\quad = - S (V\alpha\beta . \gamma S\alpha\beta\gamma),$
,, $\quad = - S (\gamma V\alpha\beta . S\alpha\beta\gamma)$
,, $\quad = - S\gamma\alpha\beta . S\alpha\beta\gamma$
,, $\quad = - (S\alpha\beta\gamma)^2.$

86°. By 54°,

$V\alpha\beta\gamma = \alpha S\beta\gamma - \beta S\gamma\alpha + \gamma S\alpha\beta = (\text{say}) \ \alpha' - \beta' + \gamma'.$
$V\beta\gamma\alpha = \beta S\gamma\alpha - \gamma S\alpha\beta + \alpha S\beta\gamma = \quad\quad \alpha' + \beta' - \gamma'.$
$V\gamma\alpha\beta = \gamma S\alpha\beta - \alpha S\beta\gamma + \beta S\gamma\alpha = \quad - \alpha' + \beta' + \gamma'.$

Therefore,

$S . V\alpha\beta\gamma V\beta\gamma\alpha V\gamma\alpha\beta = S (\alpha' - \beta' + \gamma')(\alpha' + \beta' - \gamma')(-\alpha' + \beta' + \gamma')$

,, $\quad = S \begin{vmatrix} \alpha', & -\beta', & \gamma' \\ \alpha', & \beta', & -\gamma' \\ -\alpha', & \beta', & \gamma' \end{vmatrix}$

,, $\quad = 4S\alpha'\beta'\gamma' = 4S . (\alpha S\beta\gamma . \beta S\gamma\alpha . \gamma S\alpha\beta)$
,, $\quad = 4S\alpha\beta S\beta\gamma S\gamma\alpha S\alpha\beta\gamma.$

In expanding the determinant, the cyclical order, $\alpha', \beta', \gamma',$ must be preserved.

87°. Let α be any vector, $q (= \beta\gamma)$ any quaternion, and let $Vq = \delta.$ Then,

$\alpha q + q\alpha = \alpha(Sq + Vq) + (Sq + Vq)\alpha = 2\alpha Sq + \alpha Vq + Vq . \alpha$
,, $\quad = 2\alpha Sq + \alpha\delta + \delta\alpha = 2\alpha Sq + 2S\alpha\delta$
,, $\quad = 2(\alpha Sq + S . \alpha V\beta\gamma) = 2(\alpha Sq + S\alpha\beta\gamma)$
,, $\quad = 2(\alpha Sq + S\beta\gamma\alpha)$
,, $\quad = 2(\alpha Sq + S . q\alpha).$

88°. $\alpha q\alpha = \alpha(Sq + Vq)\alpha = \alpha^2 Sq + \alpha Vq . \alpha$
,, $\quad = \alpha^2 Sq - \alpha^2 Vq + \alpha^2 Vq + \alpha Vq . \alpha$
,, $\quad = \alpha^2 Kq + \alpha(\alpha Vq + Vq . \alpha)$
,, $\quad = \alpha^2 Kq + 2\alpha S . q\alpha.$

FORMULÆ 97

89°. Let OBCA be any parallelogram, and draw the diagonals OC, AB. Let $\dfrac{OB}{OA} = q$; $\angle AOB$ being thus $\angle q$.

Then,
$(T.\overline{AB})^2 = (T.\overline{OB})^2 + (T.\overline{OA})^2 - 2(T.\overline{OB})(T.\overline{OA})\cos\angle q,$
$(T.\overline{OC})^2 = (T.\overline{OB})^2 + (T.\overline{OA})^2 + 2(T.\overline{OB})(T.\overline{OA})\cos\angle q.$

Dividing both these equations by $(T.\overline{OA})^2$,

$$\left(T\frac{AB}{OA}\right)^2 = \left(T\frac{OB}{OA}\right)^2 + 1 - 2T\frac{OB}{OA}\cos\angle q,$$

$$\left(T\frac{OC}{OA}\right)^2 = \left(T\frac{OB}{OA}\right)^2 + 1 + 2T\frac{OB}{OA}\cos\angle q.$$

But $\quad\dfrac{AB}{OA} = \dfrac{OB - OA}{OA} = \dfrac{OB}{OA} - 1 = q - 1$;

$\quad\dfrac{OC}{OA} = \dfrac{OB + OA}{OA} = \dfrac{OB}{OA} + 1 = q + 1.$

Therefore, $\quad T(q-1)^2 = 1 - 2Sq + Tq^2$;
$\quad T(q+1)^2 = 1 + 2Sq + Tq^2.$

More generally, since $T(q''+1) = 1 + 2Sq'' + T^2q''$; if $q'' = \dfrac{q'}{q}$, we have

$$T^2\left(\frac{q'}{q} + 1\right) = 1 + 2S\frac{q'}{q} + T^2\frac{q'}{q}.$$

But $\quad S\dfrac{q'}{q} = \dfrac{S . q'Kq}{T^2q}.$

Therefore,

$$T^2\left(\frac{q'}{q} + 1\right) = 1 + \frac{2S . q'Kq}{T^2q} + T^2\frac{q'}{q},$$

and $\quad T^2(q' + q) = T^2q + 2S . q'Kq + T^2q'.$

If q' degenerate into a scalar, x,
$\quad T^2(q + x) = T^2q + 2xSq + x^2.$
$\quad T^2(q - x) = T^2q - 2xSq + x^2.$

90°. Let a be any unit-vector and t any scalar. Then since a^{-t} is the conjugate of a^t,
$\quad Sa^{-t} = Sa^t$; $Sa^{-t-1} = Sa^{t+1} = -Sa^{t-1}.$

$$Va^t = a \sin\frac{t\pi}{2} = a \cos\frac{(t-1)\pi}{2} = aSa^{t-1}.$$

$Sa^{t+1} = -\sin\dfrac{t\pi}{2} = i . i \sin\dfrac{t\pi}{2} = iVi^t = jVj^t = kVk^t.$

H

Since S . $j^ik = 0$,
$$j^ik = -\text{K}.j^ik = -\text{K}k.\text{K}j^i = kj^{-i},$$
and
$$k = j^ikj^i.$$

91°. If q and r be any two quaternions,
$$(qrq^{-1})^i = qr^iq^{-1}.$$
For,
$$(qrq^{-1})^2 = qrq^{-1}.qrq^{-1} = qr^2q^{-1};$$
$$(qrq^{-1})^3 = qr^2q^{-1}.qrq^{-1} = qr^3q^{-1}$$
$$\ldots \ldots \ldots \ldots \ldots$$
$$(qrq^{-1})^i = qr^iq^{-1}.$$
Similarly, $(jkj^{-1})^i = jk^ij^{-1}$,
and $(k^ij^ikj^{-i}k^{-i})^v = k^ij^vk^vj^{-i}k^{-i}.$

92°. The proofs of the following formulæ are left to the reader:
(1). $\text{S}.\text{V}\alpha\beta\text{V}\beta\gamma = \text{S}.\alpha\beta\text{V}\beta\gamma.$
(2). $\text{S}(\alpha + \beta)(\beta + \gamma)(\gamma + \alpha) = 2\text{S}\alpha\beta\gamma.$
(3). $\text{V}(\alpha\text{V}\beta\gamma + \beta\text{V}\gamma\alpha + \gamma\text{V}\alpha\beta) = 0.$
(4). $\text{V}\alpha\beta\gamma + \text{V}\gamma\alpha\beta = 2\gamma\text{S}\alpha\beta.$
(5). $\text{S}(\alpha\text{V}\beta\gamma + \beta\text{V}\gamma\alpha + \gamma\text{V}\alpha\beta) = 3\text{S}\alpha\beta\gamma.$
(6). $\text{V}^2\alpha\beta = \text{S}^2\alpha\beta - \alpha^2\beta^2.$
(7). $\text{S}.\text{V}\beta\gamma\text{V}\gamma\alpha = \gamma^2\text{S}\alpha\beta - \text{S}\beta\gamma\text{S}\gamma\alpha.$
(8). $\text{S}(\text{V}\alpha\beta\text{V}\gamma\delta + \text{V}\alpha\gamma\text{V}\delta\beta + \text{V}\alpha\delta\text{V}\beta\gamma) = 0.$

If α be any unit-vector and t any scalar,
(9). $\alpha^{-t} = \text{S}\alpha^t - \alpha\text{S}\alpha^{t-1}.$
(10). $\alpha\text{V}\alpha^t = \text{S}\alpha^{t+1}.$
(11). $i\text{V}j^i = \text{V}k^i$; $j\text{V}k^i = \text{V}i$; $k\text{V}i^i = \text{V}j^i.$
(12). $j\text{V}i^i = -\text{V}k^i$; $k\text{V}j^i = -\text{V}i^i$; $i\text{V}k^i = -\text{V}j^i.$

CHAPTER X

INTERPRETATION OF QUATERNION EXPRESSIONS

93°. The symbol $S . a \times$ means that a is to be multiplied into some given expression, and the scalar then taken. $S . \times a$ means that some given expression is to be multiplied into a, and the scalar then taken. And similarly for $V . a \times$, &c. What is the geometric meaning of the equation

$$S a \beta \gamma = 0 ?$$

Since $\qquad S a \beta \gamma = 0, S a V \beta \gamma = 0.$
Therefore, $\qquad V \beta \gamma \perp a.$
But $\qquad V \beta \gamma \perp \beta$ and $V \beta \gamma \perp \gamma.$

Therefore, since a, β, γ are coinitial, they are coplanar.

Conversely, if a, β, γ are coplanar, then
$$S a \beta \gamma = 0.$$
For $\qquad S a \beta \gamma = S a V \beta \gamma.$

Now, since $V \beta \gamma$ is at right angles to β and γ, it is also at right angles to a, the three vectors being coplanar. Therefore, $a V \beta \gamma$ is a right quaternion, and

$$0 = S a V \beta \gamma = S a \beta \gamma.$$

94°. What is the geometric meaning of the expression $S a \beta \gamma$, if a, β, γ be diplanar, coinitial vectors ?

Let a, β, γ, fig. 27, be the three vectors, and complete the parallelopiped OD. From O draw a unit-vector, ϵ, perpendicular to the plane AOB, such that rotation round it from a to β is positive, and from C let fall a perpendicular, CP, on the plane AOB. Let $\angle AOB = \theta$; $\angle POC = \phi.$

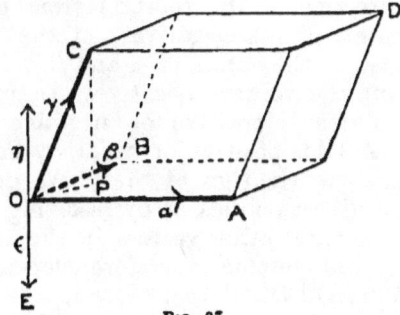

FIG. 27.

Then,

$$S\alpha\beta\gamma = S\gamma\alpha\beta = S\gamma V\alpha\beta = S \cdot \gamma (T\alpha T\beta \sin \theta \cdot \epsilon) = T\alpha T\beta \sin \theta S\gamma\epsilon$$
$$\quad = T\alpha T\beta T\gamma \sin \theta \sin \phi. \quad \ldots \ldots \ldots \ldots \quad (1)$$

But $T\alpha T\beta \sin \theta$ is the area of the parallelogram AOB, and $T\gamma \sin \phi = CP$ is the altitude of the parallelopiped OD. Therefore,

$$S\alpha\beta\gamma = \text{volume of the parallelopiped OD} \quad . \quad . \quad (2)$$

whose three coinitial edges are α, β, γ.

95°. As a confirmation of equation (2) of 94°, we may deduce the value of $S\alpha\beta\gamma$ in the form of a determinant by making use of the trinomial form of the three vectors.
Let

$$\alpha = x_1 i + y_1 j + z_1 k, \quad \beta = x_2 i + y_2 j + z_2 k, \quad \gamma = x_3 i + y_3 j + z_3 k.$$

Then,

$$S\alpha\beta\gamma = S \cdot (x_1 i + y_1 j + z_1 k)(x_2 i + y_2 j + z_2 k)(x_3 i + y_3 j + z_3 k)$$
$$\quad = - x_1(y_2 z_3 - y_3 z_2) - y_1(z_2 x_3 - z_3 x_2) - z_1(x_2 y_3 - x_3 y_2)$$
$$\quad = - \begin{vmatrix} x_1, y_1, z_1 \\ x_2, y_2, z_2 \\ x_3, y_3, z_3 \end{vmatrix} \quad \ldots \ldots \ldots \ldots \quad (1)$$

It will be observed that the sign of this determinant is negative, while the signs of (1) and (2), 94°, are positive. To explain this difference of signs, let $OB = \alpha$, $OA = \beta$ (fig. 27). Then the axis of $\alpha\beta$ will be a unit-vector, $\eta = -\epsilon$, and

$$S\alpha\beta\gamma = S\gamma V\alpha\beta = T\alpha T\beta \sin \theta S\gamma\eta = T\alpha T\beta \sin \theta \cdot T\gamma (-\sin \phi)$$
$$\quad = - T\alpha T\beta T\gamma \sin \theta \sin \phi.$$
$$\quad = - \text{volume of the parallelopiped OD.}$$

It is clear that the change of sign is due to the change in direction of the rotation from β to γ round α. In 94° this rotation was negative and the volume positive. When we change the names of α and β, this rotation becomes positive and the volume negative. In other words, the sign of the volume is positive or negative according as the pyramid OABC is positive or negative, Part I., 30° (c). We can now see why the sign of the above determinant is negative. The result was obtained by resolving each of the vectors, α, β, γ, into three other vectors in the directions of i, j, k. The sign of the volume, therefore, depended upon the sign of the pyramid OIJK (fig. 11), and the sign of this pyramid is, and must always be, negative by definition.

INTERPRETATION OF QUATERNION EXPRESSIONS

We may, therefore, write generally,

$$S\alpha\beta\gamma = \pm \text{ volume of parallelopiped OD}$$
$$\text{„} \quad = \pm 6 \times \text{ volume of pyramid OABC} \quad \cdots (2)$$

In the case of $S\gamma\beta\alpha$ everything is, of course, reversed, because $S\gamma\beta\alpha = -S\alpha\beta\gamma$.
But the rule of the pyramid holds good. $S\gamma\beta\alpha$ is positive or negative according as the pyramid OCBA is positive or negative.

96°. What is the geometric meaning of the symbol $V\alpha\beta\gamma$, when α, β, γ are the successive sides of a triangle?

Let α, β, γ represent the sides of a vector-triangle ABC, fig. 28. Circumscribe a circle to the triangle, and let the tangents at the points A, B, C meet in T_1, T_2, T_3. Let the angles of the triangle be A, B, C, and let $U\gamma\tau_2 = \eta$.

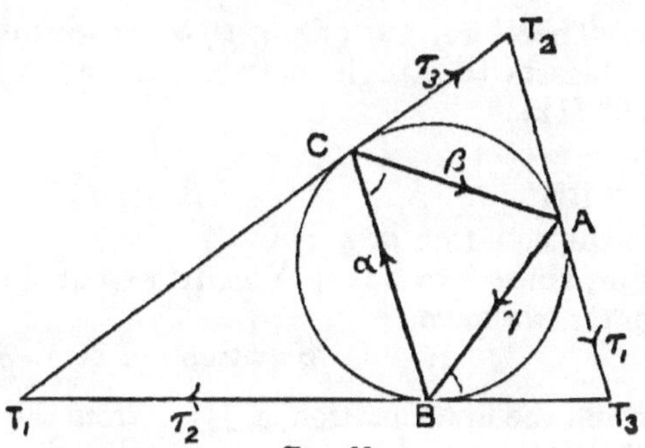

FIG. 28.

Then, since
$$\angle T_3BA = \angle C,$$
$$U\beta\alpha = -U\gamma\tau_2 ;$$
$$U\gamma U\beta\alpha = U\gamma\beta\alpha = -U\gamma U\gamma\tau_2 = -U\gamma^2 U\tau_2 = U\tau_2 ;$$
$$\gamma\beta\alpha = cba U\tau_2.$$

But $\qquad S\gamma\beta\alpha = 0$, 93°,

therefore, $\qquad \gamma\beta\alpha = V\gamma\beta\alpha = V\alpha\beta\gamma$.

Therefore, $\qquad V\alpha\beta\gamma = abc U\tau_2. \quad \cdots \cdots (1)$

The product of the three coplanar vectors, α, β, γ, then, represents a vector along the tangent to the circumcircle at B, the origin of α, whose tensor is the product of the sides of the triangle, and whose direction represents the initial direction of motion along the circumference from B through C towards A [the point T_1 is not the term of τ_2]. Were the direction of rotation round the triangle negative, we should have

$$(\text{since } \gamma\beta\alpha = V\gamma\beta\alpha = V\alpha\beta\gamma = \alpha\beta\gamma),$$
$$(-\gamma)(-\beta)(-\alpha) = -\gamma\beta\alpha = -\alpha\beta\gamma = abc(-U\tau_2),$$

a vector equal in length to $\alpha\beta\gamma$, but drawn from B in the contrary direction.

Similarly,
$$\begin{aligned}V\beta\gamma a &= bca \,.\, U\tau_3\,; \\ V\gamma a\beta &= cab \,.\, U\tau_1.\end{aligned} \right\} \quad \ldots \ldots \quad (2)$$

97°. What is the geometric meaning of
$$\delta = a\beta a^{-1}\,?$$

Multiplying a^{-1} into the equation,
$$a^{-1}\delta = \beta a^{-1};$$
therefore,
$$\frac{\beta}{a} = K\frac{\delta}{a}.$$

Therefore, 49° (*f*), a, β, δ are coinitial, coplanar vectors; a bisects the angle between β and δ; and $T\delta = T\beta$. See 75° (12).

98°. $$\beta = a\rho \,.\, \ldots \ldots \ldots (1)$$
is the equation of a Point.

For, since $\beta = Sa\rho + Va\rho$, if we equate the scalar and vector parts, we have,
$$0 = Sa\rho\,;\quad \beta = Va\rho.$$

From the first equation, $\rho \perp a$; from the second, $\beta \perp a$, $\beta \perp \rho$. Multiplying a^{-1} into the given equation,
$$\rho = a^{-1}\beta\,;$$
or, since $\beta \perp a$ and $a^{-1}\beta$ is a right quaternion,
$$\rho = Va^{-1}\beta = -VKa^{-1}\beta = -V\beta a^{-1} = -V\frac{\beta}{a}.$$

Therefore, ρ is a constant vector, and the locus of P is a point, the term of $-V\dfrac{\beta}{a}$.

The system
$$V\frac{\rho}{a} = V\frac{\beta}{a}\,;\quad S\frac{\rho}{a} = S\frac{\beta}{a}, \quad \ldots \ldots (2)$$
also expresses that the locus of P is a point. For
$$V\frac{\rho - \beta}{a} = 0\,;\quad S\frac{\rho - \beta}{a} = 0\,;$$
therefore,
$$S\frac{\rho - \beta}{a} + V\frac{\rho - \beta}{a} = \frac{\rho - \beta}{a} = 0\,;$$
" $\rho = \beta,$
" $P = B.$

INTERPRETATION OF QUATERNION EXPRESSIONS 103

99°. $$V \frac{\rho}{a} = 0, \text{ or } V a\rho = 0, \quad \ldots \ldots (1)$$

is the equation of the indefinite straight line OA.

$$K \frac{\rho}{a} = \frac{\rho}{a}. \quad \ldots \ldots (2)$$

is another form of the equation of OA. For, if $q = \frac{\rho}{a}$,

$$0 = q - Kq = 2Vq, \; 48°\; (8).$$

Therefore, $\angle q = \angle \frac{\rho}{a} = 0$ or π.

$$U\frac{\rho}{a} = \pm U\frac{\beta}{a}. \quad \ldots \ldots (3)$$

is the equation of the indefinite straight line OB in the case of the positive, or OB′ in the case of the negative sign ($\overline{OB'} = -\overline{OB}$).

If $\gamma = \overline{OC}$ be a third vector such that $\angle BOC = \angle AOB$,

$$U^2 \frac{\rho}{a} = U\frac{\gamma}{a}. \quad \ldots \ldots (4)$$

is the equation of the indefinite straight line BB. For, since

$$U\frac{\rho}{a} = \sqrt{U\frac{\gamma}{a}},$$

the angle AOC is bisected by ρ or $-\rho$, 51° (9).

$$V\frac{\rho}{a} = V\frac{\beta}{a}, \text{ or } V\frac{\rho - \beta}{a} = 0, \quad \ldots \ldots (5)$$

is the equation of an indefinite straight line drawn through B parallel to a.

What locus is represented by

$$Va\rho = \beta? \quad \ldots \ldots (6)$$

From inspection, $\beta \perp a, \beta \perp \rho$.

$V \cdot a^{-1} \times$.

$$Va^{-1}\beta = V \cdot a^{-1}Va\rho = \rho Saa^{-1} - aS\rho a^{-1} = \rho - xa,$$

where x is an indeterminate scalar. But since $\beta \perp a$,

$$Va^{-1}\beta = a^{-1}\beta = \gamma = \overline{OC},$$

some vector perpendicular to a and β. Therefore,

$$\rho = \gamma + xa,$$

and the locus of P is the indefinite straight line through C, parallel to a.

The system of equations,
$$S\epsilon\rho = 0; \quad S\epsilon\beta = 0; \quad S\beta\rho = -c \text{ (constant)} \quad . \quad . \quad (7)$$
where ϵ is a given unit-vector, expresses that the locus of P is a straight line.

The first equation restricts ρ to a fixed plane through the origin $\perp \epsilon$, which, by the second equation, contains β. From the third equation, if $T\rho = x$, and $T\beta = b$, θ being the variable angle between the two vectors, we have
$$-xb \cos\theta = -c,$$
$$x \cos\theta = \frac{c}{b}.$$

If, then, we take on β (or β produced) a point C such that
$$OC = \frac{c}{b},$$
the sought locus will be the straight line through $C \perp \beta$.

If $c = 0$,
$$S\beta\epsilon = 0; \quad S\beta\rho = 0; \quad S\epsilon\rho = 0, \quad . \quad . \quad . \quad (8)$$
expresses that the locus of P is the indefinite straight line through O, $\perp \beta$.

100°.
$$UV\frac{\rho}{a} = UV\frac{\beta}{a} \quad . \quad . \quad . \quad . \quad . \quad (1)$$
is the equation of that part of the plane AOB which lies on the same side of the indefinite straight line OA as the point B.

If $\overline{OA'} = -\overline{OA}$,
$$T(\rho + a) = T(\rho - a), \quad . \quad . \quad . \quad . \quad (2)$$
being equivalent to $AP = A'P$, is the equation of a plane through O perpendicular to a.
$$S\frac{\rho}{a} = 0, \text{ or } Sa\rho = 0, \quad . \quad . \quad . \quad . \quad (3)$$
expresses the same locus; as also does
$$K\frac{\rho}{a} = -\frac{\rho}{a} \quad . \quad . \quad . \quad . \quad . \quad . \quad (4)$$

To deduce (3) from (2),
$$T(\rho + a) = T(\rho - a),$$
$$T\frac{\rho + a}{a} = T\frac{\rho - a}{a},$$
$$T(q + 1) = T(q - 1),$$
$$1 + 2Sq + T^2q = 1 - 2Sq + T^2q, \text{ 89°},$$
$$Sq = S\frac{\rho}{a} = 0.$$

INTERPRETATION OF QUATERNION EXPRESSIONS 105

To deduce (4) from (3),

$$0 = 2S\frac{\rho}{a} = S\frac{\rho}{a} + V\frac{\rho}{a} - V\frac{\rho}{a} + S\frac{\rho}{a} = \frac{\rho}{a} + K\frac{\rho}{a}.$$

$$S\frac{\rho}{a} = 1 \quad \ldots \quad \ldots \quad (5)$$

is the equation of a plane through A perpendicular to a.

For it is equivalent to $S\frac{\rho - a}{a} = 0$, which shows that $(\rho - a) \perp a$.

$$Sa\rho = -a^2, \quad \ldots \quad \ldots \quad (6)$$

which is equivalent to $Sa(\rho - a) = 0$, gives the same locus.

$$Sa\rho = 1 \quad \ldots \quad \ldots \quad (7)$$

is the equation of a plane through A', the term of a^{-1}, perpendicular to a^{-1} or a. For it is equivalent to

$$0 = Sa\rho - 1 = S\frac{\rho}{a^{-1}} - S\frac{a^{-1}}{a^{-1}} = S\frac{\rho - a^{-1}}{a^{-1}}.$$

This plane is consequently parallel to the plane of (5) and (6).

$$S\frac{\rho}{a} = c \text{ (constant)} \quad \ldots \quad \ldots \quad (8)$$

is a plane parallel to the plane of (5).

For, $$1 = \frac{1}{c} S\frac{\rho}{a} = S\frac{\rho}{ca};$$

therefore, $$S\frac{\rho - ca}{ca} = 0.$$

Consequently $(\rho - ca) \perp ca$, or a.

$$Sa\rho = c \quad \ldots \quad \ldots \quad (9)$$

gives the same locus.

$$S\frac{\rho - \beta}{a} = 0, \text{ or, } S\frac{\rho}{a} = S\frac{\beta}{a} \quad \ldots \quad (10)$$

shows that $\rho - \beta \perp a$, or $BP \perp OA$. The locus of P, therefore, is a plane through B perpendicular to a, in some point, A'. This may seem plainer if we write the second equation,

$$T\frac{\rho}{a} SU\frac{\rho}{a} = T\frac{\beta}{a} SU\frac{\beta}{a};$$

whence $$T\rho SU\frac{\rho}{a} = T\beta SU\frac{\beta}{a},$$

or, $\qquad$ OP cos POA$'$ = OA$'$ = OB cos BOA$'$.
$$T(\rho - \beta) = T(\rho - \alpha), \quad \ldots \quad \ldots \quad (11)$$
being equivalent to BP = AP, expresses that the locus of P is a plane which bisects at right angles the straight line AB.

Squaring (11) we get as the equation of the same plane,
$$(\rho - \beta)^2 = (\rho - \alpha)^2 \quad \ldots \quad \ldots \quad (12)$$

101°. If $\qquad \left(\dfrac{\rho}{\alpha}\right)^2 = -1, \quad \ldots \quad \ldots \quad (1)$

$\dfrac{\rho}{\alpha}$ was shown (51°) to be a right quarternion such that $T\rho = T\alpha$. The locus of P, therefore, is a Circle with O as centre and $T\alpha$ as radius, the plane of the circle being perpendicular to α. Or the locus of P is a great circle of a sphere with O as centre and $T\alpha$ as radius, of which circle A is one of the poles.
$$\frac{\rho^2}{\alpha^2} = -v^2 \; ; \; v > 0 \quad \ldots \quad \ldots \quad (2)$$
give a similar locus, the radius of the circle being in this case $vT\alpha$.

If ϵ be any given unit-vector,
$$T\rho = T\alpha \; ; \; S\epsilon\rho = 0 \quad \ldots \quad \ldots \quad (3)$$
is the equation of a circle with O for centre and $T\alpha$ for radius.
$$S\rho(\rho - 2\alpha) = 0 \; ; \; UV\alpha\rho = \epsilon \quad \ldots \quad (4)$$
is the equation of a circle passing through O, with A for centre.

The system of equations,
$$\rho = \alpha^t\beta \; ; \; T\alpha = 1 \; ; \; S\alpha\beta = 0 \quad \ldots \quad (5)$$
represents a circle with O for centre and OB for radius, in a plane perpendicular to OA, t being a variable scalar.

102°. What locus is represented by
$$V\alpha\rho V\rho\beta = V^2\alpha\beta \text{ ?}$$

Since $V^2\alpha\beta$ is a scalar, $V\alpha\rho$ and $V\rho\beta$ are parallel; and consequently ρ, α and β are coplanar. Therefore,
$$\rho = x\alpha + y\beta,$$
where x and y are scalars.

$$\text{V} \cdot \alpha \times, \quad V\alpha\rho = yV\alpha\beta.$$
$$\text{V} \cdot \times \beta, \quad V\rho\beta = xV\alpha\beta.$$

Therefore, $\quad V^2\alpha\beta = V\alpha\rho V\rho\beta = xy V^2\alpha\beta$;

,, $\quad xy = 1$;

,, $\quad \rho = x\alpha + \dfrac{1}{x}\beta$,

the equation of a Hyperbola, α and β being unit-vectors along the asymptotes taken as the axes, and x and y the Cartesian co-ordinates.

103°. $\quad \rho = \alpha^t \beta$;
$\quad T\alpha = 1$; $S\alpha\beta \gtreqless 0$;

represents a plane ellipse. For,

$$\rho = \left(\cos\frac{t\pi}{2} + \alpha\sin\frac{t\pi}{2}\right)\beta = \beta\cos\frac{t\pi}{2} + \alpha\beta\sin\frac{t\pi}{2}.$$

Let $\quad \dfrac{t\pi}{2} = \theta$, and $V\alpha\beta = \overline{OC} = \gamma$.

Then, taking vectors,

$$\rho = \beta\cos\theta + \gamma\sin\theta,$$

the equation of a plane Ellipse of which O is the centre, β the major and γ the minor semi-axis, and θ the eccentric angle.

104°. $\quad \rho^2 = -1$, or, $T\rho = 1$ . . . . . . (1)

is the equation of the unit Sphere.

$$T\rho = T\alpha \ . \ . \ . \ . \ . \ . \ . \ . \ (2)$$

is the equation of a sphere with O for centre, which passes through A.

$$\left(S\frac{\rho}{\alpha}\right)^2 - \left(V\frac{\rho}{\alpha}\right)^2 = 1 \ . \ . \ . \ . \ (3)$$

gives the same locus ; for,

$1 = S^2 q - V^2 q = (Sq + Vq)(Sq - Vq) = qKq = T^2 q = \left(T\dfrac{\rho}{\alpha}\right)^2$;

whence, $T\rho = T\alpha$.

$$T(\rho - \alpha) = T\alpha \ . \ . \ . \ . \ . \ . \ (4)$$

is the equation of a sphere passing through O, with A for centre.

$$(\rho - \alpha)^2 = (\beta - \alpha)^2 . \ . \ . \ . \ . \ . \ (5)$$

or, $\quad T(\rho - \alpha) = T(\beta - \alpha)$ . . . . . . (6)

being equivalent to $AP = AB$, is the equation of a sphere

passing through B, with A for centre. O may be any point in space.

$$S\frac{\beta}{\rho} = 1, \text{ or, } S\frac{\beta-\rho}{\rho} = 0, \text{ or, } S\beta\rho = \rho^2. \quad . \quad . \quad (7)$$

is the equation of a sphere with OB for a diameter; for since $(\beta - \rho)$ is at right angles to ρ, the angle OPB is always a right angle.

$$\frac{\rho}{a} = K\frac{a}{\rho}. \quad . \quad . \quad . \quad . \quad . \quad . \quad . \quad (8)$$

gives the same locus as (2). For, multiplying by $\frac{a}{\rho}$,

$$1 = \frac{a}{\rho}\frac{\rho}{a} = \frac{a}{\rho}K\frac{a}{\rho} = T^2\frac{a}{\rho}; \text{ therefore, } T\rho = Ta.$$

105°. The system of equations,

$$S\frac{\rho}{a} = 1 \; ; \; S\frac{\beta}{\rho} = 1. \quad . \quad . \quad . \quad . \quad (1)$$

expresses that the locus of P is a circle, namely, the Circle in which the plane through A, perpendicular to a $\left(S\frac{\rho}{a} = 1\right)$ intersects the sphere with OB for a diameter $\left(S\frac{\beta}{\rho} = 1\right)$. For since P must lie at the same time upon the sphere and in the plane, its locus is necessarily the only line which the sphere and the plane have in common—the circle of intersection.

106°. $\rho = a^t \beta a^{-t},$

or, $\rho = a^{c\theta} \beta a^{-c\theta},$

where t and θ are variable, is also the equation of a Circle. What circle?

Comparing these equations with (9) of 75°, it is clear that ρ is the result of the positive conical rotation of β round a through an angle $= 2\theta = t\pi = 2t\left(\frac{\pi}{2}\right)$, i.e. twice t times the angle of a considered as a right quaternion. The locus of P, therefore, is a circle upon a sphere with $T\beta$ for radius.

107°. $$SU\frac{\rho}{a} = SU\frac{\beta}{a}$$

is the equation of one sheet of a Cone of revolution passing through B, with O for vertex and a for axis.

INTERPRETATION OF QUATERNION EXPRESSIONS 109

The other sheet is represented by

$$\mathrm{S}\,\mathrm{U}\frac{\rho}{\alpha} = -\mathrm{S}\,\mathrm{U}\frac{\beta}{\alpha};$$

both sheets by

$$\left(\mathrm{S}\,\mathrm{U}\frac{\rho}{\alpha}\right)^2 = \left(\mathrm{S}\,\mathrm{U}\frac{\beta}{\alpha}\right)^2.$$

108°. If we multiply together the two equations of 105° we get

$$\mathrm{S}\frac{\beta}{\rho}\mathrm{S}\frac{\rho}{\alpha} = 1, \quad \ldots \ldots \ldots (1)$$

the equation of the Cyclic Cone, discovered by Appolonius of Perga. It is an oblique cone, and has a circular base.

Equation (1) is evidently satisfied when the two equations of 105° are satisfied. Therefore every point of the circle represented by the equations of 105° must lie upon the locus represented by equation (1). But this equation remains essentially unchanged when ρ becomes $x\rho$, x being any scalar, positive, negative, or null. For,

$$\mathrm{S}\frac{\beta}{x\rho}\mathrm{S}\frac{x\rho}{\alpha} = \frac{1}{x}\mathrm{S}\frac{\beta}{\rho} \cdot x\mathrm{S}\frac{\rho}{\alpha} = \mathrm{S}\frac{\beta}{\rho}\mathrm{S}\frac{\rho}{\alpha} = 1.$$

Equation (1) therefore represents the cone (prolonged both ways) with O for vertex which has the circle of 105° as its base.

It becomes a cone of revolution when A (the term of α) coincides with the point in which β cuts the plane of the circle.

Any plane parallel to the plane $\mathrm{S}\frac{\rho}{\alpha} = 1$ will obviously cut either sheet of the cone cyclically. But there is another and a distinct series of planes which also cut the cone cyclically. For

$$\rho^2\mathrm{S}\frac{\beta}{\rho} = \mathrm{S}\cdot\frac{\beta}{\rho}\rho^2 = \mathrm{S}\beta\rho = \mathrm{S}\rho\beta = \mathrm{S}\frac{\rho}{\beta^{-1}};$$

therefore, $\quad \mathrm{S}\dfrac{\beta}{\rho} = \dfrac{1}{\rho^2}\mathrm{S}\dfrac{\rho}{\beta^{-1}}.$

And $\quad \mathrm{S}\dfrac{\rho}{\alpha} = \mathrm{S}\rho\alpha^{-1} = \mathrm{S}\alpha^{-1}\rho = \mathrm{S}\dfrac{\alpha^{-1}\rho^2}{\rho} = \rho^2\mathrm{S}\dfrac{\alpha^{-1}}{\rho}.$

Therefore $\quad 1 = \mathrm{S}\dfrac{\beta}{\rho}\mathrm{S}\dfrac{\rho}{\alpha} = \dfrac{1}{\rho^2}\mathrm{S}\dfrac{\rho}{\beta^{-1}} \cdot \rho^2\mathrm{S}\dfrac{\alpha^{-1}}{\rho} = \mathrm{S}\dfrac{\alpha^{-1}}{\rho}\mathrm{S}\dfrac{\rho}{\beta^{-1}},$

110 INTERPRETATION OF QUATERNION EXPRESSIONS

an equation which expresses that the locus of P is a cyclic cone with O as vertex, whose base is the circle in which a sphere with a^{-1} for a diameter $\left(S\dfrac{a^{-1}}{\rho}=1\right)$ is cut by a plane through B' (the term of β^{-1}), perpendicular to β^{-1} $\left(S\dfrac{\rho}{\beta^{-1}}=1\right)$.

109°.

$$TV\frac{\rho}{a} = TV\frac{\beta}{a}, \text{ or, } TVa\rho = TVa\beta, \text{ or, } V^2\frac{\rho}{a} = V^2\frac{\beta}{a} \quad ..(1)$$

is the equation of a Cylinder of revolution passing through B, with a along its axis. For, if $\angle \dfrac{\rho}{a} = \phi$, and $\angle \dfrac{\beta}{a} = \theta$, the given equations are equivalent to

$$T\rho \sin \phi = T\beta \sin \theta ;$$

or, if D and Q be the feet of the perpendiculars let fall from B and P respectively upon a,

$$PQ = BD.$$

CHAPTER XI

ON THE DIFFERENTIATION OF QUATERNIONS

Section 1

General Principles

110°. When we speak of a variable quaternion, we mean, in general, a quaternion whose tensor, angle and plane are variable. Hence, if q be any variable quaternion, then Tq and Uq, Sq and Vq, $\angle q$ and UVq are, in general, variable quantities.

When the plane is variable the quaternion and its differential, which is obviously a quaternion also, are diplanar.

If the plane happen to be constant, while the tensor and angle vary, the quaternion and its differential are coplanar.

The method of the ordinary Differential Calculus, in so far as it involves the commutative law of multiplication, is inapplicable to vectors and quaternions. To show this, let us examine some simple case of ordinary differentiation, say,

$$f(x) = x^2.$$

Then, $\qquad f(x + \Delta x) = (x + \Delta x)^2,$

$$\frac{f(x + \Delta x) - f(x)}{\Delta x} = \frac{(x + \Delta x)^2 - x^2}{\Delta x} = \frac{2x\Delta x + (\Delta x)^2}{\Delta x} \quad .. \text{ (A)}$$

$$\text{,,} \qquad = 2x + \Delta x;$$

and at the limit, when $\Delta x = 0$,

$$\frac{df(x)}{dx} = 2x.$$

This result, it will be observed, depends upon our having, as in (A),

$$(x + \Delta x)^2 = x^2 + 2x\Delta x + (\Delta x)^2.$$

But in the case of the equation
$$f(q) = q^2,$$
where q is any quaternion, in general,
$$(q + \Delta q)^2 \neq q^2 + 2q\Delta q + (\Delta q)^2\,;$$
because, in general, q and dq are diplanar quaternions, and the commutative law of multiplication is applicable to coplanar quaternions only. In fact,
$$(q + \Delta q)^2 = (q + \Delta q)(q + \Delta q) = q^2 + \Delta q \cdot q + q\Delta q + (\Delta q)^2.$$

In consequence of this peculiarity of quaternions, it becomes necessary to frame a definition of differentials which shall not involve the commutative law, and which shall also remain true for quaternions which degrade to vectors or to scalars.

Definition.—*Simultaneous Differentials are the Limits of equimultiples of simultaneous and decreasing Differences. Conversely, if any simultaneous Differences, of any system of Variables, tend to vanish together (according to any law), and if any equimultiples of these decreasing Differences tend altogether to any system of finite limits, then these Limits are Simultaneous Differentials of the related Variables of the System* (Hamilton).

In symbols, let
$$q, r, s \ldots \qquad \ldots \qquad \ldots \quad (1)$$
denote any system of connected variables; let
$$\Delta q, \Delta r, \Delta s \ldots \qquad \ldots \qquad \ldots \quad (2)$$
denote a system of their connected (or simultaneous) differences, so that
$$q + \Delta q,\ r + \Delta r,\ s + \Delta s \ldots \quad \ldots \quad (3)$$
shall be a new system of variables satisfying the same law as the old system (1). Then, in returning gradually from the new system to the old one, the simultaneous differences (2) can generally be made to approach together to zero, since evidently they may all vanish together. But if, while the differences themselves decrease indefinitely together, we multiply them all by some common but increasing number, n, the system of their equi multiples,
$$n\Delta q,\ n\Delta r,\ n\Delta s \ldots \quad \ldots \quad \ldots \quad (4)$$
may tend to become equal to some determined system of finite limits,
$$a, b, c \ldots \qquad \ldots \qquad \ldots \quad (5)$$

When this happens (as it can be generally made to do by a suitable adjustment of the increase of n to the decrease of Δq, &c.), the limits thus obtained are the Simultaneous Differentials of the related variables, $q, r, s \ldots$, and we have
$$a = dq,\ b = dr,\ c = ds \ldots \ldots \ldots (6)$$

A quaternion decreases as its tensor decreases, and it decreases indefinitely when its tensor tends to zero (Hamilton).

111°. As an algebraic illustration of the foregoing principles, let us investigate the differential of x^2, where x is any scalar.

Let
$$y = x^2 \ldots \ldots \ldots \ldots (1)$$
Then $y + \Delta y = (x + \Delta x)^2$,
and
$$\Delta y = 2x\Delta x + \Delta x^2 ; \ldots \ldots (2)$$
where Δx^2 represents $(\Delta x)^2$. $\Delta(x^2)$ will be represented by $\Delta \cdot x^2$; $(dx)^2$ by dx^2; $d(x^2)$ by $d \cdot x^2$. If n be an arbitrary multiplier, say a positive whole number,
$$n\Delta y = 2xn\Delta x + n^{-1}(n\Delta x)^2 \ldots \ldots (3)$$

Conceive, now, that while the simultaneous differences Δx and Δy tend together to zero (always, however, remaining connected with each other and with x by equation (2)), the number n tends to infinity, in such a manner that $n\Delta x$ tends to some finite limit, a. This will be the case if we oblige Δx to satisfy always the condition,
$$\Delta x = n^{-1}a,\ \text{or}\ n\Delta x = a \ldots \ldots (4)$$
We then have
$$n\Delta y = 2xa + n^{-1}a^2 = b + n^{-1}a^2 ;\ \text{if}\ b = 2xa ;$$
where b is finite, because x is supposed to be finite.

But as n increases indefinitely, $n^{-1}a^2$ decreases indefinitely, a being given and finite ; and the limit of $n^{-1}a^2$ is rigorously zero. We therefore have at the limit,
$$n\Delta y = b \ldots \ldots \ldots (5)$$

Since, then, a and b are the limits of equimultiples of simultaneous and decreasing differences, we have
$$dx = a ;\ dy = b = 2xa ; \ldots \ldots (6)$$
or,
$$dy = d \cdot x^2 = 2xdx \ldots \ldots \ldots (7)$$

It will be observed that the use of the word 'limit' has been extended so as to include the case of constants. A constant is here regarded as its own limit.

I

112°. As a geometric illustration of the foregoing principles, let us investigate the differential of an area, say a rectangle.

Let ABCD, fig. 29, be any given rectangle, and let BE and DG be any arbitrary, but given and finite, increments of its sides AB and AD. Complete the rectangle AF, which will thus exceed the given rectangle by the gnomon CBEFGDC.

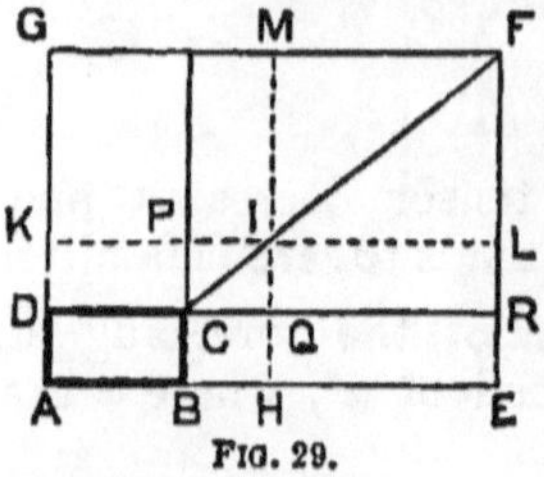

Let I be a point upon the diagonal of CF such that the line CI is an arbitrary but given submultiple of the line CF; and through I draw HM and KL parallel to AD and AB. These parallels intercept, on AD and AB produced, equisubmultiples DK and BH of the two given increments (DG and BE) of those given sides; for, obviously,

$$\frac{DK}{DG} = \frac{CI}{CF} = \frac{BH}{BE}.$$

Fig. 29.

Let the point I gradually approach C. Then the lines BH and DK, and the gnomon CBHIKDC, or the sum of the rectangles CH, CI, CK, will all indefinitely decrease, and will tend to vanish together; remaining, however, always a system of three simultaneous differences (or increments) of the two given sides, AB, AD, and of the given rectangle, AC.

The increments of the sides, being constant, are their own limits; and since (by construction) they are always equimultiples of the simultaneous and decreasing differences, BH and DK, we are justified by the definition, 110°, in taking BE and DG as the simultaneous differentials of the sides AB and AD; provided that we take the limit of the equimultiple of the gnomon CBHIKDC as the simultaneous differential of the rectangle AC.

What is the equimultiple of this gnomon, and what is the limit of the equimultiple?

The equimultiple of the gnomon is evidently

$$\frac{BE}{BH}.CBHIKDC = \frac{BE}{BH}(CH + CI + CK) = \frac{BE}{BH}(BC.BH + CP.CQ + DK.DC)$$

$$= \frac{BE}{BH}(BC.BH) + \frac{CR}{CQ}(CP.CQ) + \frac{DG}{DK}(DK.DC)$$

$$= BC.BE + DG.DC + CP.CR$$

$$= CE + CG + CL.$$

Now, the limits of CE and CG are these rectangles themselves, since they are constant; while the limit of the rectangle CL (*i.e.* its value at the instant when the point I becomes coincident with C) is exactly zero. Therefore the differential of the area, or rectangle, ABCD is the sum of the rectangles CE and CG.

These two examples show, first, that differences and differentials must not in general be confounded together; secondly, that differentials are not necessarily small; thirdly, that the differentials of quantities which vary together according to a law need not be homogeneous, it being sufficient that each separately should be homogeneous with the variable to which it corresponds, and of which it is the differential, as line of line and area of area.

Section 2

Differential of a Vector

113°. Let us apply the foregoing principles to the differentiation of a vector.

The equation
$$\rho = f(t), \quad \ldots \ldots \ldots (1)$$
where t is an independent and variable scalar, generally represents the vector of a point, P, of a curve in space (fig. 30).

If Q be another point of the same curve, we have
$$\overline{OP} + \overline{PQ} = \overline{OQ},$$
or,
$$\rho + \Delta\rho = f(t + \Delta t), \ldots (2)$$
where $\Delta\rho$ and Δt are the simultaneous differences of ρ and t.

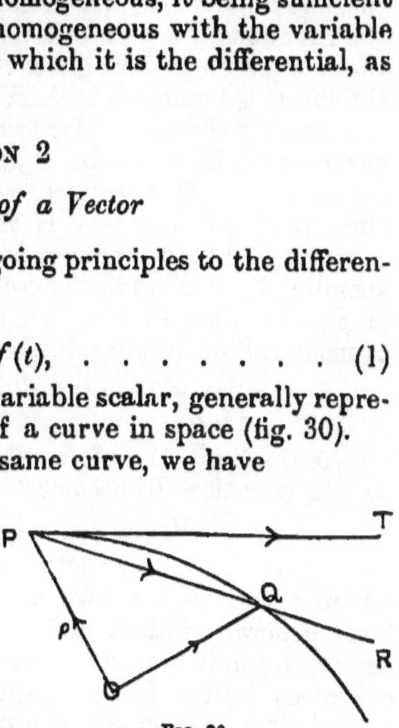

Subtracting (1) from (2),
$$\Delta\rho = f(t + \Delta t) - f(t). \ldots (3)$$

Let $\Delta\rho$, or $\overline{PQ}$, be the nth part of the vector $\overline{PR} = \sigma_n$, and let Δt be the nth part of a new scalar, u; so that
$$n\Delta\rho = n\overline{PQ} = \overline{PR}, \text{ or, } \Delta\rho = n^{-1}\sigma_n, \quad \ldots \ldots (4)$$
$$n\Delta t = u, \text{ or, } \Delta t = n^{-1}u \; : \ldots \ldots (5)$$

Then, substituting this value of Δt in (3), and multiplying it by n,
$$n\Delta\rho = n\{f(t + n^{-1}u) - f(t)\} \quad \ldots \ldots (6)$$

If the scalars t and u be constant, while n is a variable scalar, the vector ρ, and consequently the point P, will be

Fig. 30.

fixed; but the points Q and R, the differences $\Delta\rho$ and Δt, and the vector σ_n, will in general vary together.

If n increases indefinitely, the simultaneous differences $\Delta\rho$ and Δt will decrease indefinitely, and will ultimately vanish together (equations (4) and (5)). But although the chord PQ will be thus indefinitely shortened as Q moves along the curve towards P, yet its nth multiple, PR, or σ_n, will generally tend to some finite limit, depending on the supposed continuity of the function $f(t)$. In other words, R is always a point upon the line passing through the points P and Q; and when (at the limit) Q coincides with P, R will still be a point upon the line passing through these two indefinitely close points of the curve—that is, it will be a point, T, upon the tangent to the curve at P. If, therefore, we call the vector-tangent τ, it is clear that this vector τ is the limiting value of the vector $\sigma_n = n\Delta\rho$ when n increases indefinitely; while u is the corresponding limit of $n\Delta t$. Therefore τ and u are the differentials of ρ and t, since they are the limits of equimultiples of simultaneous and decreasing differences. In symbols,

$$\lim_{n=\infty} n\Delta t = u = dt \; ; \; \lim_{n=\infty} n\Delta\rho = \tau = d\rho \quad . \quad . \quad (7)$$

At the limit, therefore, whether P be a point upon a curve or not, equation (6) becomes

$$d\rho = df(t) = \lim_{n=\infty} n\{f(t + n^{-1}dt) - f(t)\} \quad . \quad . \quad (8)$$

where t and dt are two arbitrary and independent scalars, both generally finite; and $d\rho$ is, in general, a new and finite vector, depending upon those two scalars according to a law expressed by the formula, and derived from that given law, whereby the former vector ρ, or $\phi(t)$, depends upon the single scalar, t (Hamilton).

114°. As an illustration of these principles, let us differentiate

$$\rho = \tfrac{1}{2}t^2 a,$$

where a is a given and constant vector.

$$\rho = f(t) = \frac{a}{2}t^2.$$

$$\rho + \Delta\rho = \frac{a}{2}(t + \Delta t)^2,$$

$$\Delta\rho = \frac{a}{2}\{(t + \Delta t)^2 - t^2\}.$$

Let $n\Delta t = u$, a given and constant scalar.

Then, $$\Delta t = \frac{u}{n},$$

and $$\Delta\rho = \frac{a}{2}\left\{\left(t + \frac{u}{n}\right)^2 - t^2\right\} = \frac{ua}{n}\left(t + \frac{u}{2n}\right).$$

Hence, (4), $$\sigma_n = n\Delta\rho = ua\left(t + \frac{u}{2n}\right),$$

and at the limit $\tau = uta$.

But $\tau = d\rho$; $u = dt$;

therefore, $d\rho = df(t) = d \cdot \tfrac{1}{2}t^2 a = atdt$.

Section 3

The Differential of a Quaternion

115°. Let $Q = F(q, r \ldots)$,

and let $dq, dr \ldots$ be any assumed (but generally finite) and simultaneous differentials of the variables $q, r \ldots$, whether scalars, vectors, or quaternions. Then, 110°, the simultaneous differential of their function, Q, is equal to the following limit,

$$dQ = \lim_{n=\infty} \cdot n\{F(q + n^{-1}dq, r + n^{-1}dr, \ldots) - F(q, r, \ldots)\} \quad \ldots (1)$$

where n is any whole number, or other positive scalar, which increases indefinitely (Hamilton).

If the function Q involves only one variable q, or

$$Q = f(q) = fq;$$

then,

$$dQ = dfq = \lim_{n=\infty} \cdot n\{f(q + n^{-1}dq) - fq\} \quad \ldots (2)$$

116°. As an illustration, let

$$Q = q^2.$$

Then, $dQ = \lim\limits_{n=\infty} \cdot n\{(q + n^{-1}dq)^2 - q^2\}$,

,, = ,, $\cdot n\{(q + n^{-1}dq)(q + n^{-1}dq) - q^2\}$,

,, = ,, $\cdot n(n^{-1}qdq + n^{-1}dq \cdot q + n^{-2}dq^2)$,

,, = ,, $\cdot (qdq + dq \cdot q + n^{-1}dq^2)$.

Therefore, $d \cdot q^2 = qdq + dq \cdot q \ldots \ldots \ldots (1)$

118 ON THE DIFFERENTIATION OF QUATERNIONS

This expression cannot be further reduced, the quaternions q and dq being, in general, diplanar. In the special case when they happen to be coplanar, we have, 64°,

$$dq \cdot q = q\,dq,$$
and
$$d \cdot q^2 = 2q\,dq.$$

It will be observed that $n^{-1}dq^2$ vanishes at the limit, because $n^{-1}\mathrm{T}dq^2$, or $n^{-1}\mathrm{T}^2 dq$, vanishes.

If q degenerate to a vector,

$$d \cdot \rho^2 = \rho\,d\rho + d\rho \cdot \rho = 2\mathrm{S}\rho\,d\rho \;(22°) \quad \ldots \quad (2)$$

Section 4

Miscellaneous Examples

117°. $\qquad y = \sin x.$

$$dy = \lim_{n=\infty} \cdot n\left(\sin\left(x + \frac{dx}{n}\right) - \sin x\right)$$

$$,, \;=\; ,, \;\cdot\; n\left(\sin x \cos \frac{dx}{n} + \cos x \sin \frac{dx}{n} - \sin x\right).$$

But $\qquad \lim\limits_{n=\infty} \cdot n \cos \dfrac{dx}{n} = n,$

and $\qquad\quad ,, \quad n \sin \dfrac{dx}{n} = dx.$

Therefore, $\qquad dy = \cos x\,dx.$

118°. $\qquad y = \cos x.$

$$dy = \lim_{n=\infty} \cdot n\left(\cos\left(x + \frac{dx}{n}\right) - \cos x\right)$$

$$,, \;=\; ,, \;\cdot\; n\left(\cos x \cos \frac{dx}{n} - \sin x \sin \frac{dx}{n} - \cos x\right)$$

$$,, \;=\; -\sin x\,dx.$$

119°. $\qquad y = m^x,$

where m is a constant scalar.

$$dy = \lim_{n=\infty} \cdot n\left(m^{x + \frac{dx}{n}} - m^x\right)$$

$$,, \;=\; ,, \;\cdot\; m^x n\left(m^{\frac{dx}{n}} - 1\right).$$

Let $m^{\frac{dx}{n}} = 1 + \frac{1}{z}$, so that $z = \dfrac{1}{m^{\frac{dx}{n}} - 1}$.

Then, since
$$\log\left(1 + \frac{1}{z}\right)^z = z \log\left(1 + \frac{1}{z}\right),$$
we have
$$\log_m\left(1 + \frac{1}{z}\right)^z = \frac{\frac{dx}{n}}{m^{\frac{dx}{n}} - 1} = \frac{dx}{n\left(m^{\frac{dx}{n}} - 1\right)}.$$

Therefore, treating dx as a constant,
$$\lim_{n=\infty} . \frac{dx}{n\left(m^{\frac{dx}{n}} - 1\right)} = \lim_{z=\infty} . \log_m\left(1 + \frac{1}{z}\right)^z = \log_m e.$$

Consequently,
$$\lim_{n=\infty} . \frac{n\left(m^{\frac{dx}{n}} - 1\right)}{dx} = \frac{1}{\log_m e} = \log_e m.$$

Therefore,
$$\lim_{n=\infty} . n\left(m^{\frac{dx}{n}} - 1\right) = \log_e m\, dx ;$$
and
$$dy = m^x \log_e m\, dx.$$

120°. $q = \eta^x,$

where η is a constant unit-vector.

$$dq = \lim_{n=\infty} . n\left(\eta^{x + \frac{dx}{n}} - \eta^x\right),$$

$$,, = ,, . n\eta^x\left(\eta^{\frac{dx}{n}} - 1\right),$$

$$,, = ,, . n\eta^x\left(\cos\frac{\pi dx}{2n} + \eta \sin\frac{\pi dx}{2n} - 1\right), 33°, (2).$$

Now, $\quad \lim_{n=\infty} . \cos\dfrac{\pi dx}{2n} = 1 ;$

$\quad\quad\quad ,, . \sin\dfrac{\pi dx}{2n} = (\text{arc})\dfrac{\pi dx}{2n}.$

Therefore, $\qquad d\rho = \dfrac{\pi}{2}\, \eta^{x+1}\, dx.$

Had we taken $x = c\theta$, the result would have been somewhat simpler. Then,

$$dp = \lim_{n=\infty} . \; n\left\{\eta^{c\left(\theta+\frac{d\theta}{n}\right)} - \eta^{c\theta}\right\}$$

$$\;\; =\;\; ,, \quad . \; \eta^{c\theta} n\left\{\eta^{\frac{cd\theta}{n}} - 1\right\}$$

$$\;\; =\;\; ,, \quad . \; \eta^{c\theta} n\left(\cos\frac{d\theta}{n} + \eta \sin\frac{d\theta}{n} - 1\right)$$

$$\;\; = \; \eta^{c\theta}\eta\, d\theta = \eta^{c\left(\theta+\frac{\pi}{2}\right)} d\theta.$$

This result is identical with that above; because, since $x = c\theta$,

$$d\theta = \frac{1}{c}\, dx = \frac{\pi}{2}\, dx,$$

and $\qquad \eta^{c\left(\theta+\frac{\pi}{2}\right)} = \eta^{c\theta}\eta = \eta^{x+1}.$

We have here a case in which the plane and tensor are constant, and the angle alone varies. It will be observed that a unit-vector in the first power can only vary in direction, its tensor and its angle (as a versor) being constant by definition.

121°. $\qquad Q = qr.$

$$dQ = \lim_{n=\infty} . \; n\{(q + n^{-1}dq)(r + n^{-1}dr) - qr\}$$

$$\;\; =\;\; ,, \quad . \; n\{n^{-1}dq \,.\, r + n^{-1}q dr + n^{-2}dq\, dr\}$$

$$\;\; =\;\; ,, \quad (dq \,.\, r + q dr + n^{-1}dq\, dr).$$

Therefore, $\qquad dQ = d\,.\,qr = dq\,.\,r + q\,dr.$

If c be any constant quantity, evidently

$$d\,.\,cq = c\,dq\,;\; d\,.\,qc = dq\,.\,c.$$

122°. $\qquad q = \beta^x,$

where β is a constant vector.

$dq = d\beta^x = d\,(T\beta^x U\beta^x) = d\,(b^x U\beta^x)$

$\;\; = db^x \,.\, U\beta^x + b^x \,.\, dU\beta^x,\; 121°,$

$\;\; = (119°\text{ and }120°)\; b^x \log_e b\, dx \,.\, U\beta^x + b^x \,.\, \dfrac{\pi}{2}\, U\beta^{x+1}\, dx$

$\;\; = \left(\log_e b + \dfrac{\pi}{2}\, U\beta\right)\beta^x\, dx.$

123°. $Q = q^{-1}$.
By 46°, $qq^{-1} = 1$;
therefore, 121°, $qdq^{-1} + dq \cdot q^{-1} = 0$.
$q^{-1} \times$, $q^{-1}qdq^{-1} + q^{-1}dq \cdot q^{-1} = 0$,
and $d \cdot q^{-1} = -q^{-1}dq \cdot q^{-1}$.

124°. $Q = q^{\frac{1}{2}}$.
Squaring, $Q^2 = q$,
$$dq = QdQ + dQ \cdot Q = q^{\frac{1}{2}}d \cdot q^{\frac{1}{2}} + (d \cdot q^{\frac{1}{2}})q^{\frac{1}{2}}.$$
$q^{-\frac{1}{2}} \times$ and $\times Kq^{\frac{1}{2}}$,
$$q^{-\frac{1}{2}}(dq)Kq^{\frac{1}{2}} = (d \cdot q^{\frac{1}{2}})Kq^{\frac{1}{2}} + q^{-\frac{1}{2}}(d \cdot q^{\frac{1}{2}})q^{\frac{1}{2}}Kq^{\frac{1}{2}}$$
$$„ \quad = \quad „ \quad + Tq \cdot q^{-\frac{1}{2}}(d \cdot q^{\frac{1}{2}}).$$

But, 49° (b), (1),
$$Tq \cdot q^{-\frac{1}{2}} = Tq^{\frac{1}{2}}Uq^{-\frac{1}{2}} = Tq^{\frac{1}{2}}UKq^{\frac{1}{2}} = Kq^{\frac{1}{2}}.$$

Therefore,
$$q^{-\frac{1}{2}}(dq)Kq^{\frac{1}{2}} = (d \cdot q^{\frac{1}{2}})Kq^{\frac{1}{2}} + Kq^{\frac{1}{2}}(d \cdot q^{\frac{1}{2}})$$
$$„ \quad = 2Sq^{\frac{1}{2}}(d \cdot q^{\frac{1}{2}}) - \{(d \cdot q^{\frac{1}{2}})Vq^{\frac{1}{2}} + Vq^{\frac{1}{2}}(d \cdot q^{\frac{1}{2}})\} \ldots (1)$$

Again,
$$dq = d(q^{\frac{1}{2}}q^{\frac{1}{2}}) = (d \cdot q^{\frac{1}{2}})q^{\frac{1}{2}} + q^{\frac{1}{2}}(d \cdot q^{\frac{1}{2}})$$
$$„ \quad = 2Sq^{\frac{1}{2}}(d \cdot q^{\frac{1}{2}}) + \{(d \cdot q^{\frac{1}{2}})Vq^{\frac{1}{2}} + Vq^{\frac{1}{2}}(d \cdot q^{\frac{1}{2}})\} \quad \ldots (2)$$

Adding (1) and (2),
$$dq + q^{-\frac{1}{2}}(dq)Kq^{\frac{1}{2}} = 4Sq^{\frac{1}{2}}(d \cdot q^{\frac{1}{2}}),$$
and
$$d \cdot q^{\frac{1}{2}} = \frac{dq + q^{-\frac{1}{2}}(dq)Kq^{\frac{1}{2}}}{4Sq^{\frac{1}{2}}}.$$

125°. The symbols S, V, and K are commutative with d.
For $q = Sq + Vq$.
$dq = dSq + dVq$.

But, since dq is a quaternion,
$$dq = Sdq + Vdq.$$
Therefore, $dSq = Sdq$; $dVq = Vdq$, 44°.
Again, $Kq = Sq - Vq$;
therefore, $dKq = dSq - dVq = Sdq - Vdq = Kdq$.

126°. To find dTq and $dT\rho$.

$$T^2 q = qKq;$$
$$2TqdTq = \lim_{n=\infty} . n\{(q + n^{-1}dq)(Kq + n^{-1}dKq) - qKq\}$$
$$ = \phantom{\lim_{n=\infty}} . (qdKq + dq . Kq + n^{-1}dqdKq),$$
$$ = qKdq + dq . Kq,$$
$$ = (62°, (1)) \, qKdq + K . qKdq,$$
$$ = (\text{ „ } (2)) \, 2S . qKdq,$$
$$ = (\text{ „ } (3)) \, 2S (Kq . dq).$$

Therefore,
$$dTq = S\frac{Kq . dq}{Tq} = S\frac{dq . Kq}{Tq} = S\frac{dq . Tq}{Tq . Uq} = S\frac{dq}{Uq};$$
or,
$$\frac{dTq}{Tq} = S\frac{dq}{q}.$$

Similarly, if q degrade to a vector,
$$\frac{dT\rho}{T\rho} = S\frac{d\rho}{\rho}.$$

127°. To find dUq.
$$TqUq = q;$$
$$Tq . dUq + dTq . Uq = dq;$$
$$\frac{Tq . dUq}{TqUq} + \frac{dTq . Uq}{TqUq} = \frac{dq}{q};$$
$$\frac{dUq}{Uq} = \frac{dq}{q} - \frac{dTq}{Tq};$$
$$\phantom{\frac{dUq}{Uq}} = \frac{dq}{q} - S\frac{dq}{q}, \; 126°,$$
$$\phantom{\frac{dUq}{Uq}} = V\frac{dq}{q}.$$

Therefore, $$dUq = V\frac{dq}{q} . Uq.$$

128°. By the last two examples,
$$dq = dTq . Uq + Tq . dUq,$$
$$\frac{dq}{q} = \frac{dTq}{Tq} + \frac{dUq}{Uq}; \quad \ldots \ldots$$
$$\phantom{\frac{dq}{q}} = S\frac{dq}{q} + V\frac{dq}{q} \quad \ldots \ldots$$

129°. $TVqUVq = Vq,$

$TVq \cdot dUVq + dTVq \cdot UVq = dVq = Vdq$, 125°,

$$dUVq = \frac{Vdq}{TVq} - \frac{dTVq}{TVq} \cdot UVq$$

$$\;\;\;\;\; = \frac{Vdq}{Vq} UVq - S\frac{Vdq}{Vq} \cdot UVq,\; 126°,$$

$$dUVq = V\frac{Vdq}{Vq} \cdot UVq; \quad \ldots \ldots \quad (1)$$

or,

$$\frac{dUVq}{UVq} = V\frac{Vdq}{Vq}. \quad \ldots \ldots \quad (2)$$

Since $\frac{dUVq}{UVq} =$ a unit vector, it follows that

$$S\frac{dUVq}{UVq} = 0,$$

and, consequently, that $dUVq \perp UVq$. Therefore the differential of the axis lies in the plane of the quaternion.

If the plane (and consequently the axis) of the quaternion be constant, the quaternion and its differential are coplanar, and $dUVq$ vanishes. Conversely, if

$$dUVq = 0 \quad \ldots \ldots \quad (3)$$

the quaternion and its differential are coplanar.

Equation (3) is the condition of coplanarity of a quaternion and its differential.

CHAPTER XII

SCALAR AND VECTOR EQUATIONS

SECTION 1

Scalar Equations

130°. If we have two given equations,
$$S\rho\alpha = 0 \,;\ S\rho\beta = 0\,;\ \ldots\ldots \quad (1)$$
it is evident that ρ, being $\perp$ to both α and β, is parallel to $V\alpha\beta$; or,
$$\rho = xV\alpha\beta.\ \ldots\ldots\ldots \quad (2)$$
It is equally evident that x, being an indeterminate scalar, the vector ρ is indeterminate.

ρ would still be indeterminate were the given equations
$$S\alpha\rho = m\,;\ S\beta\rho = n.$$
For, in this case,
$$S\,(n\alpha - m\beta)\,\rho = 0,$$
which shows that ρ is perpendicular to $(n\alpha - m\beta)$, but shows nothing more. The conclusion is, that a vector cannot be determined from two scalar equations; a conclusion that might have been arrived at from the consideration that a vector depends upon *three* scalars.

131°. A vector can always be determined from three scalar equations. For, let the three given equations be
$$S\alpha\rho = l\,;\ S\beta\rho = m\,;\ S\gamma\rho = n.\,\ldots\ldots \quad (1)$$
Then
$$m\gamma - n\beta = \gamma S\beta\rho - \beta S\gamma\rho = V\,.\,\rho V\beta\gamma\,;$$
$$n\alpha - l\gamma = V\,.\,\rho V\gamma\alpha\,;$$
$$l\beta - m\alpha = V\,.\,\rho V\alpha\beta.$$
Therefore,
$$V\,.\,\rho l V\beta\gamma = lm\gamma - nl\beta,$$
$$V\,.\,\rho m V\gamma\alpha = mn\alpha - lm\gamma,$$
$$V\,.\,\rho n V\alpha\beta = nl\beta - mn\alpha\,;$$

SCALAR AND VECTOR EQUATIONS 125

and
$$V \cdot \rho(l V\beta\gamma + m V\gamma\alpha + n V\alpha\beta) = 0.$$
Therefore,
$$\rho \parallel (l V\beta\gamma + m V\gamma\alpha + n V\alpha\beta),$$
or,
$$\rho = x(l V\beta\gamma + m V\gamma\alpha + n V\alpha\beta).$$

$S \cdot \alpha \times$.

$$S\alpha\rho = xS\alpha(l V\beta\gamma + m V\gamma\alpha + n V\alpha\beta)$$
$$\text{,,} = xlS \cdot \alpha V\beta\gamma + xmS \cdot \alpha V\gamma\alpha + xnS \cdot \alpha V\alpha\beta$$
$$\text{,,} = xlS\alpha\beta\gamma.$$

But
$$S\alpha\rho = l;$$
therefore,
$$x = \frac{1}{S\alpha\beta\gamma};$$
therefore,
$$\rho = \frac{l V\beta\gamma + m V\gamma\alpha + n V\alpha\beta}{S\alpha\beta\gamma} \quad \ldots \ldots \quad (2)$$

This value of ρ satisfies the three given equations, but no other value of ρ will satisfy them. For, suppose the three equations to be satisfied by ρ_1 and ρ_2. Then

$$S\alpha\rho_1 = 0; \; S\alpha\rho_2 = 0;$$
therefore,
$$S \cdot \alpha(\rho_1 - \rho_2) = 0.$$
Similarly,
$$S \cdot \beta(\rho_1 - \rho_2) = 0,$$
$$S \cdot \gamma(\rho_1 - \rho_2) = 0.$$

Therefore the vector $(\rho_1 - \rho_2)$ is at once perpendicular to α, to β, and to γ. But no real and actual vector can be perpendicular at the same time to three diplanar vectors, which α, β, γ are supposed to be. Therefore $(\rho_1 - \rho_2)$ vanishes; therefore $\rho_1 = \rho_2$. Therefore, the three given equations can be satisfied by one, and only one, value of ρ. The principle that no real and actual vector can be at once perpendicular to three diplanar vectors may be put in symbols as follows:

If
$$S\alpha\sigma = 0; \; S\beta\sigma = 0; \; S\gamma\sigma = 0;$$
then
$$\sigma = 0, \text{ if } S\alpha\beta\gamma \lessgtr 0.$$

Conversely, if σ be an actual and real vector; then

$$S\alpha\beta\gamma = 0.$$

Had the three given scalar equations been of the form,

$$S\beta\gamma\rho = p; \; S\gamma\alpha\rho = q; \; S\alpha\beta\rho = r; \quad \ldots \quad (3)$$

we should have had,
$$p\alpha = \alpha S\beta\gamma\rho,$$
$$q\beta = \beta S\gamma\alpha\rho,$$
$$r\gamma = \gamma S\alpha\beta\rho;$$
$$p\alpha + q\beta + r\gamma = \alpha S\beta\gamma\rho + \beta S\gamma\alpha\rho + \gamma S\alpha\beta\rho = \rho S\alpha\beta\gamma, \; 81°,$$
and
$$\rho = \frac{p\alpha + q\beta + r\gamma}{S\alpha\beta\gamma} \quad \ldots \ldots \quad (4)$$

132°. A vector, ρ, cannot be eliminated by fewer than four equations.

If we are given only three equations,
$$S\alpha\rho = h\,;\; S\beta\rho = l\,;\; S\gamma\rho = m\,;$$
we have, 131° (2),
$$S\alpha\rho V\beta\gamma + S\beta\rho V\gamma\alpha + S\gamma\rho V\alpha\beta - \rho S\alpha\beta\gamma = 0 \quad \ldots \quad (1)$$
an equation into which the vector ρ enters once. Now, suppose we are given a fourth equation,
$$S\delta\rho = n.$$
Then, if we multiply (1) by δ and take scalars, we get
$$S\delta V\beta\gamma S\alpha\rho + S\delta V\gamma\alpha S\beta\rho + S\delta V\alpha\beta S\gamma\rho - S\delta\rho S\alpha\beta\gamma = 0,$$
$$S\alpha\rho S\beta\gamma\delta - S\beta\rho S\gamma\delta\alpha + S\gamma\rho S\delta\alpha\beta - S\delta\rho S\alpha\beta\gamma = 0,$$
$$hS\beta\gamma\delta - lS\gamma\delta\alpha + mS\delta\alpha\beta - nS\alpha\beta\gamma = 0 \quad \ldots \quad (2)$$

an equation into which the vector ρ does not enter.

Section 2

Linear Vector Equations

133°. The general form of a linear vector equation is defined to be
$$\phi\rho = \Sigma\beta S\alpha\rho + V \cdot q\rho,^* \quad \ldots \ldots \quad (1)$$
where ρ is an unknown vector, q a known quaternion, and $\alpha = (\alpha_1 + \alpha_2 + \ldots \alpha_n)$, $\beta = (\beta_1 + \beta_2 + \ldots \beta_n)$, known vectors. The symbol ϕ stands for 'function,' and $\phi\rho$ is some vector coinitial with ρ.

Similarly, if σ be any other vector,
$$\phi\sigma = \Sigma\beta S\alpha\sigma + V \cdot q\sigma \quad \ldots \ldots \quad (2)$$

---
* For proof, see Molenbroek, pp. 188-191.

If we interchange a and β, and introduce Kq instead of q, we have

$$\phi'\rho = \Sigma aS\beta\rho + V.(Kq)\rho \quad \ldots \quad (3)$$
$$\phi'\sigma = \Sigma aS\beta\sigma + V.(Kq)\sigma \quad \ldots \quad (4)$$

134°. We have now to show that
$$S\rho\phi'\sigma = S\sigma\phi\rho.$$
$$S\rho\phi'\sigma = \Sigma S\rho aS\beta\sigma + S.\rho V.(Kq)\sigma$$
$$= \Sigma S\rho aS\beta\sigma + S\rho(Kq)\sigma.$$
$$S\sigma\phi\rho = \Sigma S\sigma\beta S a\rho + S.\sigma V.q\rho.$$
$$S\sigma\beta S a\rho = S\rho aS\beta\sigma.$$
$$S.\sigma V.q\rho = S\sigma q\rho = S.\sigma(Sq+Vq)\rho = S\sigma(Sq)\rho + S.\sigma(Vq)\rho$$
$$\text{,,} \quad = SqS\rho\sigma + S.\rho\sigma Vq = S.\rho(Sq)\sigma - S.\rho(Vq)\sigma$$
$$\text{,,} \quad = S.\rho(Kq)\sigma.$$

Therefore,
$$S\sigma\phi\rho = \Sigma S\rho aS\beta\sigma + S\rho(Kq)\sigma = S\rho\phi'\sigma \quad \ldots \quad (1)$$

Functions which, like ϕ and ϕ', possess this property are called *Conjugate Functions*.

The function ϕ is said to be *Self-conjugate* when, for any two vectors, ρ and σ,
$$S\sigma\phi\rho = S\rho\phi\sigma \quad \ldots \ldots \quad (2)$$

135°. Since $\beta Sa(\rho + \sigma + ..) = \beta Sa\rho + \beta Sa\sigma + ..,$
and $\quad V.q(\rho + \sigma + ..) = V.q\rho + V.\rho\sigma + ..;$
$$\Sigma\beta Sa(\rho + \sigma + ..) + V.q(\rho + \sigma + ..)$$
$$= (\Sigma\beta Sa\rho + V.q\rho) + (\Sigma\beta Sa\sigma + V.q\sigma) + ..;$$
or, $\quad \phi(\rho + \sigma + ..) = \phi\rho + \phi\sigma + ... \quad \ldots \quad (1)$

Hence, if $\quad \rho = \sigma = \&c.$
$$\phi x\rho = x\phi\rho. \quad \ldots \ldots \ldots \quad (2)$$

$$d\phi\rho = \lim_{n \to \infty} . n \{\phi(\rho + n^{-1}d\rho) - \phi\rho\} = \lim_{n \to \infty} . n\phi \frac{d\rho}{n}$$
$$= \lim_{n \to \infty} . \phi n \frac{d\rho}{n} = \phi d\rho \quad \ldots \ldots \quad (3)$$

Since $\phi\rho$ is a vector,
$$d.\rho\phi\rho = \rho d\phi\rho + d\rho.\phi\rho \quad \ldots \ldots \quad (4)$$

136°. Let
$$\phi\rho = \delta \quad\quad\quad\quad (1)$$
where ϕ and δ are given. Then it is defined that
$$\rho = \phi^{-1}\delta \quad\quad\quad\quad (2)$$
ϕ^{-1} is a function which possesses properties corresponding to those of ϕ.

As a matter of convenience we write:
$$\phi(\phi) = \phi^2, \&c. ; \quad \phi^{-1}(\phi^{-1}) = \phi^{-2}, \&c.$$
$$\phi\phi^{-1}\delta = \phi\rho = \delta ; \quad \phi^{-1}\phi\rho = \phi^{-1}\delta = \rho \quad\quad (3)$$

According as $m \gtrless n$,
$$\phi^m \phi^{-n} = \left\{ \begin{array}{l} \phi^{m-n} \\ \phi^{-(n-m)} \end{array} \right\}$$
$$\phi^{-m}\phi^n = \left\{ \begin{array}{l} \phi^{-(m-n)} \\ \phi^{n-m} \end{array} \right\} \quad\quad\quad (4)$$

ϕ^{-1}, ϕ, ϕ^2, &c., are operators which may alter both the length and direction of any vector upon which they operate. ϕ^2 is not to be confounded with the square of $\phi,—(\phi)^2$.

137°. We cannot enter here into the general theory of vector equations; suffice it to mention a simple method for their solution suggested by Dr. Molenbroek ("Theorie, &c.," p. 245).

Let the given vector equation be
$$\phi\rho = \delta \quad\quad\quad\quad (1)$$
Then we have at once
$$S . \lambda\phi\rho = S\lambda\delta ; \ S . \mu\phi\rho = S\mu\delta ; \ S . \nu\phi\rho = S\nu\delta \quad\quad (2)$$
where λ, μ, ν are *any three noncoplanar* vectors.

But, by 134°, we also have
$$S . \rho\phi'\lambda = S\lambda\delta ; \ S . \rho\phi'\mu = S\mu\delta ; \ S . \rho\phi'\nu = S\nu\delta \quad (3)$$
Therefore, 131° (2),
$$\rho = \frac{S\lambda\delta V . \phi'\mu\phi'\nu + S\mu\delta V . \phi'\nu\phi'\lambda + S\nu\delta V . \phi'\lambda\phi'\mu}{S . \phi'\lambda\phi'\mu\phi'\nu} \quad (4)$$

As an example, let
$$V\alpha\rho\beta = \gamma.$$
Then, 78°,
$$\phi\rho = \gamma = V\alpha\rho\beta = \alpha S\beta\rho - \rho S\beta\alpha + \beta S\alpha\rho ;$$
and, 133° (3),
$$\phi'\rho = \beta S\alpha\rho - \rho SK\beta\alpha + \alpha S\beta\rho$$
$$\quad\quad = \beta S\alpha\rho - \rho S\beta\alpha + \alpha S\beta\rho = \phi\rho.$$

SCALAR AND VECTOR EQUATIONS

Since α, β, γ are any three vectors whatever, we may select them to represent respectively the λ, μ, ν of equation (2).
Hence, $S\lambda\delta = S\alpha\gamma$; $S\mu\delta = S\beta\gamma$; $S\nu\delta = \gamma^2$.

$$\phi'\lambda = \phi'\alpha = \phi\alpha = V\alpha^2\beta = \alpha^2\beta\ ;$$
$$\phi'\mu = \phi'\beta = \phi\beta = V\alpha\beta^2 = \beta^2\alpha\ ;$$
$$\phi'\nu = \phi'\gamma = \phi\gamma = V\alpha\gamma\beta.$$

$$V \cdot \phi'\mu\phi'\nu = \beta^2 V \cdot \alpha V\alpha\gamma\beta = \beta^2 V\alpha\,(\alpha\gamma\beta - S\alpha\gamma\beta)$$
$$= \alpha^2\beta^2 V\gamma\beta - \beta^2 S\alpha\gamma\beta \cdot \alpha.$$
$$\text{,,} \quad = \alpha\beta^2 S\alpha\beta\gamma - \alpha^2\beta^2 V\beta\gamma\ ;$$

$$V \cdot \phi'\nu\phi'\lambda = \alpha^2 V(V\alpha\gamma\beta \cdot \beta) = \alpha^2 V\,\{(\alpha\gamma\beta - S\alpha\gamma\beta)\beta\}$$
$$\text{,,} \quad = \alpha^2\beta^2 V\alpha\gamma - \beta\alpha^2 S\alpha\gamma\beta = \beta\alpha^2 S\alpha\beta\gamma - \alpha^2\beta^2 V\gamma\alpha\ ;$$

$$V \cdot \phi'\lambda\phi'\mu = \alpha^2\beta^2 V\beta\alpha = -\alpha^2\beta^2 V\alpha\beta.$$

$$S \cdot \phi'\lambda\phi'\mu\phi'\nu = S\,(\alpha^2\beta \cdot \beta^2\alpha \cdot V\alpha\gamma\beta) = \alpha^2\beta^2 S \cdot \beta\alpha V\alpha\gamma\beta$$
$$\text{,,} \quad = \alpha^2\beta^2 S\beta\alpha\,(\alpha\gamma\beta - S\alpha\gamma\beta) = \alpha^2\beta^2 S\alpha\beta S\alpha\beta\gamma.$$

Therefore, (4),

$$\rho = \frac{S\gamma\alpha\,(\alpha\beta^2 S\alpha\beta\gamma - \alpha^2\beta^2 V\beta\gamma) + S\beta\gamma\,(\beta\alpha^2 S\alpha\beta\gamma - \alpha^2\beta^2 V\gamma\alpha) - \gamma^2 \cdot \alpha^2\beta^2 V\alpha\beta}{\alpha^2\beta^2 S\alpha\beta S\alpha\beta\gamma}$$

$$\text{,,} = \frac{(\alpha\beta^2 S\gamma\alpha + \beta\alpha^2 S\beta\gamma)\,S\alpha\beta\gamma - \alpha^2\beta^2\,(S\alpha\gamma V\beta\gamma + S\beta\gamma V\gamma\alpha + S\gamma\gamma V\alpha\beta)}{\alpha^2\beta^2 S\alpha\beta S\alpha\beta\gamma}$$

$$\text{,,} = \frac{\alpha^2\beta^2(\alpha^{-1}S\gamma\alpha + \beta^{-1}S\beta\gamma)\,S\alpha\beta\gamma - \alpha^2\beta^2 \cdot \gamma S\alpha\beta\gamma}{\alpha^2\beta^2 S\alpha\beta S\alpha\beta\gamma},\ 82°\ (1),$$

$$\text{,,} = \frac{\alpha^{-1}S\gamma\alpha + \beta^{-1}S\beta\gamma - \gamma}{S\alpha\beta}.$$

CHAPTER XIII

ILLUSTRATIONS IN QUATERNIONS

SECTION 1

Plane Trigonometry

138°. The simple relation between the three vector-sides of a triangle, fig. 31,

$$a + \beta + \gamma = o,$$

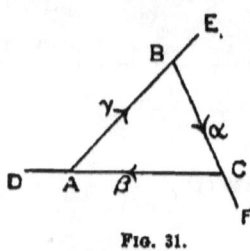

Fig. 31.

conducts at once to the three fundamental equations of plane trigonometry.

For, since $-\gamma = a + \beta$,

$$\gamma^2 = a^2 + \beta^2 + 2S a\beta,$$

or, $\quad c^2 = a^2 + b^2 - 2ab \cos C \quad . . \quad (1)$

It will be observed that ACF is the angle between a and β, and that $(\pi - \text{ACF}) = \angle \text{C}$.

Operating upon $-\gamma = a + \beta$, with $S . \gamma \times$,

$$-\gamma^2 = S\gamma a + S\gamma \beta,$$

Hence, $\quad c^2 = ca \cos B + bc \cos A$;

or, $\quad c = a \cos B + b \cos A. \quad . . . \quad (2)$

Operating with $V . \beta \times$,

$$- V\beta\gamma = V\beta a + V\beta^2 \text{ ;}$$

or, $\quad V\gamma\beta = V\beta a$;

or, $\quad TV\gamma\beta . UV\gamma\beta = TV\beta a . UV\beta a = TV\beta a . UV\gamma\beta$;

Therefore, $\quad TV\gamma\beta = TV\beta a$;

or, $\quad c \sin A = a \sin C \quad . . . . . \quad (3)$

It will be observed that $UV\gamma\beta = UV\beta a$.

139°. Let $\angle\, C = 90°$. Then,
$$-a = \beta + \gamma$$
$$-1 = \frac{\beta}{a} + \frac{\gamma}{a}$$

Taking the scalars,
$$-1 = S\frac{\beta}{a} + S\frac{\gamma}{a} = \frac{c}{a}\cos CBE = -\frac{c}{a}\cos B\,;$$

or, $\qquad\qquad\qquad \cos B = \frac{a}{c}$ . . . . (1)

Taking the vectors,
$$0 = V\frac{\beta}{a} + V\frac{\gamma}{a} = TV\frac{\beta}{a} \cdot UV\frac{\beta}{a} + TV\frac{\gamma}{a} \cdot UV\frac{\gamma}{a}$$
$$= TV\frac{\beta}{a} \cdot UV\frac{\beta}{a} - TV\frac{\gamma}{a} \cdot UV\frac{\beta}{a}$$
$$,, = \frac{b}{a} - \frac{c}{a}\sin CBE = b - c\sin B\,;$$

or, $\qquad\qquad\qquad \sin B = \frac{b}{c}$ . . . . (2)

140°. To find the sine and cosine of the sum of two angles. Let a, β, γ be three coinitial, coplanar unit-vectors, β lying between γ and a; and let $\angle\, AOB = \theta$, $\angle\, BOC = \phi$. Then,

$$\frac{\gamma}{a} = \cos(\theta + \phi) + \epsilon\sin(\theta + \phi).$$

$$\frac{\gamma}{\beta} = \cos\phi + \epsilon\sin\phi.$$

$$\frac{\beta}{a} = \cos\theta + \epsilon\sin\theta.$$

But $\qquad\qquad\qquad \frac{\gamma}{a} = \frac{\gamma}{\beta}\cdot\frac{\beta}{a}\,;$

therefore,
$$\cos(\theta+\phi) + \epsilon\sin(\theta+\phi) = (\cos\phi + \epsilon\sin\phi)(\cos\theta + \epsilon\sin\theta)$$
$$= \cos\phi\cos\theta + \epsilon(\sin\phi\cos\theta + \cos\phi\sin\theta) - \sin\phi\sin\theta.$$

Equating successively the vector and scalar parts,
$$\sin(\theta + \phi) = \sin\theta\cos\phi + \cos\theta\sin\phi \quad . . \quad (1)$$
$$\cos(\theta + \phi) = \cos\theta\cos\phi - \sin\theta\sin\phi \quad . . \quad (2)$$

To find the sine and cosine of the difference of two angles,

Let the angle between γ and a be ψ. Then,

$$\frac{\beta}{\gamma} = \cos(\psi - \theta) - \epsilon \sin(\psi - \theta),$$

$$\frac{\beta}{a} = \cos\theta + \epsilon \sin\theta,$$

$$\frac{a}{\gamma} = \cos\psi - \epsilon \sin\psi.$$

But
$$\frac{\beta}{\gamma} = \frac{\beta}{a} \cdot \frac{a}{\gamma}.$$

Therefore, as above,

$$\sin(\psi - \theta) = \sin\psi \cos\theta - \cos\psi \sin\theta \quad \ldots \quad (3)$$
$$\cos(\psi - \theta) = \cos\psi \cos\theta + \sin\psi \sin\theta \quad \ldots \quad (4)$$

Section 2

Spherical Trigonometry

141°. Let ABC, fig. 32, be any spherical triangle, its angles and sides being, as in the case of a plane triangle, A, B, C, a, b, c. Let the sphere be a unit-sphere, with O as centre, and let $\overline{OA} = a$, $\overline{OB} = \beta$, $\overline{OC} = \gamma$. Let L, M, N be respectively the positive poles of $\widehat{AB}$, $\widehat{BC}$, $\widehat{AC}$; L, M, and N corresponding to the points P, Q, R of 75°.

Let $\overline{OL} = \lambda$, $\overline{OM} = \mu$, $\overline{ON} = \nu$.

We evidently have,

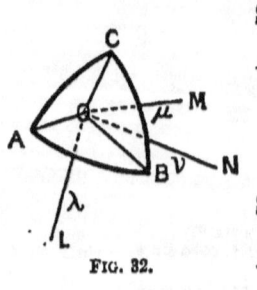

Fig. 32.

$$S\frac{\gamma}{a} = \cos b \,; \quad S\frac{\gamma}{\beta} = \cos a \,; \quad S\frac{\beta}{a} = \cos c \,;$$

$$V\frac{\gamma}{a} = \nu \sin b \,; \quad V\frac{\gamma}{\beta} = \mu \sin a \,;$$

$$V\frac{\beta}{a} = \lambda \sin c \,;$$

$$S \cdot V\frac{\gamma}{\beta} V\frac{\beta}{a} = \sin c \sin a \cos B \,;$$

$$V \cdot V\frac{\gamma}{\beta} V\frac{\beta}{a} = \sin c \sin a \, V\mu\lambda$$

$$= \beta \sin c \sin a \sin B.$$

Since
$$\frac{\gamma}{a} = \frac{\gamma}{\beta} \frac{\beta}{a}, \quad \ldots \quad \ldots \quad (1)$$

SPHERICAL TRIGONOMETRY

we have, by 60° (1),

$$S\frac{\gamma}{a} = S\frac{\gamma}{\beta} S\frac{\beta}{a} + S \cdot V\frac{\gamma}{\beta} V\frac{\beta}{a}; \quad \ldots \quad (2)$$

or, substituting the above values of these symbols,

$$\cos b = \cos c \cos a + \sin c \sin a \cos B; \quad \ldots \quad (3)$$

one form of the ordinary fundamental equation of spherical trigonometry.

142°. Taking the vectors of equation (1) of 141°,

$$V\frac{\gamma}{a} = S\frac{\beta}{a} V\frac{\gamma}{\beta} + S\frac{\gamma}{\beta} V\frac{\beta}{a} + V \cdot V\frac{\gamma}{\beta} V\frac{\beta}{a}, \; 60° \, (1), \; \cdot \; (1)$$

and substituting the values of these symbols given in 141°,

$\nu \sin b = \mu \cos c \sin a + \lambda \sin c \cos a + \beta \sin c \sin a \sin B.$ (2)

Let $\rho = \overline{OP}$ be any unit-vector. Dividing each term of this equation by ρ, taking scalars, and rearranging the terms,
$\sin c \sin a \sin B \cos PB$
$= \sin b \cos PN - \sin c \cos a \cos PL - \cos c \sin a \cos PM$ (A)

Let P coincide with M. Then,
$\cos MB = 0$; $\cos MN = \cos C$; $\cos ML = -\cos B$;
$$\cos MM = 1 \; ; \; \text{and}$$
$\sin b \cos C = \cos c \sin a - \sin c \cos a \cos B.$ . . (3)

143°. It is evident that if A and M be joined by the arc of a great circle, this arc will cut $\widehat{BC}$ at right angles in a point P_1; or $\widehat{AP_1}$ is the arcual perpendicular let fall from A upon $\widehat{BC}$. Let $\widehat{BP_2}$ and $\widehat{CP_3}$ be respectively the arcual perpendiculars let fall from B on $\widehat{CA}$ and from C on $\widehat{AB}$. Let the point P, equation (A), coincide with A, and we have

$\cos AB = \cos c$; $\cos AN = 0$; $\cos AL = 0$;
$$\cos AM = - \sin AP_1 \; ;$$
and $\quad \sin AP_1 = \sin c \sin B.$
$\quad$ Similarly, $\quad \sin BP_2 = \dfrac{\sin c \sin a}{\sin b} \sin B \quad \Big\} \; \cdot \; (1)$
$\quad \sin CP_3 = \sin a \sin B$

Since $\quad V\alpha\beta = \lambda \sin c$ and $V\beta\gamma = \mu \sin a,$
$V \cdot V\alpha\beta V\beta\gamma = \sin c \sin a \, V\lambda\mu = -\beta \sin c \sin a \sin B.$

But, 80° (1), $\quad\quad\quad V \cdot V\alpha\beta V\beta\gamma = -\beta S\alpha\beta\gamma$.

Therefore, $\quad\quad\quad S\alpha\beta\gamma = \sin c \sin a \sin B \quad \ldots \quad (2)$

It may be similarly shown, by using $V \cdot V\beta\gamma V\gamma\alpha$ and $V \cdot V\gamma\alpha V\alpha\beta$, that $\quad \sin a \sin b \sin C = S\alpha\beta\gamma = \sin b \sin c \sin A. \quad (3)$

Therefore,

$$\sin a : \sin b : \sin c = \sin A : \sin B : \sin C \quad . \quad (4)$$

The equations of (1), therefore, become

$$\left.\begin{array}{l} \sin AP_1 = \sin b \sin C \\ \sin BP_2 = \sin c \sin A \\ \sin CP_3 = \sin a \sin B \end{array}\right\} \quad \ldots \quad (5)$$

144°. Let the point P, equation (A), coincide with I, the centre of the small circle inscribed in the triangle ABC; and let the arcual perpendiculars let fall from I upon the sides cut the sides, BC in P_1, CA in P_2, AB in P_3. Let $r = \widehat{IP_1} = \widehat{IP_2} = \widehat{IP_3}$. Then, bearing in mind that the arcs (of great circles) IP_3, IP_1, and P_2I, produced, pass through L, M, N respectively, we have, from equation (A),

$$\sin c \sin a \sin B \cos IB$$
$$= \sin b \cos IN - \sin c \cos a \cos IL - \cos a \sin c \cos IM.$$

Since IBP_3 is a right-angled triangle, we have, by equation (3) of 141°,

$$\sin c \sin a \sin B = S\alpha\beta\gamma, (2) \text{ of } 143°;$$
$$\cos IB = \cos r \cos P_3B = \cos r \cos (s - b),$$

where $s = \frac{1}{2}(a + b + c)$;

$$\cos IN = \cos \left(\tfrac{\pi}{2} - r\right) = \sin r;$$
$$\cos IL = \cos \left(\tfrac{\pi}{2} + r\right) = -\sin r; \quad \cos IM = -\sin r.$$

Therefore,

$$\cos r \cos (s - b) S\alpha\beta\gamma = \sin r \{\sin b + \sin (c + a)\}$$
$$\quad\quad\quad\quad\quad\quad\quad\quad = 2 \sin r \sin s \cos (s - b);$$
$$\tan r = \frac{S\alpha\beta\gamma}{2 \sin s} = \frac{\sin a \sin b \sin C}{2 \sin s} \quad \ldots \quad (1)$$

145°. If the points L, M, N, fig. 32, be connected by arcs of great circles, we obtain a triangle exactly corresponding to PQR of 75°. Consequently,

$$\angle L = \angle P = \angle q = \frac{OB}{OA}; \quad \angle M = \angle Q = \angle q' = \angle \frac{OC}{OB};$$

$$\angle N = \angle R = (\pi - \angle q'q),$$

and $\quad \angle q'q = \angle \frac{OC}{OA} = (\pi - \angle N).$

Now, $\quad\quad\quad\quad \dfrac{OC}{OB} \dfrac{OB}{OA} = \dfrac{OC}{OA};$

Therefore,

$$\mu^{cM}\lambda^{cL} = \nu^{c(\pi - N)} = \nu^\pi \cdot \nu^{-cN} = (-1)\nu^{-cN}; \quad \ldots \quad (1)$$

$$,, \quad\quad \nu^{cN}\mu^{cM}\lambda^{cL} = -1 \quad \ldots \ldots \quad (2)$$

As a verification, multiply (2) into $\overline{OA}$. Then

$$-\overline{OA} = \nu^N\mu^{cM}\lambda^{cL} \cdot \overline{OA} = \nu^{cN}\mu^{cM} \cdot \overline{OB} = \nu^{cN} \cdot \overline{OC};$$

$$,, \quad = \nu^{c(\pi - COA)} \cdot \overline{OC} = -\overline{OA}.$$

Equation (2) may evidently be written,

$$-\frac{OA}{OC}\frac{OC}{OB}\frac{OB}{OA} = -1.$$

146°. Since equations (1) and (2) of 145° are perfectly general, we may write for *any* triangle, ABC,

$$\beta^{cB}\alpha^{cA} = \gamma^{c(\pi - C)} \quad \ldots \ldots \quad (1)$$

$$\gamma^{cC}\beta^{cB}\alpha^{cA} = -1 \quad \ldots \ldots \quad (2)$$

the fundamental quaternion equation of Spherical Trigonometry. As the left member of (2) reverses the direction of any vector it operates upon, by causing it to revolve successively through the three angles of the triangle in a certain order, it is evident that the sum of the vector-angles of a spherical triangle, *taken in a certain order*, is equivalent to π.

If the radius of the sphere becomes infinitely long, the triangle ABC becomes plane, and $\gamma = \beta = \alpha$. Consequently (2) becomes

$$\gamma^{cC}\beta^{cB}\alpha^{cA} = \gamma^{c(A+B+C)} = -1 = \gamma^\pi;$$

Therefore, $\quad\quad A + B + C = \pi \quad\quad$ (Dr. Odstrčil).

147°. Reverting to (1) of 146°,
$(\cos B + \beta \sin B)(\cos A + \alpha \sin A) = -\cos C + \gamma \sin C,$
or,
$\cos A \cos B + \alpha \sin A \cos B + \beta \cos A \sin B + \beta\alpha \sin A \sin B$
$$= -\cos C + \gamma \sin C \quad \ldots \quad (1)$$
Taking the scalars,
$\cos C = -\cos A \cos B - \sin A \sin B \cdot S\beta\alpha$
$\quad\quad\,, \; = -\cos A \cos B + \sin A \sin B \cos c \;\; \ldots (2)$
another form of the fundamental equation of Spherical Trigonometry.

148°. Taking the vectors of equation (1) of the last article,
$\gamma \sin C = \alpha \sin A \cos B + \beta \cos A \sin B + \sin A \sin B \cdot V\beta\alpha \;\; (1)$

Let P be any point upon the sphere, and let T be the foot of the arcual perpendicular let fall from P upon AB; PT being considered as positive when P and C lie upon the same side of AB, but negative otherwise. Then, dividing each term of (1) by $\rho = \overline{OP}$, and taking scalars,

$\sin A \sin B \sin c \sin PT$
$= \sin C \cos PC - \sin A \cos B \cos PA - \cos A \sin B \cos PB \quad$ (B)

If P coincide with B,
$\sin C \cos a = \cos A \sin B + \sin A \cos B \cos c \;\; \ldots \;\; (2)$

149°. Let Q be the centre of the small circle circumscribing the triangle ABC; let $\widehat{QA} = \widehat{QB} = \widehat{QC} = R$; and let QT be the arcual perpendicular from Q upon AB. Let the spherical excess be E, and $A + B + C = 2S$; so that
$$2S = A + B + C = \pi + E.$$
Then, if the point P, equation (B), coincide with Q, that equation becomes
$\sin A \sin B \sin c \sin QT$
$= \sin C \sin QC - \sin A \cos B \cos QA - \cos A \sin B \cos QB \;\; (1)$
Since $QA = QB = QC$, it is easy to see that
$2\angle QBT = A + B - C = 2(S - C),$ and $\angle QBT = S - C;$
and since BTQ is a right-angled triangle, we have, by (4) of 143°,
$$\sin QT = \sin R \sin QBT = \sin R \sin (S - C).$$

SPHERICAL TRIGONOMETRY 137

Also the right member of equation (1) is

$$\cos R \{\sin C - \sin(A+B)\} = \cos R \{-2 \cos \frac{\pi + E}{2} \sin(S-C)\}$$

$$\text{,,} \qquad = 2 \cos R \sin \tfrac{1}{2} E \sin(S-C).$$

Therefore equation (1) becomes

$$\sin A \sin B \sin c \sin R \sin(S-C) = 2 \cos R \sin \tfrac{1}{2} E \sin(S-C)$$

and $\qquad \cot R = \dfrac{\sin A \sin B \sin c}{2 \sin \tfrac{1}{2} E} \quad \ldots \quad (2)$

150°. Let CC' be a perpendicular from C upon the plane AOB; to find $\gamma' = \overline{OC'}$, the orthogonal projection of γ upon that plane.

$$\gamma' = \gamma - \overline{C'C} = \gamma + \lambda \sin COB.$$

But $\quad \sin COB = \sin CP_3 = \sin a \sin B$, (5) of 143°.

Therefore, substituting for γ its value in equation (1) of 148°, we have

$$\gamma' = \frac{a \sin A \cos B + \beta \cos A \sin B - \lambda \sin A \sin B \sin c}{\sin C} + \frac{\lambda \sin c \sin a \sin B}{\sin c}$$

$$\text{,,} = \frac{a \sin A \cos B + \beta \cos A \sin B}{\sin C} \quad \ldots \quad \ldots \quad (1)$$

151°. The three arcual perpendiculars, AP_1, BP_2, CP_3, let fall from the corners of a spherical triangle upon the opposite sides are concurrent.

CP_3 and AP_1 must intersect in some point P, OP being consequently the line of intersection of the planes COP_3 and AOP_1. Draw $\overline{OP_3} = \rho_3$ and $\overline{OP_1} = \rho_1$. Then, γ', the orthogonal projection of γ on the plane AOB, and a', the orthogonal projection of a on the plane BOC, lie respectively along ρ_3 and ρ_1. Let $\rho_3 = y\gamma'$, $\rho_1 = za'$; and let L, M, N be respectively the positive poles of AB, BC, AC. Then, by 79°,

$$x\,\overline{OP} = V \cdot V\gamma \rho_3 V \rho_1 a.$$

$$V\gamma\rho_3 = yV\gamma\gamma' = ((1) \text{ of } 150°) y \frac{V\gamma a \sin A \cos B + V\gamma\beta \cos A \sin B}{\sin C}$$

$$\text{,,} \quad = -\frac{y \cos A \cos B}{\sin C}(\mu \tan B + \nu \tan A) \quad \ldots \quad (1)$$

$$V\rho_1 a = zVa'a = z\frac{V\beta a \sin B \cos C + V\gamma a \cos B \sin C}{\sin A}$$

$$\text{,,} \quad = -\frac{z \cos B \cos C}{\sin A}(\nu \tan C + \lambda \tan B) \quad \ldots \quad (2)$$

138   SPHERICAL TRIGONOMETRY

Therefore, (1) and (2),

$V \cdot V\gamma\rho_2 V\rho_1 a = \frac{yz \cos A \cos^2 B \cos C}{\sin C \sin A}$ $(\mu\nu \tan B \tan C + \mu\lambda \tan^2 B + \nu\lambda \tan A \tan B)$

" $= \frac{1}{2}yz \cot A \sin 2B \cot C (a \tan A + \beta \tan B + \gamma \tan C) = x \overline{OP};$

or, putting p for $\dfrac{yz \cot A \sin 2B \cot C}{2x}$,

$$\overline{OP} = p(a \tan A + \beta \tan B + \gamma \tan C).$$

If the expressions for the vectors along the lines of intersection of the planes AOP_1 and BOP_2, BOP_2 and COP_3, be worked out, they will be found to be of the form:

$$\overline{OQ} = q(a \tan A + \beta \tan B + \gamma \tan C),$$
$$\overline{OR} = r(a \tan A + \beta \tan B + \gamma \tan C).$$

Therefore, p, q, r being scalars, $\overline{OP}, \overline{OQ}, \overline{OR}$ are parallel; and, consequently, the terms of their unit-vectors coincide. Therefore the three altitudes, which pass through the terms of these unit-vectors, are concurrent.

152°. What is the geometric signification of the symbol $\beta a^{-1}\gamma$, when a, β, γ are vectors drawn from the centre of a unit-sphere to the corners of a spherical triangle, ABC? Let the sides, as usual, be a, b, c, and let

$$\left. \begin{array}{l} \cos a = S\gamma\beta^{-1} = -S\beta\gamma = l; \\ \cos b = Sa\gamma^{-1} = -S\gamma a = m; \\ \cos c = S\beta a^{-1} = -Sa\beta = n. \end{array} \right\} \quad \ldots \quad (1)$$

Let it be supposed that l, m, n are each greater than zero, or that each side of the triangle is less than a quadrant.

Let δ, ϵ, ζ be three vectors, such that

$$\left. \begin{array}{l} \delta = V\beta a^{-1}\gamma = V\gamma a^{-1}\beta \\ \epsilon = V\gamma\beta^{-1}a = Va\beta^{-1}\gamma \\ \zeta = Va\gamma^{-1}\beta = V\beta\gamma^{-1}a \end{array} \right\} \quad \ldots \quad (2)$$

Then, 78°,

$V\beta a^{-1}\gamma = \beta S a^{-1}\gamma - a^{-1}S\beta\gamma + \gamma S\beta a^{-1}$
" $= aS\beta\gamma - \beta S\gamma a - \gamma Sa\beta,$ since a is unit-vector,
" $= m\beta + n\gamma - la;$

and similarly for $V\gamma\beta^{-1}a$ and $Va\gamma^{-1}\beta$.

Hence,

$$\left. \begin{array}{l} \delta = m\beta + n\gamma - la, \\ \epsilon = n\gamma + la - m\beta, \\ \zeta = la + m\beta - n\gamma. \end{array} \right\} \quad \ldots \ldots \quad (3)$$

SPHERICAL TRIGONOMETRY

To find the lengths of these vectors,

$$\zeta^2 = -T^2\delta = (m\beta + n\gamma - la)^2 = -(l^2 + m^2 + n^2 - 2lmn).$$

It will be found that ϵ^2 and ζ^2 have each the same value. Therefore,

$$T\delta = T\epsilon = T\zeta = \sqrt{(l^2 + m^2 + n^2 - 2lmn)} = \text{(say) } t \quad . \quad . \quad (4)$$

This common length, t, is less than unity. For, let

$$v = S\alpha\beta\gamma = -S\alpha^{-1}\beta\gamma = S\beta\alpha^{-1}\gamma.$$

Then, since $t = T\delta = TV\beta\alpha^{-1}\gamma$, we have

$$t^2 + v^2 = (TV\beta\alpha^{-1}\gamma)^2 + (S\beta\alpha^{-1}\gamma)^2 = (S\beta\alpha^{-1}\gamma)^2 - (V\beta\alpha^{-1}\gamma)^2$$
$$= T^2\beta\alpha^{-1}\gamma = 1.$$

Now, v is different from zero, because the three vectors are diplanar. Therefore $t < 1$.

Dividing the three vectors by their tensor, t, we obtain three unit-vectors:

$$\overline{OD} = t^{-1}\delta = U\delta; \quad \overline{OE} = t^{-1}\epsilon = U\epsilon; \quad \overline{OF} = t^{-1}\zeta = U\zeta,$$

whose terms are the corners of a new triangle, DEF, upon the sphere.

We have now to inquire what relation this new triangle bears to the original triangle, ABC.

By (3), $\qquad \epsilon + \zeta = 2l\alpha$;

Therefore, $\qquad l^{-1}\epsilon + l^{-1}\zeta = 2\alpha$;

,, $\overline{OA}$ bisects the angle between the unit-vectors $\overline{OE}$ and $\overline{OF}$. Consequently, the point

A lies upon and bisects $\widehat{EF}$.

Similarly, $\quad$ B ,, ,, ,, ,, $\widehat{FD}$,

$\qquad\qquad$ C ,, ,, ,, ,, $\widehat{DE}$.

Fig. 33 shows the two triangles.

To establish a relation between the sides of the two triangles, let

$$EF = 2a'; \quad FD = 2b'; \quad DE = 2c'.$$

Then

$$tU\epsilon + tU\zeta = \epsilon + \zeta = 2l\alpha = 2a\cos a, \quad (1).$$

Dividing across by a and taking scalars,

$$t\left(S\frac{U\epsilon}{a} + S\frac{U\zeta}{a}\right) = 2\cos a;$$

But $\quad S\dfrac{U\epsilon}{a} = S\dfrac{U\zeta}{a}$, since $\widehat{EF}$ is bisected in A;

therefore, $\quad 2t\, S\dfrac{U\epsilon}{a} = 2\cos a\,;$

or,
Similarly,
$$\left.\begin{array}{l}\cos a = t\cos a' \\ \cos b = t\cos b' \\ \cos c = t\cos c'\end{array}\right\} \quad \ldots \ldots (5)$$

To establish a relation between $a, \beta \ldots \epsilon, \zeta$. From the equality of the angles EOA, AOF, &c., we have at once
$$a\epsilon = \zeta a\,;\ \beta\zeta = \delta\beta\,;\ \gamma\delta = \epsilon\gamma \quad \ldots \ldots (6)$$
If we write the first equation as $\epsilon a = a\zeta$, 41°, and multiply both sides into a^{-1}, we get
$$\epsilon = a\zeta a^{-1}\,;$$
a confirmation of 97°.

Had we multiplied by a^{-1}, instead of into a^{-1},
$$\zeta = a^{-1}\epsilon a.$$
From the second equation of (6), multiplied into β^{-1},
$$\delta = \beta\zeta\beta^{-1}.$$
Substituting the above value of ζ,
$$\delta = \beta a^{-1}\epsilon a\beta^{-1} = \frac{\beta}{a}\,\epsilon\,\frac{a}{\beta} = q\epsilon q^{-1} \ \ldots \ldots (7)$$

Consequently, δ is generated by the conical rotation of ϵ round the axis of q, or βa^{-1}, through $2\angle q$, 75°. A geometric illustration of (7) will presently be given.

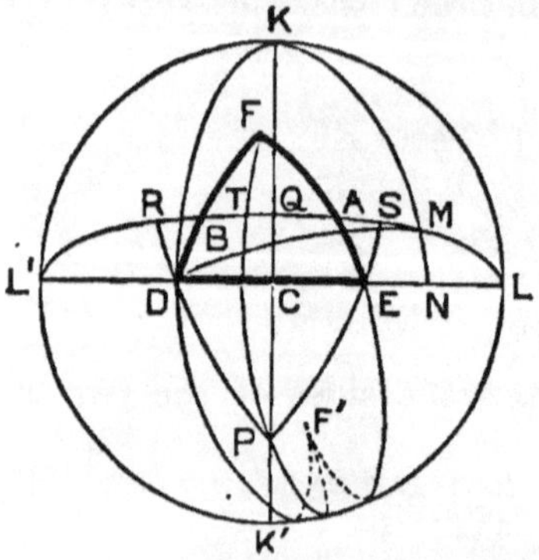

Fig. 33 is the orthographic projection of a sphere upon a tangent plane at C. Consequently, C is the centre of the circle KL. O is not seen, because the projection of OC upon the tangent plane is the point C.

Let us introduce a new vector,

FIG. 33.

$$\lambda = la - m\beta = \tfrac{1}{2}(\epsilon - \delta),\ (3)\ldots(8)$$

$S\,.\,\gamma\times.\quad 2S\gamma\lambda = S\gamma\epsilon - S\gamma\delta = (2)\,S\gamma V a\beta^{-1}\gamma - S\gamma V\beta a^{-1}\gamma$

$\quad\quad\ \ ,,\ \ = S\gamma a\beta^{-1}\gamma - S\gamma\beta a^{-1}\gamma = \gamma^2 Sa\beta^{-1} - \gamma^2 S\beta a^{-1}$

$\quad\quad\ \ ,,\ \ = \gamma^2(Sa\beta^{-1} - Sa\beta^{-1}) = 0$

SPHERICAL TRIGONOMETRY

Therefore $\gamma \perp \lambda$; and if L be the term of the unit-vector of λ, or if $OL = U\lambda$,

$$\widehat{CL} = \frac{\pi}{2} \quad \ldots \ldots \ldots (9)$$

The point L lies to the right of EF, as shown in fig. 33, because (by definition, (8)) 2λ is the diagonal of the parallelogram of which ϵ and $-\delta$ are the coinitial sides.
λ lies in the plane OAB, because, by definition, $\lambda = l\alpha - m\beta$;
„ „ ODE, „ „ $\lambda = \frac{1}{2}(\epsilon - \delta)$;
therefore λ lies along the intersection of the planes OAB and ODE; or, L is the point in which the arcs BA and DE produced meet. The arcs AB and ED produced meet in L', the point upon the sphere diametrically opposite to L; and CL' is a quadrant.

To find $T\lambda$:
$$\lambda^2 = (l\alpha - m\beta)^2,$$
$$T^2\lambda = l^2 + m^2 - 2lmn = t^2 - n^2.$$

But, (5), $\quad t^2 = \frac{\cos^2 c}{\cos^2 c'}$; $n^2 = S^2 \alpha\beta = \cos^2 c$;

therefore,
$$T^2\lambda = \frac{\cos^2 c}{\cos^2 c'} - \cos^2 c = \frac{\cos^2 c \sin^2 c'}{\cos^2 c'} = t^2 \sin^2 c',$$

$$T\lambda = \sqrt{(t^2 - n^2)} = t \sin c' \quad \ldots \ldots (10)$$

Let P be the positive pole of BA, and let the arcs drawn from P to D, E, F cut the great circle through B and A in R, S, T. Then, since FD and EF are bisected respectively in B and A, and since the angles at R, S, T are right angles, from a comparison of the triangles BDR and BFT, TFA and ASE, we find that

$$RB = BT \; ; \; AS = TA \; ;$$
$$RB + AS = BA \; ; \; RS = 2BA \quad \ldots \ldots (11)$$

Also, $\quad DR = FT = ES;$
consequently, $\quad PD = PE \quad \ldots \ldots (12)$

Let F' be the point upon the sphere diametrically opposite to F, and join the two points by the arc of a great circle passing through P. Then

$$PF' = \pi - PF = \pi - \left(\frac{\pi}{2} + FT\right) = \frac{\pi}{2} - DR = PD \ldots (13)$$

We can now illustrate equation (7) geometrically. Since

$$PF' = PD = PE,$$

P may be regarded as the interior pole of a small circle passing through D, E, F'. Let OE revolve conically round OP, its term moving negatively round the circumference of this small circle. When OE becomes coincident with OD, E will have revolved through an arc which, measured on the great circle through B and A, is

$$SR = 2AB.$$

Or, if P' be the positive pole of AB, OD is the result of the positive conical rotation of OE round OP', the axis of βa^{-1}, through $2\angle AOB = 2\angle \beta a^{-1}$. Hence,

$$\delta = \beta a^{-1} (\epsilon) a \beta^{-1}.$$

Let the arc of a great circle passing through P and C cut RS in Q. Then, from the equality of the triangles PDC, PCE, the angles at C are right angles. Therefore, if PQ be produced both ways, it will meet the great circle of which C is a pole in two points, K, K', which are respectively the negative and positive poles of $\widehat{DE}$.

Since $\angle DPC = \angle CPE$, RS is bisected in Q, and

$$QR = \tfrac{1}{2} SR = AB \quad \ldots \ldots \quad (14)$$

Finally, since the angles at C are right, and LC is a quadrant (9), L is the positive pole of CQ, and

$$\widehat{LQ} = \frac{\pi}{2} \ldots \ldots \ldots \quad (15)$$

L' is the negative pole of CQ.

Let two new points, M and N, be now determined by the conditions,

$$\left. \begin{array}{l} LM = AB = QR \\ LN = CD \end{array} \right\} \quad \ldots \ldots \quad (16)$$

Then, since LC and LQ are quadrants, ND and MR are also quadrants. Also, since the angle at R is a right angle, M is the pole of RD and MD is a quadrant. But DK is also a quadrant. Therefore D is the pole of KMN, and $\angle$ LNM is a right angle. Hence, fig. 33, if

$$U\kappa = \overline{OK},\ U\lambda = \overline{OL},\ U\mu = \overline{OM}\ ;$$

$$\frac{\beta}{a} = \beta a^{-1} = \frac{U\mu}{U\lambda}\ ;\ \gamma = \frac{U\lambda}{U\kappa}\ ;\ \ \ \ \ \ (17)$$

therefore, $\qquad \beta a^{-1}\gamma = \dfrac{U\mu}{U\kappa} \ \ \ \ \ \ \ \ (18)$

The symbol $\beta a^{-1} \gamma$, therefore, represents a versor whose representative arc is KM, whose angle is KDM, and whose axis is OD.

Since $\qquad \angle MDR = \dfrac{\pi}{2} = \angle L'DK,$

we have $\qquad \angle KDM = \angle L'DR = \angle EDP\ .\ .\ (19)$

We may therefore write,

$$\beta a^{-1}\gamma = \cos EDP + \overline{OD} \sin EDP\ .\ .\ .\ (20)$$

153°. To investigate an expression for the area of a spherical triangle.

Since F and F' are diametrically opposite points, every great circle which passes through the one passes through the other. If, therefore, the arcs FD and FE be produced, as shown in fig. 33, they will both pass through F'.

It has just been shown that

$$\angle L'DR = \angle EDP = \angle DEP\ ;$$

therefore, $\qquad 2L'DR = EDP + DEP.\ \ \ \ \ \ (a)$

But, since $\qquad PD = PE = PF',$

we have $\qquad \angle PDF' + \angle PEF' = \angle DF'E = \angle F',$

or, $\qquad PDF' + PEF' - F' = 0.$

Adding this null quantity to the right member of (a),

$$2L'DR = (EDP + PDF') + (DEP + PEF') - F'\ ;$$

or, since $\angle F' = \angle F$,

$$2L'DR = EDF' + DEF' - F$$
$$\qquad\ \ = (\pi - D) + (\pi - E) - F = 2\pi - (D + E + F).$$

Therefore,

$$\angle \beta a^{-1}\gamma = EDP = L'DR = \pi - \tfrac{1}{2}(D + E + F).$$

Now, since the radius of the sphere is unity,
Area of DEF = Spherical Excess = $(D + E + F) - \pi = E$.

[N.B.—The two E's have different meanings, the first denoting one of the angles of the triangle, the second denoting the spherical excess. It is with the latter *only* that we deal in what follows.]

Therefore, $\quad \angle \beta a^{-1}\gamma = L'DR = \tfrac{1}{2}\pi - \tfrac{1}{2}E$,

and, (20) of 152°, $\beta a^{-1}\gamma = \sin \tfrac{1}{2}E + U\delta \cos \tfrac{1}{2}E$ . . . (1)

Now, $\qquad \beta a^{-1}\gamma = S\beta a^{-1}\gamma + V\beta a^{-1}\gamma$;

and, introducing the notation of 152°,

$S\beta a^{-1}\gamma = Sa\beta\gamma = v$,

$V\beta a^{-1}\gamma = TV\beta a^{-1}\gamma \cdot UV\beta a^{-1}\gamma = tU\delta$, 152° (4) and (2).

Therefore, $\qquad \beta a^{-1}\gamma = v + tU\delta$ . . . . . . (2)

Equating the scalar and vector parts of (1) and (2),

$$\cos \tfrac{1}{2}E = t \quad \ldots \ldots \quad (3)$$
$$\sin \tfrac{1}{2}E = v.$$

But v, or $Sa\beta\gamma$, is positive or negative according as rotation from a to β round γ is negative or positive, 95°. In general, therefore,

$$\sin \tfrac{1}{2}E = \pm v = \pm Sa\beta\gamma \quad \ldots \quad (4)$$

This equation is the quaternion expression for Keogh's theorem: The sine of half the spherical excess is the volume of the parallelopiped, the three edges of which are the radii drawn from the centre of the sphere to the middle points of the sides of the triangle (DEF).

Bearing in mind that by 152° (3),

$$\begin{aligned} a &= \tfrac{1}{2}l^{-1}(\epsilon + \zeta), \\ \beta &= \tfrac{1}{2}m^{-1}(\zeta + \delta), \\ \gamma &= \tfrac{1}{2}n^{-1}(\delta + \epsilon)\,; \end{aligned} \Biggr\} \quad \ldots \ldots \quad (5)$$

we have, (4),

$$\sin \tfrac{1}{2}E = Sa\beta\gamma = \frac{S(\epsilon + \zeta)(\zeta + \delta)(\delta + \epsilon)}{8lmn} = \frac{S\delta\epsilon\zeta}{4lmn}, \quad \ldots \quad (6)$$

and, (3), $\qquad \cos \tfrac{1}{2}E = \frac{4lmn}{4lmn}t\,; \quad \ldots \ldots \quad (7)$

therefore, $\qquad \tan \tfrac{1}{2}E = \frac{S\delta\epsilon\zeta}{4lmnt} \quad \ldots \ldots \quad (8)$

But, since $m = -S\gamma a$, (1) of 152°,

$4lmn = -4nlS\gamma a = -S(2n\gamma \cdot 2la) = -S(\delta + \epsilon)(\epsilon + \zeta)$, by (5),

„ $= -S(\epsilon^2 + \epsilon\zeta + \zeta\delta + \delta\epsilon) = t^2 - S(\epsilon\zeta + \zeta\delta + \delta\epsilon)$, by (4) of 152°.

Therefore,

$$\tan \tfrac{1}{2}E = \frac{S\delta\epsilon\zeta}{4lmnl} = \frac{S\delta\epsilon\zeta}{t^3 - tS(\epsilon\zeta + \zeta\delta + \delta\epsilon)} \quad \cdot \cdot \quad (9)$$

$$\text{„} \quad = \frac{SU\delta\epsilon\zeta}{1 - SU\epsilon\zeta - SU\zeta\delta - SU\delta\epsilon}, \quad \cdot \cdot \cdot \quad (10)$$

a general expression for the tangent of half the spherical opening at O of any triangular pyramid, ODEF, whatever be the lengths of its edges, Tδ, Tϵ, Tζ.

Applying equation (9) to the triangle ABC, we have at once,

$$\tan \tfrac{1}{2}E = \frac{S\alpha\beta\gamma}{1 - S\beta\gamma - S\gamma\alpha - S\alpha\beta} = \frac{\sin a \sin b \sin C}{1 + \cos a + \cos b + \cos c}, \text{ by (4) of 143°} \cdot \cdot \cdot \quad (11)$$

154°. In (20) of 152° we obtained a versor whose angle was half the area of the triangle DEF, (1) of 153°. To obtain a versor whose angle is the area of this triangle, we have only to take the negative square of equation (1) of 153°. Then

$$-(\beta\alpha^{-1}\gamma)^2 = -(\sin \tfrac{1}{2}E + U\delta \cos \tfrac{1}{2}E)^2,$$

or, $\qquad \dfrac{\beta}{\alpha}\dfrac{\gamma}{\beta}\dfrac{\alpha}{\gamma} = \cos E - U\delta \sin E \quad \cdot \cdot \cdot \cdot \quad (1)$

Articles 152°, 153°, 154° are almost entirely from Hamilton.

155°. The Chordal Triangle of a spherical triangle is the plane triangle formed by joining its corners by cords of the sphere.

Let ABC be a spherical triangle such that

$$\angle C = \angle A + \angle B;$$

then the chordal triangle is right-angled at C.

For, draw an arc of a great circle from C, cutting $\widehat{AB}$ in D, so that $\qquad \angle DAC = \angle DCA$.

Then, with the usual notation for a spherical triangle, but calling the three equal arcs, DA, DB, DC, t, we have

$$1 + \cos 2t = 2 \cos^2 t;$$

and $\qquad 0 = \sin^2 t (\cos CDB + \cos CDA);$

L

adding,

$1 + \cos 2t = (\cos^2 t + \sin^2 t \cos CDB) + (\cos^2 t + \sin^2 t \cos CDA)$
   $= \cos a + \cos b$, 141°, (3);
$-\cos 2t + \cos a + \cos b = 1 = OC^2 = -\gamma^2$;
$S a\beta - S\beta\gamma - S\gamma a + \gamma^2 = 0$;
$S(a - \gamma)(\beta - \gamma) = 0$;

therefore, (chord) CA $\perp$ (chord) CB,
and the chordal triangle is right-angled at C.

156°. To find the angle at which two opposite sides of a spherical quadrilateral meet when produced, in terms of the sides and diagonals (Gauss).

Let ABDE, fig. 33, be the quadrilateral, and let BA and DE produced meet in L. Let θ be the angle between σ and τ, the axes respectively of βa and $\epsilon\delta$; the angle between the planes OAB and ODE, that is, the angle at L, being consequently $(\pi - \theta)$. Then, 84°,

$S \cdot V\beta a V\epsilon\delta = S\beta\delta S a\epsilon - S\beta\epsilon S a\delta$
$= \cos BD \cos EA - \cos BE \cos DA$.

Now, $V\beta a = \sigma \sin AB$; $V\epsilon\delta = \tau \sin DE$;
therefore, $S \cdot V\beta a V\epsilon\delta = \sin AB \sin DE \cdot S\sigma\tau$
   „ = „   „ $\cdot \cos(\pi - \theta)$
   „ = „   „ $\cdot \cos L$.

Therefore,
$$\cos L = \frac{\cos BD \cos EA - \cos BE \cos DA}{\sin AB \sin DE}.$$

Section 3

The Triangle

157°. The sum of the angles of a plane triangle is π. Let ϵ be a unit-vector at C, fig. 31, $\perp$ the plane of the triangle ABC, such that rotation round it from Ua to $U\beta$ is positive; let $\angle BAD = A'$, $\angle CBE = B'$, $\angle ACF = C'$. Then

$\epsilon^{C'} Ua = U\beta$,
$\epsilon^{A'}\epsilon^{C'} Ua = \epsilon^{A'} U\beta = U\gamma$,
$\epsilon^{B'}\epsilon^{A'}\epsilon^{C'} Ua = \epsilon^{B'} U\gamma = Ua$,
$\epsilon^{B'}\epsilon^{A'}\epsilon^{C'} = \epsilon^{(A' + B' + C')} = 1 = \epsilon^{2n\pi}$,

where n is an integer.

THE TRIANGLE

Now, during the triple operation of version represented by $\epsilon^{\iota(A'+B'+C')}$, U_a has evidently made one, and only one, complete revolution of a circle. Therefore $n = 1$, and

$$\epsilon^{\iota(A'+B'+C')} = \epsilon^{\iota(2\pi)};$$

therefore, $\quad\quad\quad A' + B' + C' = 2\pi.$

But $\quad (A + A') + (B + B') + (C + C') = 3\pi.$

Therefore, $\quad\quad\quad A + B + C = \pi.$

158°. The square on the hypotenuse of a right-angled triangle is the sum of the squares on the sides.

Let the hypotenuse $\overline{AB} = \gamma$, $\overline{BC} = a$, $\overline{CA} = \beta$.

Then $\quad -\gamma = a + \beta,$

$\quad\quad \gamma^2 = (a + \beta)^2 = a^2 + \beta^2 + 2Sa\beta$

$\quad\quad\quad\, = a^2 + \beta^2$ (since $Sa\beta = 0$).

Therefore, $\quad\quad AB^2 = BC^2 + CA^2.$

Given the base, the difference of the base angles, and the rectangle under the sides, to construct the triangle. Let A'PA, fig. 34, be the required triangle, O being the middle point of the given base A'A. Draw AB, making $\angle OAB = $ given difference of base angles, and of such a length that $OA \cdot AB = $ the given rectangle under the sides, A'P . PA. Draw OB, OP, and let

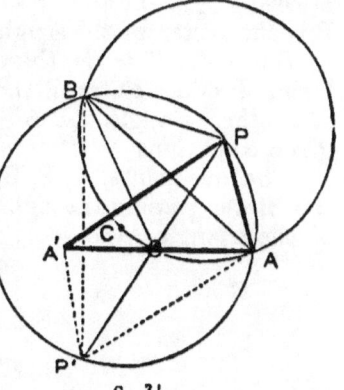

G. 31.

$$\overline{OA} = a,\ \overline{OB} = \beta,\ \overline{OP} = \rho.$$

The problem resolves itself into finding ρ.

Since $A'P \cdot PA = OA \cdot AB,$

$$A'P : A'O = AB : AP.$$

Further, $\angle OA'P = \angle PAB$. Therefore, the triangles OA'P, PAB are similar, and

$$\frac{\rho + a}{a} = \frac{\beta - a}{\rho - a},$$

$$\frac{\rho + a}{a}(\rho - a) = \beta - a,$$

$$\frac{\rho + a}{a}\frac{\rho - a}{a} = \frac{\beta - a}{a},$$

$$\left(\frac{\rho}{a} + 1\right)\left(\frac{\rho}{a} - 1\right) = \quad ,,$$

$$\left(\frac{\rho}{a}\right)^2 = \left(\frac{\rho}{a} + 1\right)\left(\frac{\rho}{a} - 1\right) + 1 = \frac{\beta - a}{a} + 1 = \frac{\beta}{a}.$$

Therefore ρ bisects the angle between a and β, and $r^2 = ab$, since $\rho^2 = \frac{\beta}{a}a^2$. Hence the construction. Bisect the given base A'A in O; draw AB making $\angle$ OAB = given difference of base angles, and of such a length that OA . AB = given rectangle under the sides; and draw OB. Draw OP bisecting $\angle$ AOB, and of such a length that $OP^2 = OA . AB$. P is the vertex of the sought triangle.

Since $(\pm\rho)^2 = \beta a$, there is another solution of the problem. Produce PO until OP' = OP, and P' will be the vertex of another triangle, AP'A', which it is easy to show fulfils the given conditions.

The four points, A, P, B, P', are concyclic; C, the centre of the circle passing through them, lying upon the circumcircle of the triangle AOB.

SECTION 4

The Circle

159°. Let $\overline{OA} = a$, $\overline{OB} = \beta$, $\overline{OC} = \gamma$, be *any* three vectors. Then,

$$K\frac{\beta}{a} = \frac{a^{-1}}{\beta^{-1}};$$

therefore,

$$K\frac{\beta}{a} \pm 1 = \frac{a^{-1}}{\beta^{-1}} \pm 1.$$

THE CIRCLE

But
$$K\frac{\beta}{a} \pm 1 = K\frac{\beta \pm a}{a} = \frac{a^{-1}}{(\beta \pm a)^{-1}};$$

and
$$\frac{a^{-1}}{\beta^{-1}} \pm 1 = \frac{a^{-1} \pm \beta^{-1}}{\beta^{-1}};$$

therefore,
$$\frac{a^{-1} \pm \beta^{-1}}{\beta^{-1}} = \frac{a^{-1}}{(\beta \pm a)^{-1}} \quad \ldots \quad (1)$$

Similarly,
$$\frac{\gamma^{-1} \pm \beta^{-1}}{\beta^{-1}} = \frac{\gamma^{-1}}{(\beta \pm \gamma)^{-1}} \quad \ldots \quad (2)$$

Adopting the negative signs, dividing (2) by (1), and taking the conjugates,

$$K\frac{\gamma^{-1}-\beta^{-1}}{a^{-1}-\beta^{-1}} = K\left(\frac{\gamma^{-1}}{(\beta-\gamma)^{-1}} \cdot \frac{(\beta-a)^{-1}}{a^{-1}}\right) = K\frac{(\beta-a)^{-1}}{a^{-1}} K\frac{\gamma^{-1}}{(\beta-\gamma)^{-1}}$$

$$,, \quad = \quad \frac{a}{\beta-a} \cdot \frac{\beta-\gamma}{\gamma} = \frac{a}{\beta-a} \cdot \frac{\gamma-\beta}{-\gamma} = \frac{OA}{AB} \cdot \frac{BC}{CO} \quad \ldots \quad (3)$$

whatever the vectors a, β, γ may be.

Now, in Pt. I., 29°, it was defined that

$$(OABC) = \frac{OA}{AB} \frac{BC}{CO},$$

where O, A, B, C are any four collinear points. Let O, A, B, C now be *any* four points, $\frac{OA}{AB}$ and $\frac{BC}{CO}$ being, consequently, quaternions.

Definition.

$$(OABC) = \frac{OA}{AB} \frac{BC}{CO} \quad \ldots \ldots \quad (4)$$

is the Anharmonic Quaternion Function of the group of four points, O, A, B, C, *or of the* (*plane or gauche*) *quadrilateral* OABC (Hamilton).

We may therefore write equation (3) as,

$$K\frac{\gamma^{-1}-\beta^{-1}}{a^{-1}-\beta^{-1}} = (OABC) \quad \ldots \quad (5)$$

If $\overline{OA'}$, $\overline{OB'}$, $\overline{OC'}$ be the reciprocals of $\overline{OA}$, $\overline{OB}$, $\overline{OC}$, fig. 35,

$$(OABC) = K\frac{\gamma^{-1}-\beta^{-1}}{a^{-1}-\beta^{-1}} = K\frac{B'C'}{B'A'} \quad \ldots \quad (6)$$

In the particular case when A', B', C' are collinear, (OABC) is a negative scalar.

160°. If $\overline{OA'}$, $\overline{OB'}$ be the reciprocals of any two vectors, $\overline{OA}$, $\overline{OB}$, fig. 35, then $A'B' \parallel OT$, the tangent at O to the circle passing through O, A and B. For, by 96°,

$$\overline{OT} = \beta(\alpha - \beta)(-\alpha) = \alpha^2\beta - \beta^2\alpha.$$

$$B'A' = \alpha^{-1} - \beta^{-1} = -\frac{U\alpha}{T\alpha} + \frac{U\beta}{T\beta} = \frac{1}{\alpha^2 b^2}(\alpha^2\beta - b^2\alpha).$$

Therefore, $\overline{B'A'} \parallel \overline{OT}.$

If a circle be circumscribed to $OA'B'$, the tangent to this new circle at O will be parallel to BA.

161°. If any three coinitial vectors, $\overline{OA}$, $\overline{OB}$, $\overline{OC}$, be chords of one common circle, the terms of their coinitial reciprocals, $\overline{OA'}$, $\overline{OB'}$, $\overline{OC'}$ are collinear, fig. 35.

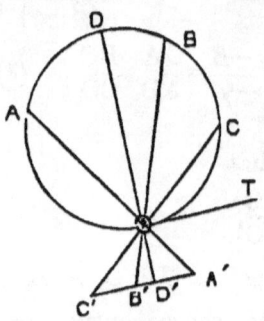

FIG. 35.

For it has been shown, 160°, that $B'A' \parallel OT$, the tangent at O. And it may similarly be shown that $C'B' \parallel OT$. Therefore A', B', C' are collinear.

The indefinite straight line $A'B'$ is evidently the locus of the terms of the reciprocals of all the vector-chords of the circle which have O for origin.

Conversely, if the terms of three vectors, $\overline{OA'}$, $\overline{OB'}$, $\overline{OC'}$, are collinear, their coinitial reciprocals, $\overline{OA}$, $\overline{OB}$, $\overline{OC}$ (if not parallel), are chords of one common circle, or the points O, A, B, C are concyclic.

Let $\angle OAB = \theta$; $\angle BCO = \phi$. Then, since A', B', C' are collinear, $\dfrac{B'C'}{B'A'}$ is a negative scalar, $-t$, and

$$(OABC) = \frac{OA}{AB} \cdot \frac{BC}{CO} = K\frac{B'C'}{B'A'} = K(-t) = -t;$$

$$\frac{AO}{AB} = -t\frac{CO}{CB} = t\left(-\frac{CO}{CB}\right).$$

Therefore,

$$U\frac{AO}{AB} = U\left(-\frac{CO}{CB}\right) = U\frac{OC}{CB};$$

$$\epsilon^{\iota\theta} = \epsilon^{\iota(\pi - \phi)},$$

and $\theta + \phi = \pi.$

THE CIRCLE 151

Therefore, the quadrilateral OABC is inscribed in a circle, or the points O, A, B, C are concyclic.

It is clear that for any circular group, O ... C, we have

$$U \frac{AO}{AB} = \pm U \frac{OC}{CB}. \quad \ldots \ldots \quad (1)$$

the upper or lower sign being taken according as the quadrilateral OABC is uncrossed or crossed. And conversely, if we are given such an equation as (1), connecting a group of points that are not collinear, we know that the group is circular.

162°. Let
$$(OABC) = K \frac{B'C'}{B'A'} = -1.$$

From this equation it follows that A', B', C' are collinear; that O, A, B, C are concyclic; and that $A'B' = B'C'$. Consequently,

$$\beta^{-1} = \tfrac{1}{2}(\gamma^{-1} + a^{-1}) \quad \ldots \ldots \quad (1)$$

The vector β is defined to be the Harmonic Mean between the two vectors γ and a.

Multiplying 2β into (1),

$$2 = \beta(\gamma^{-1} + a^{-1}); \text{ and, } \beta = \frac{2}{\gamma^{-1} + a^{-1}}.$$

Therefore,

$$\frac{\beta}{\gamma} = \frac{2}{(a^{-1} + \gamma^{-1})\gamma} = \frac{2}{a^{-1}\gamma + 1} = \frac{2a}{\gamma + a}; \quad \ldots \quad (2)$$

$$\frac{\beta}{a} = \frac{2}{(a^{-1} + \gamma^{-1})a} = \frac{2}{1 + \gamma^{-1}a} = \frac{2\gamma}{\gamma + a}. \quad \ldots \quad (3)$$

From (2) and (3),

$$\frac{2a}{\gamma + a}\gamma = \beta = \frac{2\gamma}{\gamma + a}a \quad \ldots \ldots \quad (4)$$

If E be the middle point of the chord AC, fig. 35,

$$\gamma + a = \overline{2OE} = 2\epsilon, \ldots \ldots \quad (5)$$

and
$$\frac{a}{\epsilon}\gamma = \beta = \frac{\gamma}{\epsilon}a. \ldots \ldots \quad (6)$$

Therefore, as in algebra, the harmonic mean between any two vectors is the fourth proportional to their semisum and themselves.

By (5) and (6),

$$\beta - \epsilon = \frac{a}{\epsilon}\gamma - \tfrac{1}{2}(\gamma+a) = (7)\frac{a}{\epsilon}(2\epsilon-a) - \frac{2\epsilon-a}{2} - \frac{a}{2} = 2a - \frac{a^2}{\epsilon} - \epsilon\,;$$

$$\frac{\beta-\epsilon}{-\epsilon} = 1 - \frac{2a}{\epsilon} + \frac{a^2}{\epsilon^2} = \left(\frac{\epsilon-a}{\epsilon}\right)^2.$$

Therefore, $\dfrac{EB}{EO} = \dfrac{EC^2}{EO^2}$, and $EC^2 = EO\,.\,EB$, . . . (7)

or, EC is the mean proportional between EO and EB.
Conversely, if any three vectors, EO, EB, EC, be in continued proportion, and we draw $EA = CE$; the points O, A, B, C will form a Circular Harmonic Group. The points A, P, B, P', fig. 34, are an example of such a group.

If $(OABC) = -1$,

$$(OBAC) = K\frac{A'C'}{A'B'} = 2K\frac{A'B'}{A'B'} = 2\,;$$

and $\qquad (OBAC) = \dfrac{OB}{BA}\dfrac{AC}{CO}.$

Therefore, taking tensors,

$\qquad\qquad OC\,.\,BA = \tfrac{1}{2}(OB\,.\,CA).$

Similarly, $\qquad CB\,.\,AO = $ „   „   .

Therefore the rectangles under the opposite sides of an inscribed quadrilateral are each equal to one half the rectangle under its diagonals, if $(OABC) = -1$.

Let F be the cross of the tangents at O and B, fig. 35. Then it is easy to prove that F lies upon AC produced. Similarly, the cross of the tangents at A and C lies upon OB produced. Therefore the diagonals, OB and AC, are Conjugate Chords,—each passes through the pole of the other.

163°. If ABCD be a quadrilateral, plane or gauche,

$$(ABCD) = \frac{AB}{BC}\frac{CD}{DA} = \frac{AB}{BC}\frac{BC}{BC}\frac{CD}{DA}\frac{DA}{DA} = \frac{AB\,.\,BC\,.\,CD\,.\,DA}{BC^2\,.\,DA^2}\,;$$

or,

$v^2(ABCD) = AB\,.\,BC\,.\,CD\,.\,DA = $ continued product of the
$\qquad\qquad\qquad\qquad$ sides, ... (1)

where $v^2 = BC^2\,.\,DA^2$ is a positive scalar.

If the quadrilateral be plane and inscribed in a circle, the anharmonic function, (ABCD), 159° (4), is a scalar, m, which is positive or negative according as the quadrilateral is crossed or not. Hence, in this case, (1) becomes
$$\overline{AB} \cdot \overline{BC} \cdot \overline{CD} \cdot \overline{DA} = \pm mv^2 = \pm t \quad . \quad . \quad (2)$$
In general, the product of the successive sides of an n-gon inscribed in a circle is a scalar if n be even, and a vector-tangent to the circle at the initial point of the n-gon if n be odd.

164°. Some of the equations of the circle have been given in 101°. If $\overline{OE} = \epsilon$ be any given unit-vector ; $\overline{OK} = \kappa$, the vector of any given point in the plane through $E \perp \epsilon$; and $\overline{KA} = a$, a constant vector in that plane ; then
$$(\rho - \kappa)^2 = a^2 \; ; \; S\frac{\rho}{\epsilon} = 1 \quad . \quad . \quad . \quad . \quad . \quad (1)$$
is the equation of a circle passing through A, with K for centre.

If $T\kappa = c$, these equations become
$$\rho^2 - 2S\kappa\rho = c^2 - a^2 \; ; \; S\frac{\rho}{\epsilon} = 1 \quad . \quad . \quad . \quad (2)$$
If O be on the circle,
$$\rho^2 - 2S\kappa\rho = 0 \; ; \; UV\kappa\rho = \eta \quad . \quad . \quad . \quad . \quad (3)$$
where η is some other given unit-vector.

The first equation of (3) may be written :
$$S\rho(\rho - 2\kappa) = 0 \; ;$$
therefore the angle of a semicircle is $\frac{1}{2}\pi$.

165°. Let $OD = \delta$ be a diameter of the circle, fig. 35 ; and let DO produced cut $C'A'$ in D'. Then, 161°, $\overline{OD'} = \delta^{-1}$; and since $A'D' \parallel OT$, if τ be the vector along OT,
$$V\tau(\delta^{-1} - a^{-1}) = 0.$$
Therefore, $\qquad V\tau\delta^{-1} = V\tau a^{-1},$
or, since $\tau\delta^{-1}$ is a right quaternion,
$$\tau\delta^{-1} = V\tau a^{-1},$$
$$K\tau\delta^{-1} = \delta^{-1}\tau = KV\tau a^{-1} = -V\tau a^{-1},$$
and $\qquad \delta = \dfrac{-\tau}{V\tau a^{-1}} \quad . \quad . \quad . \quad . \quad . \quad . \quad . \quad (1)$

the expression for the diameter passing through O.

166°. It has been assumed that the tangent is perpendicular to the radius drawn to the point of contact. This may be shown by differentiating the equation,

$$\rho^2 - 2S\kappa\rho = 0, \text{ (3) of } 164°.$$

Then
$$2S\rho d\rho - 2S\kappa d\rho = 0,$$
$$S(\rho - \kappa)d\rho = 0.$$

Therefore the radius drawn to the point of contact, $\rho - \kappa$, is perpendicular to $d\rho$, the vector-tangent.

167°. Let $O\bar{A} = a$ be the vector of any point upon a circle whose centre is O, and let ρ be the vector of a variable point upon the tangent at A. Then, η being a given unit-vector perpendicular to the plane of the circle,

$$\left. \begin{array}{ll} Sa(\rho - a) = 0, & UVa\rho = \eta, \\ Sa\rho = -a^2, & UVa\rho = \eta, \end{array} \right\} \quad \cdots \quad (1)$$

or,

are the equations of the tangent at A.

If the circle be a great circle of a sphere, equation (1) is the equation of a tangent to the sphere at A.

$$Sa\rho = -a^2 \quad \cdots \cdots \cdots (2)$$

is the equation of the tangent plane to the sphere at A, since it represents all the tangents that can be drawn at A.

168°. From O, the centre of a given circle, draw a straight line, cutting the circle in A, to a given external point, E; let T, T' be the points in which the tangents from E touch the circle; and let TT' cut OA in D. Let $\overline{OA} = a$, $\overline{OD} = \delta$, $OE = \epsilon$, and let ρ be the vector of a variable point in TT'. Then D and E are inverse points with respect to the circle, and

$$OD \cdot OE = OA^2; \quad OD = \frac{a^2}{e}.$$

Therefore,
$$\delta = T\delta U\delta = \frac{a^2}{e}U\epsilon = \frac{a^2}{e^2}\epsilon. \quad \cdots \quad (1)$$

But
$$0 = S\delta(\rho - \delta), \text{ or, } S\delta\rho = -d^2.$$

Substituting in this last equation the value of δ, (1),

$$\frac{a^2}{e^2}S\epsilon\rho = -\frac{a^4}{e^2},$$

and
$$S\epsilon\rho = -a^2.$$

THE CIRCLE

Hence, if η be a given unit-vector perpendicular to the plane of the circle,
$$S\epsilon\rho = -a^2\ ;\ UV\epsilon\rho = \eta\ .\ \ .\ \ .\ \ .\ \ .\ (2)$$
are the equations of the chord of contact of the two tangents from E.

If the circle be a great circle of a sphere,
$$S\epsilon\rho = -a^2\ .\ \ .\ \ .\ \ .\ \ .\ \ .\ \ .\ (3)$$
is the equation of the polar plane of E.

169°. The join of the points of intersection of two circles is perpendicular to the join of their centres.

Let the circles intersect in A and A'; let their centres be K and K'; let $\overline{KK'} = \gamma$, $\overline{AA'} = \delta$. Then,
$$(\overline{KA} - \gamma)^2 = \overline{K'A}{}^2 = \overline{K'A'}{}^2 = (\overline{KA'} - \gamma)^2,$$
and
$$S(\overline{KA}\cdot\gamma) = S(\overline{KA'}\cdot\gamma)\ ;$$
$$S(\overline{KA'} - \overline{KA})\gamma = 0,$$
$$S\gamma\delta = 0.$$
Therefore, $\gamma \perp \delta$.

SECTION 5
Conic Sections

170°. To find the locus of a point such that the ratio of its distances from a given point and a given straight line is constant.

Let F be the given point and QR the given straight line, fig. 36. Let P be any point, and let PQ and FR be perpendicular to QR. Let $\overline{FP} = \rho$; $\overline{FR} = \mu$, $\overline{RQ} = y\nu$; $\overline{PQ} = x\mu$. This last assumption limits the locus of P to the plane containing QR which passes through F. Then, if e be a scalar representing the constant ratio,
$$e = \frac{T\rho}{T\cdot\overline{PQ}}\ ;\ e^2 = \frac{T^2\rho}{T^2\cdot\overline{PQ}} = \frac{\rho^2}{x^2\mu^2}\ ;$$
$$\rho^2 = e^2 x^2 \mu^2.$$
$$\overline{FP} + \overline{PQ} = \overline{FQ} = \overline{FR} + \overline{RQ},$$
$$\rho + x\mu = \mu + y\nu\ ;$$
$S\cdot\mu\times.\quad S\mu\rho + x\mu^2 = \mu^2 + yS\mu\nu$
$\quad\quad\quad\ ,,\ \quad\ \ = \mu^2$, since $S\mu\nu = 0.$

Therefore, $x^2\mu^4 = (\mu^2 - S\mu\rho)^2$,

But $x^2 = \dfrac{\rho^2}{e^2\mu^2}$;

therefore, $\mu^2\rho^2 = e^2(\mu^2 - S\mu\rho)^2$ . . . . . (1)

the general focal equation of a Conic Section, which is an ellipse, parabola, or hyperbola according as $e \lessgtr 1$.

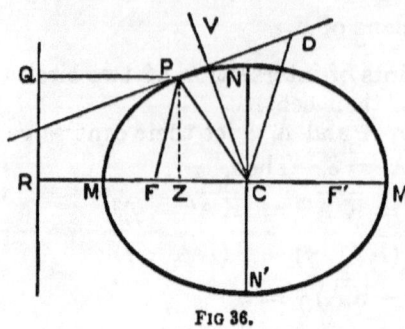

FIG 36.

The point F is a focus, and QR is the directrix.

171°. To find the points in which the conic cuts μ, or $\overline{\text{FR}}$, fig. 36.

Let $x\mu$ be substituted for ρ in the general equation, and we get

$$x = \frac{e}{1+e}, \text{ or } -\frac{e}{1-e}.$$

Therefore,

$$\overline{\text{FM}} = \frac{e\mu}{1+e}; \quad \overline{\text{FM}'} = -\frac{e\mu}{1-e}.$$

$$\overline{\text{M'M}} = \overline{\text{M'F}} + \overline{\text{FM}} = \left(\frac{e}{1-e} + \frac{e}{1+e}\right)\mu = \frac{2e\mu}{1-e^2};$$

hence, $\mu = \dfrac{1-e^2}{2e}\overline{\text{M'M}} = \dfrac{1-e^2}{2e}\text{T}.\overline{\text{M'M}}.\text{U}\mu.$

Let $\text{T}.\overline{\text{M'M}} = 2m$, and

$$\text{T}\mu = \text{FR} = \frac{1-e^2}{e}m.$$

$$\text{T}.\overline{\text{FM}} = \frac{e}{1+e}\text{T}\mu = (1-e)m.$$

$$\text{T}.\overline{\text{FM}'} = \frac{e}{1-e}\text{T}\mu = (1+e)m.$$

Let C be the middle point of MM'. Then

$$\text{T}.\text{CF} = m - (1-e)m = em.$$

$$\text{T}.\overline{\text{CR}} = em + \frac{1-e^2}{e}m = \frac{m}{e}.$$

$$\text{T}.\overline{\text{MR}} = \frac{m}{e} - m = \frac{1-e}{e}m;$$

CONIC SECTIONS 157

Collecting these results, we have, for the ellipse and hyperbola,

$$CF = em = CF';$$

$$CR = \frac{m}{e};$$

$$FM' = (1 + e)m = F'M;$$

$$FM = \pm(1 - e)m = F'M';$$

$$FR = \pm\frac{1 - e^2}{e}m;$$

$$MR = \pm\frac{1 - e}{e}m;$$

the positive signs being taken for the ellipse, the negative for the hyperbola.

For the parabola, $e = 1$, and

$$x = \tfrac{1}{2} \text{ or } \infty.$$

Therefore the point M', and consequently C, is at infinity; and

$$\overline{FM} = \tfrac{1}{2}\mu = \overline{MR}.$$

172°. To transform the focal equation of the ellipse and hyperbola into their central equation.

Let the focal equation be written,

$$\mu_1{}^2\rho_1{}^2 = e^2(\mu_1{}^2 - S\mu_1\rho_1)^2,$$

as we are about to change the origin, and thereby change the meaning, of μ and ρ.

Let $CM = \mu$; $CP = \rho$, fig. 36. Then,

$$\mu_1 = \overline{FR} = \frac{1 - e^2}{e}\mu;$$

$$\rho_1 = \overline{FP} = \overline{FC} + \overline{CP} = \rho - e\mu.$$

Substituting these values of μ_1 and ρ_1 in the general focal equation, we get

$$\mu^2\rho^2 - e^2S^2\mu\rho = \mu^4(1 - e^2); \quad . \quad . \quad . \quad (1)$$

the general equation of a central conic.

This equation may be written,

$$1 = \frac{\mu^2\rho^2 - e^2S^2\mu\rho}{\mu^4(1 - e^2)} = \frac{\mu^2\rho^2 - e^2S\rho\mu S\mu\rho}{\mu^4(1 - e^2)} = S_\rho\left(\frac{\mu^2\rho - e^2\mu S\mu\rho}{\mu^4(1 - e^2)}\right).$$

But the quantity in brackets is of the same form as the right-hand member of equation (1), 133°. Therefore, if we put

$$\phi\rho = \frac{\mu^2\rho - e^2\mu S\mu\rho}{\mu^4(1 - e^2)}, \quad \ldots \ldots (2)$$

we get, as the equation of a central conic,

$$S\rho\phi\rho = 1. \ldots \ldots \ldots (3)$$

Let ρ be parallel to μ, or $x\rho = \mu$. Then

$$\phi\rho = \frac{\mu^2 - e^2x^2\rho^2}{\mu^4(1 - e^2)}\rho.$$

If $\rho \perp \mu$, or $S\mu\rho = 0$,

$$\phi\rho = \frac{\rho}{\mu^2(1 - e^2)}.$$

Hence the coinitial vector $\phi\rho$ is parallel to ρ when ρ is parallel to either the major or minor axis of the ellipse, or the transverse or conjugate axis of the hyperbola.

173°. To find the points in which the conic cuts the line NN' drawn through C perpendicular to MM', fig 36.

$$\mu^2\rho^2 - e^2S^2\mu\rho = \mu^4(1 - e^2).$$

But in this particular case $S\mu\rho = 0$. Therefore,

$$\rho^2 = \mu^2(1 - e^2) \quad . \quad . \quad . \quad (1)$$

Let n be the tensor of ρ, and we have

$$n^2 = m^2(1 - e^2) \quad . \quad . \quad . \quad (2)$$

and

$$e^2 = \frac{m^2 - n^2}{m^2} \quad . \quad . \quad . \quad (3)$$

Obviously, n^2 in (2) is positive for the ellipse and negative for the hyperbola. Further, in this latter case, since $e > 1$,

$$n = \pm m\sqrt{(1 - e^2)}$$

gives an imaginary value for n; or, the conjugate axis does not meet the hyperbola in real points.

CN = CN' = n, the square root of n^2, without regard to sign; and NN' is called an axis of the curve.

The vector $\overline{CN}$ will be designated by ν, for both the ellipse and the hyperbola.

174°. It has been shown that, if ρ be the vector of a plane curve, $d\rho$ is a vector successive to ρ, along the tangent at P, 113°. Differentiating the equation $S\rho\phi\rho = 1$ we get

$$dS\rho\phi\rho = Sd\,(\rho\phi\rho) = S\,(d\rho \cdot \phi\rho) + S\,(\rho \cdot d\phi\rho) = 0.$$

But $S\,(d\rho \cdot \phi\rho) = S\,(\rho \cdot \phi d\rho)\,;$
and $S\,(\rho \cdot d\phi\rho) = S\,(\rho \cdot \phi d\rho)\,;$
therefore, $S\rho\phi d\rho = 0.$

Now, since $d\rho$ is parallel to the tangent at P, if $\overline{CD}\,(=\pi)$, fig. 36, be the vector of *any* point upon the tangent,

$$\pi = \rho + x d\rho$$

and $$d\rho = \frac{1}{x}\,(\pi - \rho).$$

Therefore, $S\rho\phi\,(\pi - \rho) = 0 = S\,(\pi - \rho)\,\phi\rho,$ . . (1)
or, $S\rho\phi\pi = S\pi\phi\rho = S\rho\phi\rho = 1.$ . . . (2)

Equation (2) is the general equation of the Tangent of a central conic.

Since $\pi - \rho$ is parallel to the tangent, equation (1) shows that $\phi\rho = CV$ is perpendicular to the tangent, or parallel to the normal at the point of contact, fig. 36.

175°. The locus of the middle points of parallel chords of a central conic is a straight line.

Let any number of chords be drawn parallel to any given diameter, 2γ, and let σ be the vector of the middle point of any one of them, $2x\gamma$. Then the vectors of the extremities of this chord,

$$\sigma + x\gamma\,;\quad \sigma - x\gamma,$$

are vectors of points upon the conic. Therefore,

$$S\,.\,(\sigma + x\gamma)\,\phi\,(\sigma + x\gamma) = 1,$$
$$S\,.\,(\sigma - x\gamma)\,\phi\,(\sigma - x\gamma) = 1.$$

Equating the left-hand numbers of these two equations, and bearing in mind that $\phi\,(\sigma + x\gamma) = \phi\sigma + x\phi\gamma$, 135° (1), (2),

$$S\sigma\phi\gamma + S\gamma\phi\sigma = 0.$$

But $S\gamma\phi\sigma = S\sigma\phi\gamma\,;$
therefore, $S\sigma\phi\gamma = 0.$

Now, σ lies in the plane of the conic. The locus, therefore, is that of equation (8), 99°—*i.e.*, a straight line through the origin (C, the centre of the conic) perpendicular to $\phi\gamma$. Therefore the locus of the middle points of all chords of a central conic parallel to any diameter, 2γ, is another diameter, say $2\tilde{c}$, which is at right angles to $\phi\gamma$, or parallel to the tangent through either extremity of 2γ.

176°. By the last article, if ν_1 be a diameter which bisects all chords parallel to μ_1,
$$S\nu_1\phi\mu_1 = 0.$$
But $\qquad S\nu_1\phi\mu_1 = S\mu_1\phi\nu_1 = 0 \; ; \quad \ldots \quad (1)$

therefore μ_1 bisects all chords parallel to ν_1 ; and as ν_1 is parallel to the tangent at the term of μ_1, so μ_1 is parallel to the tangent at the term of ν_1.

Diameters which possess this property are called Conjugate Diameters.

177°. The system
$$\rho = V a^{c\theta}\mu \; ; \; T a = 1 \; ; \; S a\mu \neq 0, \quad \ldots \quad (1)$$
represents a plane ellipse, θ being the eccentric angle and μ and $V a\mu \; (= \nu)$ the major and minor axes, 103°.

$\rho = V a^{c\theta}\mu = V(\cos\theta + a\sin\theta)\mu = V(\mu\cos\theta + a\mu\sin\theta)$

$\quad = \mu\cos\theta + \nu\sin\theta \; . \; . \; . \; . \; . \; . \; . \; . \; . \; . \; . \; . \; (2)$

Differentiating (1),

$\dfrac{d\rho}{d\theta} = V a^{c(\theta + \frac{1}{2}\pi)}\mu \; . \; . \; . \; . \; . \; . \; . \; . \; . \; . \; . \; . \; . \; . \; (3)$

$\quad = V a^{\frac{1}{2}c\pi} a^{c\theta}\mu = V a (\cos\theta + a\sin\theta)\mu$

$\quad = V(a^2\mu\sin\theta + a\mu\cos\theta) = -\mu\sin\theta + \nu\cos\theta \; . \; . \; (4)$

Since the value of $\dfrac{d\rho}{d\theta}$ in (3) (which is parallel to the conjugate of ρ, 176°) is the value of ρ in (1), when θ becomes $(\theta + \frac{1}{2}\pi)$; it follows that any two expressions for ρ in which θ differs by $\frac{1}{2}\pi$, represent conjugate diameters. For example, if we substitute $(\theta + \frac{1}{2}\pi)$ for θ in (2), we obtain (4).

178°. From (2) and (4) of 177°,

$$4TV\rho \frac{d\rho}{d\theta} = 4TV(\mu\cos\theta + \nu\sin\theta)(-\mu\sin\theta + \nu\cos\theta)$$

$$\quad = 4TV\mu\nu.$$

In words, the area of the parallelogram circumscribing an ellipse and touching it at the extremities of conjugate diameters is constant.

CONIC SECTIONS   161

179°. Let DD' be any diameter of a central conic. Then, if E be any point upon the conic, DE and $D'E$ are Supplemental Chords.

Let C be the centre of the conic; $\overline{CE} = \rho$; $\overline{DD'} = 2\delta$. Then,
$$\overline{DE} = \delta + \rho, \quad \overline{ED'} = \delta - \rho,$$

and $S \cdot (\delta + \rho) \phi (\delta - \rho) = S \cdot (\delta + \rho)(\phi\delta - \phi\rho)$
$$= S\delta\phi\delta - S\delta\phi\rho + S\rho\phi\delta - S\rho\phi\rho.$$

But
$$-S\delta\phi\rho + S\rho\phi\delta = -S\rho\phi\delta + S\rho\phi\delta = 0\,;$$
and $\qquad\qquad S\delta\phi\delta - S\rho\phi\rho = 1 - 1 = 0.$

Therefore, $\qquad S \cdot (\delta + \rho) \phi (\delta - \rho) = 0.$

Therefore, if ϵ and ζ be two diameters parallel respectively to the supplemental chords $(\delta + \rho)$ and $(\delta - \rho)$,
$$S\epsilon\phi\zeta = 0.$$

Therefore diameters parallel to supplementary chords are conjugate.

180°. From T, any point exterior to a central conic, draw tangents touching the conic in P and R. Let C (as usual) be the centre of the conic; draw PR, cutting CT in Q, and let $\overline{CT} = \pi$. Then the equation of the tangent, 174°,
$$S\rho\phi\pi = 1,$$

is satisfied by the values of ρ for the points P and R. And this equation is also the equation of a straight line, 99°. It must, therefore, be the equation of the straight line passing through the points P and R—*i.e.*, the equation of the chord of contact. Writing σ for ρ (to avoid confusion with the ρ of the conic), we have
$$S\sigma\phi\pi = 1 \quad \ldots \quad \ldots \quad \ldots \quad (1)$$

as the equation of the chord of contact, or of the Polar of the point T.

181°. To find the locus of T, the cross of the tangents, if the chord of contact always passes through a fixed point, A.

Let σ be the vector of the point A. Then, since A lies on the chord of contact,
$$S\sigma\phi\pi = 1,$$
and $\qquad\qquad S\pi\phi\sigma = 1.$

M

Therefore, 99°, the locus of T is a straight line perpendicular to $\phi\sigma$—*i.e.*, parallel to the tangent at the point where CA produced meets the conic.

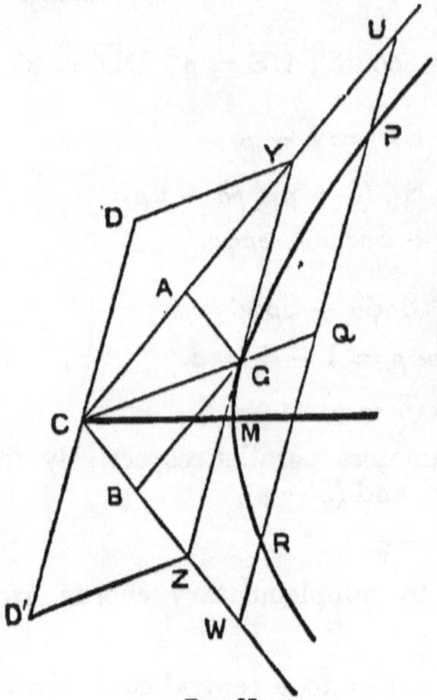

182°. The equation,

$$\rho = t\alpha + t^{-1}\beta \quad .. \quad (1)$$

represents a hyperbola, 102°; α and β being unit-vectors along the asymptotes CY and CZ respectively, and t and t^{-1} the Cartesian co-ordinates, fig. 37.

For the tangent at G,

$$\tau = d\rho = (\alpha - t^{-2}\beta)\, dt,$$

or,

$$\frac{d\rho}{dt} = \alpha - t^{-2}\beta \quad .. \quad (2)$$

If π be the vector of a variable point upon τ,

Fig. 37.

$$\pi = \rho + x\frac{d\rho}{dt} = t\alpha + t^{-1}\beta + x\alpha - xt^{-2}\beta = (t+x)\alpha + t^{-2}(t-x)\beta.$$

If $\pi = \overline{CY}$,

$$t^{-2}(t-x) = 0\ ; \text{ or, } x = t, \text{ and } \overline{CY} = 2t\alpha.$$

If $\pi = \overline{CZ}$,

$$t + x = 0\ ; \text{ or, } x = -t, \text{ and } \overline{CZ} = 2t^{-1}\beta.$$

Therefore,

$$\overline{GY} = \overline{CY} - \rho = t\alpha - t^{-1}\beta = \rho - \overline{CZ} = \overline{ZG} \quad .. \quad (3)$$

Therefore the intercept of the tangent between the asymptotes is bisected in the point of contact.

Obviously, any diameter, CG produced, bisects the intercept between the asymptotes of all lines drawn ∥ the tangent at its vertex; or, UQ = QW.

183°. From (2) of 182° it follows that, if any diameter, CG, be the intermediate diagonal of a parallelogram whose coinitial sides, CA, CB, lie along the asymptotes, the other diagonal, AB, is parallel to the tangent at G.

For, since $\overline{CA} + \overline{CB} = \overline{CG} = t\alpha + t^{-1}\beta,$

we have $\overline{CA} = t\alpha \; ; \; \overline{CB} = t^{-1}\beta,$

and $\overline{BA} = t\alpha - t^{-1}\beta.$

But, 182° (2), $\dfrac{d\rho}{dt} = \alpha - t^{-2}\beta = t^{-1}(t\alpha - t^{-1}\beta) = t^{-1}\overline{BA}.$

Therefore, $\overline{BA} \parallel d\rho.$

184°. It is evident that if we complete the parallelograms CGYD and CGZD', DD' and CG will be conjugate diameters; or, the asymptotes have the same direction as the diagonals of parallelograms whose adjacent sides are any pair of conjugate diameters.

185°. Any diameter of a hyperbola, CG, bisects all chords parallel to the tangent at its vertex (G); for example, RP which is cut in Q by CG.

For, let $\overline{CP} = v\alpha + v^{-1}\beta.$ Then,

$v\alpha + v^{-1}\beta = CQ + \overline{QP} = x(t\alpha + t^{-1}\beta) + y(t\alpha - t^{-1}\beta)\, 182°\,(1),\,(3).$

Therefore, $t(x + y) = v = \dfrac{t}{x - y},$

and $x^2 - y^2 = 1.$

Therefore, for every point, as Q, determined by x, there are two points, R and P, determined by the two corresponding values of y, which values are equal with opposite signs (Hardy).

Since UQ = QW, 182°, and PQ = QR, it follows that UP = RW, or, the intercepts of the secant between the hyperbola and its asymptotes are equal.

186°. The area of the triangle formed by the asymptotes and any tangent is constant. For, since $CY = 2t\alpha$, $\overline{CZ} = 2t^{-1}\beta$, we have at once,

$V(2t\alpha \,.\, 2t^{-1}\beta) = 4V\alpha\beta = $ constant vector-area.

187°. The general focal equation of the parabola is, (1) of 170°,

$$\mu^2\rho^2 = (\mu^2 - S\mu\rho)^2, \qquad \ldots \ldots \quad (1)$$

which may also be written,
$$S\rho\left\{\frac{\rho-\mu^{-1}S\mu\rho}{\mu^2}+2\mu^{-1}\right\}=1.$$

Let
$$\phi\rho=\frac{\rho-\mu^{-1}S\mu\rho}{\mu^2}\quad\ldots\ldots\quad(2)$$

and the equation of the parabola becomes
$$S\rho\,(\phi\rho+2\mu^{-1})=1\quad\ldots\ldots\quad(3)$$

Operating on equation (2) with $S\,.\,\mu\times$,
$$S\mu\phi\rho=S\mu\rho-S\mu\rho=0\quad\ldots\ldots\quad(4)$$

Therefore $\phi\rho$, which is coinitial with ρ, is $\perp$ the axis of the parabola.

$S\,.\,\rho\times$,
$$S\rho\phi\rho=\frac{\rho^2-\mu^{-2}S^2\mu\rho}{\mu^2}=\mu^2\,(\phi\rho)^2=1-2S\mu^{-1}\rho.\quad(5)$$

188°. Differentiating equation (3) of 187°,
$$0=S\,(d\rho\,.\,\phi\rho)+S\,(\rho\,.\,d\phi\rho)+2S\mu^{-1}d\rho$$
$$\text{,,}\ =S\,(\rho\,.\,\phi d\rho)+S\,(\rho\,.\,\phi d\rho)+2S\mu^{-1}d\rho$$
$$\text{,,}\ =2S\rho\phi d\rho+2S\mu^{-1}d\rho,$$
or,
$$S\rho\phi d\rho+S\mu^{-1}d\rho=0.$$

If π be the vector of any point upon the tangent,
$$\pi=\rho+xd\rho,$$
and
$$d\rho=\frac{\pi-\rho}{x}.$$

Hence, $\quad\dfrac{1}{x}\{S\rho\phi\,(\pi-\rho)+S\mu^{-1}\,(\pi-\rho)\}=0,$

and $\quad S\rho\phi\pi-S\rho\phi\rho+S\mu^{-1}\pi-S\mu^{-1}\rho=0,\quad\ldots\quad(1)$

the focal equation of the tangent.

Since, equation (5) of 187°,
$$S\rho\phi\rho=1-2S\mu^{-1}\rho,\text{ and }S\rho\phi\pi=S\pi\phi\rho,$$
$$S\pi\,(\phi\rho+\mu^{-1})+S\mu^{-1}\rho=1,\quad\ldots\ldots\quad(2)$$

another form of the equation of the tangent.

Equation (1) is evidently equivalent to
$$S\,(\pi-\rho)\,(\phi\rho+\mu^{-1})=0.$$

But $(\pi-\rho)$ is a vector along the tangent. Therefore,
$$\phi\rho+\mu^{-1}\quad\ldots\ldots\quad(3)$$

CONIC SECTIONS

is a vector along the normal; and if σ be the vector of any point on the normal, its equation is

$$\sigma = \rho + x(\phi\rho + \mu^{-1}). \quad \ldots \ldots \quad (4)$$

189°. Let $\overline{PA}$ be $\perp \mu \ (= \overline{FR})$, fig. 38, and let equation (2) of 187° be written,

$$\rho = \overline{FA} + \overline{AP} = \mu^{-1}S\mu\rho + \mu^2\phi\rho.$$

Since $\overline{FP} = \rho$, and $\phi\rho \perp \mu$, (4) of 187°; this equation gives us

$$\overline{FA} = \mu^{-1}S\mu\rho\ ;$$
$$\overline{AP} = \mu^2\phi\rho \quad . \quad . \quad (1)$$

Since π in equation (2) of 188° is *any* vector drawn from the focus to the tangent, it may represent $\overline{FT} = x\mu$. Substituting this value of π in that equation, we have

$$x = 1 - S\mu^{-1}\rho.$$

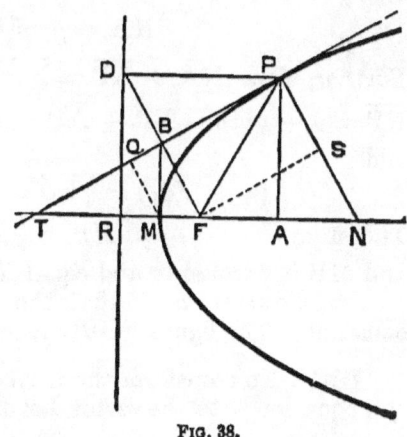

Fig. 38.

Hence,

$$\pi = \overline{FT} = x\mu = \mu - \mu S\mu^{-1}\rho.$$
$$\overline{MT} = \overline{FT} - \overline{FM} = \tfrac{1}{2}\mu - \mu S\mu^{-1}\rho = \tfrac{1}{2}\mu - \mu^{-1}S\mu\rho$$
$$\text{''} \ = (\text{by (1)}) \ \overline{FM} - \overline{FA} = \overline{AF} + FM\ ;$$

therefore, $\quad\quad\quad \overline{MT} = \overline{AM}. \quad \ldots \ldots \quad (2)$

Since $\quad\quad\quad \overline{FT} = \mu - \mu^{-1}S\mu\rho,$

we have $\quad (\overline{FT})^2 = (\mu - \mu^{-1}S\mu\rho)^2 = \dfrac{\mu^4 - 2\mu^2 S\mu\rho + S^2\mu\rho}{\mu^2}$

$$\text{''} \ = \dfrac{(\mu^2 - S\mu\rho)^2}{\mu^2} = \rho^2, \ (1) \text{ of } 187°.$$

Therefore, $\quad\quad\quad FT = FP \quad \ldots \ldots \quad (3)$

Consequently, if PD be a line parallel to the axis, meeting the directrix in D, the tangent PT bisects the angle FPD; and FD is perpendicular to, and is bisected by, the tangent.

By (3) of 188° $(\phi\rho + \mu^{-1})$ is a vector along the normal. Therefore,
$$y(\phi\rho + \mu^{-1}) = \overline{PN} = \overline{PA} + \overline{AN}$$
$$" \quad = -\mu^2\phi\rho + z\mu, (1).$$
Therefore, $(y + \mu^2)\phi\rho = (-y + z\mu^2)\mu^{-1}$;
,, $\quad y = -\mu^2$; $y = z\mu^2$;
,, $\quad z = -1$;
,, $\quad NA = \mu = FR$ . . . . . . (4)

Further, since $\overline{NA} + \overline{AP} = \overline{NP}$,
$$\overline{NP} = \mu + \mu^2\phi\rho = \overline{FR} + \overline{AP} = \overline{FR} + \overline{RD} = \overline{FD}, \ldots (5)$$
and
$$\tfrac{1}{2}(\mu + \mu^2\phi\rho) = \tfrac{1}{2}\overline{FD} = \overline{FB} = \overline{FM} + \overline{MB}.$$
Therefore, $\quad \overline{MB} = \tfrac{1}{2}\mu^2\phi\rho,$ . . . . . . (6)
and MB is parallel to and equal to half AP.

It follows from (4) that the subnormal of a parabola is constant. The figure FDPN is evidently a rhombus.

190°. To transform the focal equation of the parabola to the equation with the vertex for origin; let the focal equation be written,
$$\mu_1^2\rho_1^2 = (\mu_1^2 - S\mu_1\rho_1)^2,$$
as we are about to change the meaning of both μ and ρ. Then,
$$\mu_1 = \overline{FR} = -2\overline{MF} = -2\mu,$$
$$\rho_1 = \overline{FP} = \overline{FM} + \overline{MP} = \rho - \mu.$$
Substituting these values of μ_1 and ρ_1 in equation (1) of 187°,
$$\rho^2 - 4S\mu\rho - \mu^{-2}S^2\mu\rho = 0, \ldots (1)$$
the equation of the parabola with the vertex for origin.

This equation may be written,
$$S\rho(\rho - \mu^{-1}S\mu\rho - 4\mu) = 0.$$
Let $\quad \phi\rho = \rho - \mu^{-1}S\mu\rho,$ . . . . . . (2)
and we have, for the equation of the parabola with the vertex for origin,
$$S\rho(\phi\rho - 4\mu) = 0 \ldots \ldots (3)$$
As before, $\quad S\mu\phi\rho = 0;$ . . . . (4)
but, in this case, $\quad S\rho\phi\rho = (\phi\rho)^2.$ . . . . (5)

CONIC SECTIONS

The equation of the tangent will be found to be

$$S\pi\phi\rho - S\rho\phi\rho + 2S\mu\rho - 2S\mu\pi = 0,$$
or, $$S\pi(\phi\rho - 2\mu) - 2S\mu\rho = 0, \quad \bigg\} \quad . . . . (6)$$

and the vector along the normal

$$\phi\rho - 2\mu. \quad . . . . (7)$$

As a verification of equation (1); let i and j be unit-vectors along the axis and tangent at the vertex, and let $\mu = mi$. Then $\rho = xi + yj$; $S\mu\rho = -mx$; and,

$$y^2 = 4mx, \quad . . . . (8)$$

the Cartesian equation.

191°. To find the locus of the intersection of the normal and the perpendicular upon it from the focus, FS, fig. 38.

Since $FS \perp PN$, if $\overline{FS} = \sigma$,

$$S\rho\sigma = \sigma^2 \quad . . . . (1)$$

$$\sigma = \overline{FP} + \overline{PS} = \overline{FP} + \tfrac{1}{2}PN$$

$$,, = \rho - \tfrac{1}{2}\mu^2(\phi\rho + \mu^{-1}), \text{ by (5) of 190°.} . \quad (2)$$

S . μ ×. $\quad S\mu\sigma = S\mu\rho - \tfrac{1}{2}\mu^2(S\mu\phi\rho + 1).$
But $\quad S\mu\phi\rho = 0;$
therefore, $\quad S\mu\rho = S\mu\sigma + \tfrac{1}{2}\mu^2. \quad . . . . . . (3)$
S . ρ ×. $\quad S\rho\sigma = \rho^2 - \tfrac{1}{2}\mu^2(S\rho\phi\rho + S\mu^{-1}\rho).$

Subtracting (1) from this equation,

$$\rho^2 - \sigma^2 = \tfrac{1}{2}\mu^2(S\rho\phi\rho + S\mu^{-1}\rho).$$

Now, (5) of 187°,

$$S\rho\phi\rho = \frac{\mu^2 - 2S\mu\rho}{\mu^2}.$$

Therefore,

$$\rho^2 - \sigma^2 = \tfrac{1}{2}\mu^2 \left(\frac{\mu^2 - S\mu\rho}{\mu^2}\right) = \frac{\mu^2 - S\mu\rho}{2}$$

$$,, = \frac{\mu^2 - 2S\mu\sigma}{4}, \text{ by (3)}.$$

Multiplying this equation by μ^2, and transposing,

$$\mu^2\sigma^2 + \frac{\mu^4 - 2\mu^2 S\mu\sigma}{4} = \mu^2\rho^2 = \mu^4 - 2\mu^2 S\mu\rho + S^2\mu\rho, \text{ (1) of 187°,}$$

$$,, = \mu^4 - 2\mu^2(S\mu\sigma + \tfrac{1}{2}\mu^2) + (S\mu\sigma + \tfrac{1}{2}\mu^2)^2, \text{by (3)}$$

and $\quad \mu^2\sigma^2 = -\tfrac{1}{2}\mu^2 S\mu\sigma + S^2\mu\sigma \quad . . . . . (4)$

This is the equation of a parabola with its vertex for origin, whose axis is parallel to the axis of the given parabola; for, if we substitute $-8\mu_1$ for μ, we get

$$\sigma^2 - 4S\mu_1\sigma - \mu_1^{-2}S^2\mu_1\sigma = 0,$$

which is the same form as (1) of 190°.

The focus of the given parabola is the vertex of this parabola. For, let $\sigma = t\mu$. Substituting this value of σ in (4), we get

$$\frac{t\mu^4}{2} = 0, \text{ or, } t = 0.$$

Therefore the curve passes through the origin of μ,—i.e. the focus of the given parabola.

Let F' (measured to the right of F, fig. 38) be the focus of the new parabola; l' the tensor of its latus rectum; l the tensor of the latus rectum of the given parabola. Then, since

$$T\mu = 8T\mu_1,$$

we have
$$FR = 8FF',$$
$$\tfrac{1}{2}l = 8(\tfrac{1}{4}l') = 2l',$$
$$l = 4l';$$

or, the latus rectum of the given parabola is four times the latus rectum of the new parabola.

The reader will remember that in the equation of the given parabola, the focus being the origin, μ is the vector $\overline{FR}$ drawn from the focus to the directrix. In the equation of the new parabola, the vertex being the origin, μ_1 is the vector $\overline{FF'}$ drawn from the vertex F to the focus F'—i.e. in the opposite direction to μ.

192°. To find the locus of the intersection of the tangent and the perpendicular upon it from the vertex, MQ, fig. 38.

Since the vector of the sought locus is always parallel to the normal at the point of contact, we have, (7) of 190°,

$$\pi = x(\phi\rho - 2\mu). \quad \ldots \ldots \quad (1)$$

$S . \mu^{-1} \times .$ $\qquad S\mu^{-1}\pi = -2x,$

and $\qquad x = -\dfrac{S\mu^{-1}\pi}{2} = -\dfrac{S\mu\pi}{2\mu^2}; \; S\mu\pi = -2x\mu^2. \ldots (2)$

$S . \times \phi\rho .$ $\qquad S\pi\phi\rho = x(\phi\rho)^2.$

Also, (3) of 190°,

$$S\mu\rho = \frac{S\rho\phi\rho}{4} = \frac{(\phi\rho)^2}{4}.$$

Substituting these values of $S\mu\pi$, $S\pi\phi\rho$ and $S\mu\rho$ in (6) of 190°,

$$(\phi\rho)^2 = \frac{Sx\mu^2}{1-2x}.$$

Squaring (1), $\quad (\phi\rho)^2 = \dfrac{\pi^2}{x^2} - 4\mu^2.$

Therefore, $\quad \pi^2 = 2x\pi^2 + 4x^2\mu^2.$

Substituting the value of x from (2),

$$\mu^2\pi^2 = (S\mu\pi - \pi^2)S\mu\pi;$$

the equation of a cissoid, as will be shown in the following article.

Section 6

Various Curves

193°. The Cissoid of Diocles is the locus of a point, P, fig. 39, where the radius-vector of a circle, OR, is cut by an ordinate so that $OQ = SB$.

Let C be the centre of the circle; $\overline{OC} = a$; $\overline{OQ} = ya$; $\overline{OP} = \rho$; $\overline{OR} = x\rho$.
Then, since $\overline{OR} - \overline{OC} = \overline{CR}$,

$$(x\rho - a)^2 = \overline{CR}^2 = -a^2,$$

and the equation of the circle is

$$x\rho^2 - 2Sa\rho = 0 \quad \ldots \quad (1)$$

By similar triangles,

$$\frac{OQ}{OS} = \frac{OP}{OR},$$

$$\frac{ya}{2a - ya} = \frac{\rho}{x\rho};$$

hence,
$$(1 + x)y = 2 \quad \ldots \quad (2)$$

From (1),
$$x = \frac{2Sa\rho}{\rho^2}.$$

Again,

$$\rho = \overline{OQ} + \overline{QP} = ya + \overline{QP}.$$

$S \cdot a \times.\quad Sa\rho = ya^2;$

and $\quad y = \dfrac{Sa\rho}{a^2}.$

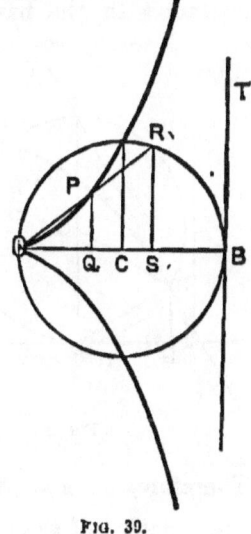

Fig. 39.

Substituting these values of x and y in (2), we get

$$2a^2\rho^2 = (\rho^2 + 2S a\rho) Sa\rho; \quad \ldots \quad (3)$$

the equation of the cissoid.

The cusp of the cissoid, O, coincides with the vertex M; the point B coincides with R; and BT, the tangent to the circle ORB, coincides with the directrix of the parabola, 192°, Consequently, the vertex being the origin, $OC = a$ (in the foregoing calculation) $= \tfrac{1}{2}\overline{MR} = -\tfrac{1}{2}\mu$, in 192°. Substituting this value of a in (3), we get

$$\mu^2 \rho^2 = (S\mu\rho - \rho^2) S\mu\rho ;$$

the equation there deduced.

194°. The Cycloid is the path described by a point on the circumference of a circle which rolls in a fixed plane upon a fixed straight line, called the base.

Let APR be any position of the generating circle, fig. 40, A being the point of contact of the circle with the base, AB. On the base take the point O, such that $AO =$ arc AP. Then, obviously, O is the position of the tracing point, P, when in contact with the base. Draw OD and PQ perpendicular to the base; draw the diameter of the circle, AC, and CP, AP; and suppose OP to be drawn. Let $CA = c$, $\angle PCA = \theta$; and let α and β be vectors in the directions OB, OD, such that $T\alpha = T\beta = c$. Then,

$$\overline{OP} = \overline{OQ} + \overline{QP}.$$

$\overline{OQ} = \overline{OA} - \overline{QA}$
,, $= (\text{arc AP} - c \sin \theta) U\alpha$
,, $= (c\theta - c \sin \theta) U\alpha$
,, $= (\theta - \sin \theta) \alpha ;$
$\overline{QP} = (c - c \cos \theta) U\beta$
,, $= (1 - \cos \theta) \beta.$

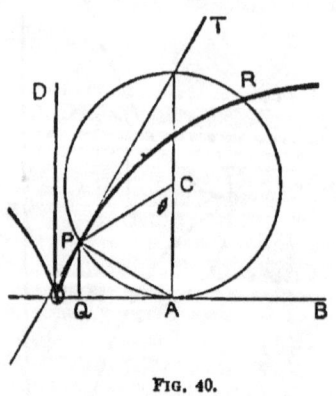

Fig. 40.

Therefore, $\quad \rho = (\theta - \sin \theta) \alpha + (1 - \cos \theta) \beta, \quad \ldots \quad (1)$

the equation of the cycloid.

For the tangent at P we have

$$\frac{d\rho}{d\theta} = (1 - \cos \theta) \alpha + \beta \sin \theta. \qquad (2)$$

THE LOGARITHMIC SPIRAL   171

Let $\overline{PA} = \nu$. Then

$$\nu = \overline{OA} - \rho = \theta a - (\theta - \sin\theta)a - (1 - \cos\theta)\beta$$
$$\;\;\, = a\sin\theta - (1 - \cos\theta)\beta.$$

$S\nu\frac{d\rho}{d\theta} = S\{a\sin\theta - (1-\cos\theta)\beta\}\{(1-\cos\theta)a + \beta\sin\theta\}$
$\;\;\; = S\{-c^2\sin\theta(1-\cos\theta) + a\beta\sin^2\theta - \beta a(1-\cos\theta)^2 + c^2\sin\theta(1-\cos\theta)\}$
$\;\;\; = 0.$

Therefore, $\nu \perp \dfrac{d\rho}{d\theta}$, or AP is normal to the cycloid at P . . (3)

Let us assume Hamilton's formula for the vector of curvature,

$$\pi = -\frac{\rho'^3}{V\rho''\rho'},$$

where ρ' and ρ'' are the first and second derivatives of ρ, and the origin of π is the centre of curvature. Then

$\rho'^2 = \left(\dfrac{d\rho}{d\theta}\right)^2 = \{(1-\cos\theta)a + \beta\sin\theta\}^2 = -2c^2(1-\cos\theta)\{(1-\cos\theta)a + \beta\sin\theta\}$;
$\rho'' = a\sin\theta + \beta\cos\theta$;
$V\rho''\rho' = c^2(1-\cos\theta)\epsilon$, where ϵ is a unit-vector coinitial with and $\perp a$ and β, such that rotation round it from a to β is positive ;

$$\pi = -2\{a\sin\theta - (1-\cos\theta)\beta\} = -2\nu. \quad . . (4)$$

Therefore the length of the radius of curvature is twice the length of the normal, PA.

195°. If a vector, ρ, revolve round its origin in a plane, and if equal angular motions of ρ correspond to equal multiplications of $T\rho$; then the locus of P is a Logarithmic-Spiral, and its equation evidently is

$$\rho = a^t\beta ; \quad \ldots \ldots \ldots (1)$$
$$Ta \gtrless 1 \; ; \; Sa\beta = 0.$$

For, let OB, OC, &c., fig. 41, be a number of equiangular rays, $\angle BOC = \angle COD = \angle DOE = \&c. = \theta$; let $\overline{OB} = \beta$; and let a be a vector perpendicular to the plane BOE, drawn from O towards us. Then

$\overline{OB} = \rho_0 = a^0\beta = \beta,$
$\overline{OC} = \rho_1 = a^{c\theta}\beta = a^{c\theta}T\beta \cdot Ua^{c\theta}U\beta,$
$\overline{OD} = \rho_2 = a^{2c\theta}\beta = a^{2c\theta}T\beta \cdot Ua^{c(\theta+\theta)}U\beta,$
$\overline{OE} = \rho_3 = a^{3c\theta}\beta = a^{3c\theta}T\beta \cdot Ua^{c(\theta+2\theta)}U\beta$; and ultimately,
$\overline{OP} = \rho\;\; = a^{nc\theta}\beta = a^t\beta.$

THE LOGARITHMIC SPIRAL

The scalar exponent may, of course, be either positive or negative.

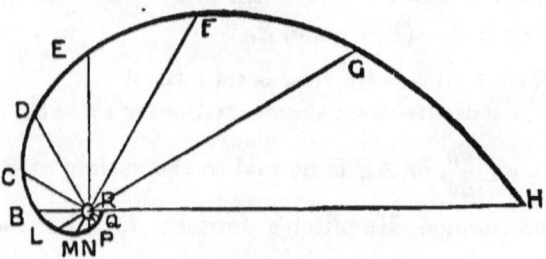

Fig. 41.

Suppose, for instance, that, as in fig. 41,
$$t = \tfrac{1}{3}; \quad OA = 2\tfrac{1}{3}; \quad OB = 10 \text{ mm}.$$
Then
$$\phi = \angle QOR = \angle POQ = \&c. \ldots = \angle FOG = \angle GOH = 30°;$$
and
$$T\rho_1 = OC = Ta^{\frac{1}{3}}T\beta = 10\,(2\tfrac{1}{3})^{\frac{1}{3}} = 10\sqrt{2};$$
$$T\rho_2 = OD = Ta^{\frac{1}{3}}T\rho_1 = 10\sqrt{2}\sqrt{2};$$
$$T\rho_3 = OE = Ta^{\frac{1}{3}}T\rho_2 = 10\sqrt{2}\sqrt{2}\sqrt{2}; \text{ and so on.}$$

For the points L, M, &c., we have
$$\rho = a^{-t}\beta;$$
$$T\rho'_1 = OL = \frac{T\beta}{Ta^t} = \frac{10}{\sqrt{2}}; \text{ and so on.}$$
$$d\rho = (a^t dUa^t + da^t \cdot Ua^t)\beta,$$
$$\text{,,} = (121°)(\log a + \tfrac{\pi}{2}Ua)\,a^t\beta dt = (\log a + \tfrac{\pi}{2}Ua)\,\rho dt, \ldots (2)$$

the vector-tangent of the spiral.

Hence, $\quad \rho d\rho = \rho^2 \log a \cdot dt + \dfrac{\pi}{2a}\rho a \rho dt;$

$$S\rho d\rho = \rho^2 \log a \cdot dt \text{ (since } S\rho a\rho = 0\text{)};$$
$$V\rho d\rho = \frac{\pi}{2a}V\rho a\rho \cdot dt = -\frac{\pi}{2a}\rho^2 a dt;$$
$$TV\rho d\rho = \frac{\pi \rho^2 dt}{2}.$$

THE HELIX 173

Therefore, if $\angle \rho d\rho = \theta$,

$$\tan \theta = \frac{TV\rho d\rho}{S\rho d\rho} = \frac{\pi\rho^2 dt}{2\rho^2 \log a \cdot dt} = \frac{\pi}{2} \frac{1}{\log a}; \quad . . . (3)$$

or, the angle between the vector of any point upon the logarithmic spiral and the tangent at that point, is constant. It will be observed that in this expression for $\tan \theta$, a is the tensor of a versor perpendicular to the plane of the spiral. In the ordinary polar equation,

$$\tan \theta = \frac{1}{\log a},$$

a is a constant line in the plane of the spiral.

196°. A Helix is the path generated by a point, P, upon the rim of a very thin circular disc, fig. 42 (*a*), which revolves (like a wheel) at a constant velocity, and at the same time moves at a constant velocity along a very thin, straight, and fixed wire, OA_4, which passes through its centre, the plane of the disc being

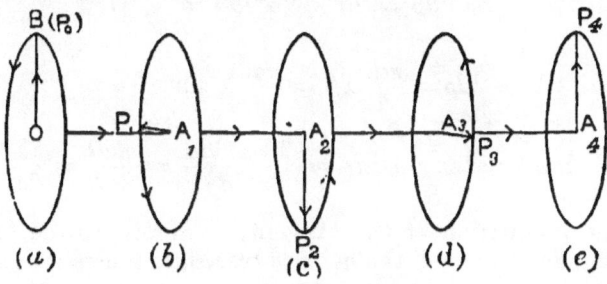

Fig. 42.

always perpendicular to the wire. The point P is supposed to take the same time to rotate through one quadrant of the circle that the centre of the disc takes to move in a straight line from O to A_1, or A_1 to A_2, &c. Fig. 42 (*a*) shows the position of B, the term of a given vector β, before motion has taken place. Let a be a unit-vector in the direction OA_1, and let $T \cdot \overline{OA_1} = T \cdot \overline{A_1A_2} = \&c. = c.$

Then $\overline{OP_1} = \overline{OA_1} + \overline{A_1P_1},$

or, $\rho_1 = ca + a\beta;$

$\overline{OP_2} = \overline{OA_2} + \overline{A_2P_2};$

or, $\rho_2 = 2ca + a^2\beta;$

and, ultimately,

$$\rho = cta + a^t\beta, \quad \ldots \ldots \ldots (1)$$

$$\mathrm{T}a = 1 \;;\; \mathrm{S}a\beta = 0,$$

where t is a variable scalar.

It is evident that this is a helix upon the cylinder,

$$\mathrm{TV}a\rho = \mathrm{TV}a\beta, \quad \ldots \ldots (2)$$

of 109°. The mathematical pitch of the screw is the ratio of the rectilinear velocity of the centre of the circle to the angular velocity of P. The mechanical pitch is the rectilinear distance passed through by the centre of the circle in the time that P takes to make one complete revolution of a circle, that is, OA_4.

$$d\rho = ca\,dt + \frac{\pi}{2}a^{t+1}\beta\,dt\;;\; \ldots (3)$$

$$\mathrm{S}a^{-1}d\rho = c\,dt\;;\; \mathrm{V}a^{-1}d\rho = \frac{\pi\,dt}{2}a^t\beta\;;\; \ldots (4)$$

$$\mathrm{TV}a^{-1}d\rho = \frac{\pi\,dt}{2}\mathrm{T}\beta = \frac{\pi\,dt}{e}b, \text{ since } \mathrm{T}a = 1\;;$$

$$\tan\theta = \tan\angle a^{-1}d\rho = \frac{\mathrm{TV}a^{-1}d\rho}{\mathrm{S}a^{-1}d\rho} = \frac{\pi b\,dt}{2c\,dt} = \frac{\pi b}{2c}. \quad (5)$$

The inclination of the tangent, therefore, to the axis of the cylinder on which the helix is traced, is constant.

If $\phi = \frac{\pi}{2} - \theta,$ $\qquad \cot\phi = \frac{\pi b}{2c} \quad \ldots \ldots (6)$

is the expression for the constant angle at which the helix cuts any circle traced upon the cylinder. πb is the semi-circumference of the cylinder; $2c = OA_2$, that is, half the interval between the two spires, B and P_4.

If a series of vectors be drawn from O, in both directions, parallel to a series of tangents, the locus of the vectors will obviously be a cone of revolution whose equation is,

$$\mathrm{SU}a^{-1}d\rho = \pm\cos\theta. \quad \ldots \ldots (7)$$

The normal plane is the plane perpendicular to the tangent at the point of contact.

Let BPP', fig. 43, be a helix, and let CD be the normal

plane at P to the tangent PT. Let the plane cut the axis of the cylinder in Q ; let $\overline{OA} = a$, $\overline{OQ} = x$, $a = \gamma$, $\overline{PT} = \tau$. Since τ is $\perp$ the plane CD,

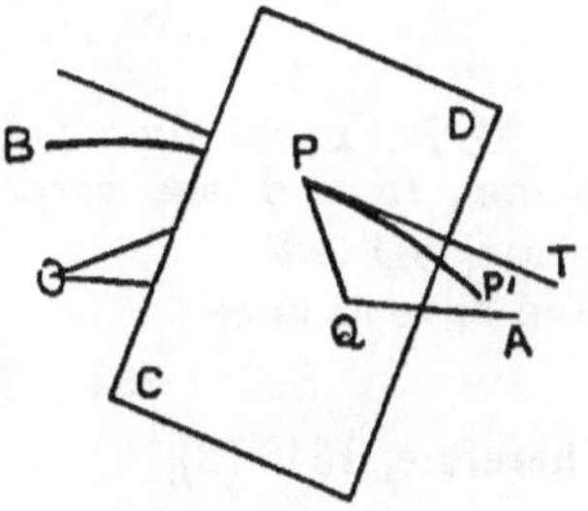

$$S(\gamma - \rho)\,d\rho = 0 \quad . \quad . \quad (8)$$

is the equation of the normal plane.
Since the equation of the helix is

$$\rho = cta + a'\beta,$$

with the conditions

$$Ta = 1 \; ; \; Sa\beta = 0 \; ;$$

FIG. 43.

$\rho^2 = (cta + a'\beta)(cta + a'\beta) = -c^2 t^2 + cta^{t+1}\beta + cta'\beta a + a'\beta a'\beta,$
$\quad = -c^2 t^2 + cta^t(a\beta + \beta a) + V^2 a'\beta,$
$\quad = c^2 t^2 - T^2 a'\beta,$
$\quad = \beta^2 - c^2 t^2 \; . \; . \; . \; . \; . \; . \; . \; . \; . \; . \; . \; . \; (9)$

Therefore, $\quad S\rho d\rho = -c^2 t\,dt.$
But, (8), $\quad S\rho d\rho = S\gamma d\rho = xSad\rho = -xc\,dt$, (4).
Therefore, $\quad x = ct \; ; \; \gamma = cta \; ; \; Sa\gamma = cta^2.$
Also, (1), $\quad Sa\rho = Sa(cta + a'\beta)$
$\quad\quad\quad = cta^2 + Sa^{t+1}\beta = cta^2. \; . \; . \; . \; (10)$
Therefore, $\quad Sa\gamma - Sa\rho = Sa(\gamma - \rho) = 0 \; ;$
„ $\quad \gamma - \rho = \overline{PQ} \perp a. \; . \; . \; . \; . \; . \; (11)$

In words, PQ is perpendicular to the axis of the cylinder, or is a normal to the cylinder.

It follows that the locus of all the perpendiculars let fall from the helix upon the axis of the cylinder is a screw-surface, or helicoid, bounded by the surface of the cylinder, and containing the helix itself ; its equation being of the form,

$$\rho = cta + ua'\beta, \quad . \quad . \quad . \quad . \quad . \quad (12)$$

where t and u are independent variables. Or, reverting to the conception of a moving circle, we may say that u is a function of the velocity of rotation of the circumference of the circle, and t is a function of the velocity of translation of its centre, the two velocities being absolutely independent.

To gain a definite idea of the shape of this surface, we have only to imagine that the cylinder is upright, and that a corkscrew staircase is constructed round the axis. The (smooth) bottom surface of the staircase is a helicoid.

Section 7

The Plane

197°. Three given coinitial vectors, α, β, γ, terminate in a plane; to find the perpendicular from the origin upon the plane, $OD = \delta$.
We have at once
$$S\alpha\delta^{-1} = 1 \; ; \; S\beta\delta^{-1} = 1 \; ; \; S\gamma\delta^{-1} = 1 \; ;$$
therefore, 131° (2),
$$\delta = \frac{S\alpha\beta\gamma}{V(\beta\gamma + \gamma\alpha + \alpha\beta)}.$$
Since $\delta V(\beta\gamma + \gamma\alpha + \alpha\beta) = $ a scalar, $V(\beta\gamma + \gamma\alpha + \alpha\beta) \parallel \delta$.

198°. To find the condition that four points shall be coplanar. Let the vectors of the four points be $\alpha, \beta, \gamma, \rho$. If the point P lie in the plane passing through the points A, B, C, which are supposed to be non-collinear, then
$$S \cdot (\alpha - \rho)(\beta - \rho)(\gamma - \rho) = 0,$$
or, $\qquad S\beta\gamma\rho + S\gamma\alpha\rho + S\alpha\beta\rho - S\alpha\beta\gamma = 0.$

The geometric meaning of this equation is obvious.

As a verification, let $\rho = xi + yj + zk$; $\alpha = x_1 i + y_1 j + z_1 k$; &c., &c. Then
$$0 = x(y_1 z_2 - y_2 z_1 + y_2 z_3 - y_3 z_2 + y_3 z_1 - y_1 z_3) + \&c. \; ;$$
or,
$$0 = \begin{vmatrix} x & , & y & , & z & , & 1 \\ x_1 & , & y_1 & , & z_1 & , & 1 \\ x_2 & , & y_2 & , & z_2 & , & 1 \\ x_3 & , & y_3 & , & z_3 & , & 1 \end{vmatrix}$$

For another solution, see Part I., 38°.

199°. The intersection of two planes is a straight line.[1] For let $OA = \alpha$, $OB = \beta$ lie in one plane, and $OC = \gamma$, $OD = \delta$ lie in the other. Then, 79°, the intersection of the two planes is $V \cdot V\alpha\beta V\gamma\delta$, that is, a straight line.

---

[1] As the point of intersection of two lines is called their *cross*, I venture to suggest that the line of intersection of two planes might be called their *cut*.

200°. The condition that three planes shall intersect in one common straight line.

Let the equations of the three planes, P_1, P_2, P_3, be respectively,
$$S\alpha\rho = p \,;\, S\beta\rho = q \,;\, S\gamma\rho = r \,;$$

and let σ be a vector along their common line of intersection. Then, since α is perpendicular to P_1, it is perpendicular to σ. Similarly, β and γ are perpendicular to σ.

Therefore, $$S\alpha\beta\gamma = 0,$$
and $$pV\beta\gamma + qV\gamma\alpha + rV\alpha\beta = 0.$$

This is the condition that the three planes should be parallel to the same straight line.

201°. To find the condition that four planes shall meet in a point.

Let the equations of the given planes be
$$S\alpha\rho = h \,;\, S\beta\rho = l \,;\, S\gamma\rho = m \,;\, S\delta\rho = n.$$

For the point of intersection, the variables of the first three equations must have a common value,
$$\rho = \frac{hV\beta\gamma + lV\gamma\alpha + mV\alpha\beta}{S\alpha\beta\gamma}.$$

But since the fourth plane passes through the same point, this value of ρ must be also a value of its variable. Therefore, substituting this value of ρ in the fourth equation, we get
$$n = S\delta\rho = \frac{hS\delta V\beta\gamma + lS\delta V\gamma\alpha + mS\delta V\alpha\beta}{S\alpha\beta\gamma},$$
or,
$$hS\beta\gamma\delta - lS\gamma\delta\alpha + mS\delta\alpha\beta - nS\alpha\beta\gamma = 0\,;$$
the sought condition.

Section 8

The Tetrahedron

202°. To find the diameter of the sphere circumscribing a given tetrahedron.

This will be given in the Section on the sphere, 211°.

203°. If two pairs of opposite edges of a tetrahedron, OABC, be at right angles, the third pair will be also at right angles. Let $OA \perp BC$, $OB \perp CA$. Then

$$S\alpha(\gamma - \beta) = 0,$$
$$S\beta(\gamma - \alpha) = 0.$$

Subtracting, $\quad S\gamma(\alpha - \beta) = 0,$

that is, $\quad OC \perp AB.$

204°. To find the condition that the perpendiculars from the corners of a tetrahedron, OABC, upon the opposite faces shall be concurrent.

Let $xV\beta\gamma$ and $yV\gamma\alpha$, the respective perpendiculars from A and B upon the opposite faces, intersect in P. Then, since $(\beta - \alpha)$, $V\beta\gamma$ and $V\gamma\alpha$ are coplanar, $V . V\beta\gamma V\gamma\alpha$ is perpendicular to $\beta - \alpha$. Therefore,

$$S(\beta - \alpha) V . V\beta\gamma V\gamma\alpha = 0,$$
$$S(\beta - \alpha)(-\gamma S\alpha\beta\gamma) = 0,$$
$$(S\gamma\alpha - S\beta\gamma) S\alpha\beta\gamma = 0.$$

Therefore, $\quad 0 = S\gamma\alpha - S\beta\gamma = S\gamma(\alpha - \beta),\ \ldots\ \ldots\ (1)$

that is, $\quad OC \perp AB.$

We get corresponding results in the other cases; therefore the sought condition is that the opposite edges shall be at right angles.

205°. If the opposite edges of a tetrahedron be at right angles, then the sums of the squares of the opposite edges are equal.

For, by (1) of 204°, we have

$$S\beta\gamma = S\gamma\alpha,$$
$$T\beta \cos BOC = T\alpha \cos AOC,$$

$$OB \frac{OB^2 + OC^2 - BC^2}{2OB . OC} = OA \frac{OC^2 + OA^2 - CA^2}{2OC . OA};$$

consequently,
$$OB^2 + CA^2 = OA^2 + BC^2.$$

We get corresponding results in the other cases; therefore, &c., &c.

This is another form of the condition of 204°.

206°. The sum of the vector-areas of the faces of a tetrahedron, OABC, is zero.

$$OBC = \tfrac{1}{2}V\beta\gamma;\ \ OCA = \tfrac{1}{2}V\gamma\alpha;\ \ OAB = \tfrac{1}{2}V\alpha\beta.$$

THE TETRAHEDRON

As we have taken the positive areas of these three faces as seen by an observer standing upon the point O, *i.e.* from the outside of the tetrahedron; we must take the positive area of the remaining face from a corresponding point of view —exterior to the solid. Accordingly,

$$ACB = \tfrac{1}{2}V(\gamma - a)(\beta - a) = -\tfrac{1}{2}V(\beta\gamma + \gamma a + a\beta).$$

Therefore,

$$OBC + OCA + OAB + ACB$$
$$= \tfrac{1}{2}V\beta\gamma + \tfrac{1}{2}V\gamma a + \tfrac{1}{2}V a\beta - \tfrac{1}{2}V(\beta\gamma + \gamma a + a\beta) = 0.$$

In general, the sum of the vector-areas of the faces of any polyhedron is zero.

Let O be any point within the polyhedron, and let it be divided into a number of tetrahedra by planes passing through O. Then the sum of the faces of each separate tetrahedron is zero. Adding, the sum of the faces of all the tetrahedra is zero, that is, the sum of the internal faces, *plus* the sum of the external faces, is zero. But the internal areas, taken two and two, cancel each other, since each two adjacent areas have the same vector-expressions with opposite signs. Therefore the sum of the external faces, that is, the sum of the vector-areas of the faces of the original polyhedron, is zero.

Section 9

The Sphere

207°. If a quadrilateral be not inscriptible in a circle, then, whether it be plane or gauche, we can always circumscribe two circles, OAB, OBC, about the two triangles formed by drawing the diagonal OB, fig. 44.

We then have, 96°,

$$\overline{OA}.\overline{AB}.\overline{BO} = \overline{OT};$$
$$\overline{OB}.\overline{BC}.\overline{CO} = \overline{OU};$$

therefore,

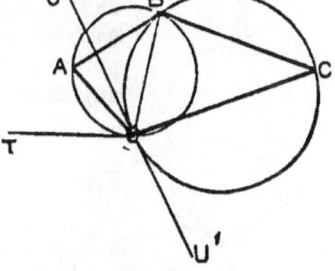

Fig. 44.

$$\overline{OA}.\overline{AB}.\overline{BC}.\overline{CO}. = \frac{\overline{OT}.\overline{OU}}{OB^2},$$

where both members of the equation are quaternions.

If the quadrilateral be plane, the axis of $\overline{OA}.\overline{AB}.\overline{BC}.\overline{CO}$ (or of $\overline{OT}.\overline{OU}$) is perpendicular to the plane of the two tangents, TOU, and therefore to the plane OABC. If the quadrilateral be gauche, this axis will still be perpendicular to the plane of the two tangents, and will be consequently normal at O to the sphere circumscribing the quadrilateral.

In both cases the direction of the axis is such that rotation round it from OT to OU is positive.

The angle of the quaternion $\overline{OA}.\overline{AB}.\overline{BC}.\overline{CO}$ is the supplement of the angle TOU, and is consequently the angle TOU' contained by OT and a tangent OU', the opposite of OU; or the angle between the planes OAB and OCB, or between the arcs OAB and OCB (we write OCB, not OBC, because $\overline{OU'} = \overline{OC}.\overline{CB}.\overline{BO}$).

208°. Since $\overline{OA}.\overline{AB}.\overline{BC}.\overline{CO}$ differs from the anharmonic function (OABC) by a scalar only, 163°, (1), we have

$$\angle \, (OABC) = \angle \, \frac{OA\ BC}{AB\ CO} = \angle \, (\overline{OA}.\overline{AB}.\overline{BC}.\overline{CO}).$$

And since $\quad \angle\, a\beta\gamma\delta = \angle\, \beta\gamma\delta a = $ &c., 76° (5),

we have for the successive sides of any quadrilateral, plane or gauche,

$\angle\,(\overline{OA}.\overline{AB}.\overline{BC}.\overline{CO}) = \angle\,(\overline{AB}.\overline{BC}.\overline{CO}.\overline{OA}) = $ &c.; .. (1)

$\angle\,(OABC) = \angle\,(ABCO) = \angle\,(BCOA) = \angle\,(COAB)$; .. (2)

and also for the four reciprocal anharmonics,

$\angle\,(OCBA) = \angle\,(AOCB) = \angle\,(BAOC) = \angle\,(CBAO)$ .. (3)

If, then, we are given four points, A, B, C, D, coplanar or in space, fig. 45, connected by four circles, each of which passes through three of the points; we have the following equality of angles :

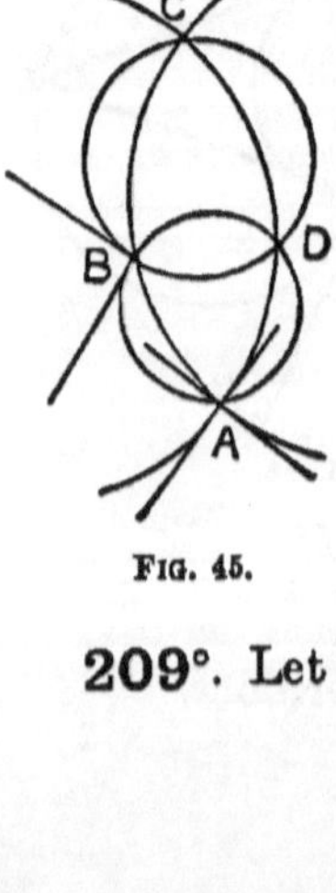

$$\angle\, A = \angle\, B = \angle\, C = \angle\, D.$$

For

$\angle\, A = \angle\,(ABCD); \quad \angle\, B = \angle\,(BCDA);$

$\angle\, C = \angle\,(CDAB); \quad \angle\, D = \angle\,(DABC);$

Fig. 45.

and the angles of these four anharmonic quaternions are equal by (2), (Hamilton).

209°. Let ABCDE be any pentagon, plane or gauche,

inscribed in a sphere, and let the two diagonals AC, AD be drawn. We then have the three equations,

$$\overline{AB} \cdot \overline{BC} \cdot \overline{CA} = \overline{AT},$$
$$\overline{AC} \cdot \overline{CD} \cdot \overline{DA} = \overline{AU},$$
$$\overline{AD} \cdot \overline{DE} \cdot \overline{EA} = \overline{AV},$$

where $\overline{AT}, \overline{AU}, \overline{AV}$ are three tangents to the sphere at A. Multiplying the three equations together,

$$\overline{AB} \cdot \overline{BC} \cdot \overline{CD} \cdot \overline{DE} \cdot \overline{EA} = \frac{\overline{AT} \cdot \overline{AU} \cdot \overline{AV}}{AC^2 \cdot AD^2} \quad . . \quad (1)$$

Now, the product $\overline{AT} \cdot \overline{AU} \cdot \overline{AV}$ is some fourth coplanar vector $\overline{AW}$, which, being coplanar with the three tangents, is itself a tangent at A. Therefore the product of the five successive sides of a pentagon, plane or gauche, inscribed in a sphere, is a tangential vector drawn from the point at which the pentagon begins and ends.

In general, the product of the successive sides of any n-gon inscribed in a sphere is a quaternion whose axis is normal to the sphere at the initial point of the n-gon, when n is even; and is a vector tangential to the sphere at the same point, when n is odd.

210°. The last equation, 209° (1), may be written:

$$\overline{OA} \cdot \overline{AB} \cdot \overline{BC} \cdot \overline{CP} \cdot \overline{PO} = x\xi,$$

where P is a variable point upon the sphere. Hence, taking scalars,

$$0 = Sa(\beta - a)(\gamma - \beta)(\rho - \gamma)(-\rho),$$

or, $\quad \rho^2 Sa\beta\gamma = a^2 S\beta\gamma\rho + \beta^2 S\gamma a\rho + \gamma^2 Sa\beta\rho; \quad . . \quad (1)$

the equation of a sphere, O being a point upon its surface.

To verify the equation, we have only to observe that it is satisfied by assigning to ρ the successive values, o, a, β, γ. Hence, if the vector of any point in space, in terms of three given diplanar vectors, a, β, γ, be

$$\rho = xa + y\beta + z\gamma;$$

the equation $\quad \rho^2 = xa^2 + y\beta^2 + z\gamma^2$

expresses that the vectors a, β, γ, ρ terminate in the surface of a sphere which passes through O.

Let $\overline{OA}, \overline{OB}, \overline{OC}$, &c., be any chords of a sphere, and let $\overline{OD}$ be a diameter, fig. 35 of 161°. Then, 160°, $a^{-1} - \delta^{-1} = \tau_1,$

a tangent at O; $\beta^{-1} - \delta^{-1} = \tau^2$, another tangent at O; &c., &c. But these tangents are coplanar; therefore $a^{-1} - \delta^{-1}$, $\beta^{-1} - \delta^{-1}$, &c., are coplanar; therefore $\beta^{-1} - a^{-1}$, $\gamma^{-1} - a^{-1}$, &c., lie in a plane parallel to the tangent plane at O. Therefore, if ρ be the vector of a variable point, P, upon the sphere,

$$S(\beta^{-1} - a^{-1})(\gamma^{-1} - a^{-1})(\rho^{-1} - a^{-1}) = 0 \quad . \quad (2)$$

is the equation of a sphere passing through the five points O, A, B, C, P. It is not difficult to transform (2) into (1). Since $S\dfrac{\delta - \rho}{\rho} = 0$,

and
$$\left.\begin{array}{l} S\delta\rho^{-1} = 1 \\ \rho^2 = S\delta\rho \end{array}\right\} \quad \ldots \ldots \quad (3)$$

are equations of the sphere.

If the origin be any point in space, κ the vector of the centre, and a any given vector radius,

$$\left.\begin{array}{l} T(\rho - \kappa) = Ta \\ (\rho - \kappa)^2 = a^2 = C \end{array}\right\} \quad \ldots \ldots \quad (4)$$

are also equations of the sphere.

If $T\kappa = c$, this last equation may be written:

$$\rho^2 = 2S\kappa\rho = c^2 - a^2 \quad \ldots \ldots \quad (5)$$

211°. By 82°,

$$\delta S a\beta\gamma = S\delta a V\beta\gamma + S\delta\beta V\gamma a + S\delta\gamma V a\beta.$$

But, by (3) of 210°,

$$S\delta a = a^2 \;;\; S\delta\beta = \beta^2 \;;\; S\delta\gamma = \gamma^2.$$

Therefore,

$$\delta = \frac{a^2 V\beta\gamma + \beta^2 V\gamma a + \gamma^2 V a\beta}{S a\beta\gamma} \;; \quad \ldots \quad (1)$$

the expression for the diameter of the sphere circumscribing the tetrahedron OABC.

212°. The equations of the tangent and tangent plane have been given in 167°; that of the polar plane in 168°.

213°. To find the equation of the curve formed by the intersection of a plane and a sphere.

From the centre, O, of the sphere let fall a perpendicular $\overline{OD} = \delta$ upon the given plane. Let ρ be the variable vector of the sphere; σ a vector in the given plane drawn from D to meet ρ in the line of intersection whose equation is required. Then, if a be the radius of the sphere,

$$\rho^2 = -a^2;$$

but $\rho = \delta + \sigma;$

therefore, $(\delta + \sigma)^2 = -a^2,$

and $\sigma^2 = -(a^2 - d^2).$

The locus, therefore, is the circle,

$$\sigma^2 = -(a^2 - d^2), \; S\delta\sigma = 0,$$

with D for centre and $\sqrt{a^2 - d^2}$ for radius.

214°. To find the curve in which the spheres intersect. Let the equations of the two spheres be, 210° (5),

$$\rho^2 - 2S\kappa_1\rho = C_1^2 - a_1^2,$$
$$\rho^2 - 2S\kappa_2\rho = C_2^2 - a_2^2.$$

For every point of the curve of intersection the variables must have one common value. We may consequently equate the two equations, thus obtaining

$$S(\kappa_1 - \kappa_2)\rho = \tfrac{1}{2}\{(a_1^2 - a_2^2) + (C_2^2 - C_1^2)\} = C. \ldots (1)$$

Now, this is the equation of a plane $\perp (\kappa_1 - \kappa_2)$, 100° (9). Therefore the line of intersection of the two spheres is the common line of intersection of this plane with the two spheres. But the intersection of a sphere and a plane is a circle. Therefore the line of intersection of two spheres is a circle.

Equation (1) is the equation of the Radical Plane of the two spheres.

215°. If three spheres intersect one another, their three planes of intersection pass through one common straight line.

If the equations of the three spheres be

$$\rho^2 - 2S\kappa_1\rho = C_1,$$
$$\rho^2 - 2S\kappa_2\rho = C_2,$$
$$\rho^2 - 2S\kappa_3\rho = C_3,$$

the equations of the three planes of intersection will be

$$S(\kappa_1 - \kappa_2)\rho = \tfrac{1}{2}(C_2 - C_1), \text{ or } P_1,$$
$$S(\kappa_2 - \kappa_3)\rho = \tfrac{1}{2}(C_3 - C_2), \; ,, \; P_2,$$
$$S(\kappa_3 - \kappa_1)\rho = \tfrac{1}{2}(C_1 - C_3), \; ,, \; P_3;$$

where $P_1 \perp (\kappa_1 - \kappa_2)$, $P_2 \perp (\kappa_2 - \kappa_3)$, $P_3 \perp (\kappa_3 - \kappa)$.

Now,

$(C_2-C_1)\nabla(\kappa_2-\kappa_3)(\kappa_3-\kappa_1)+(C_3-C_2)\nabla(\kappa_3-\kappa_1)(\kappa_1-\kappa_2)+(C_1-C_3)\nabla(\kappa_1-\kappa_2)(\kappa_2-\kappa_3)=0.$

Therefore P_1, P_2, P_3 intersect in one common straight line, 200°.

216°. To find the locus of a point, the sum of the squares of whose distances from n given points is constant.

Let ρ be the vector of the sought point; $a_1, a_2 \ldots a_n$ the vectors of the given points. Then
$$(\rho - a_1)^2 + (\rho - a_2)^2 + \&c. = \Sigma(\rho - a)^2 = -C.$$
But
$$(\rho - a_1)^2 = \rho^2 - 2Sa_1\rho + a_1^2,$$
$$(\rho - a_2)^2 = \rho^2 - 2Sa_2\rho + a_2^2,$$
$$\cdots\cdots\cdots\cdots\cdots$$
$$(\rho - a_n)^2 = \rho^2 - 2Sa_n\rho + a_n^2.$$
Therefore, $\quad \Sigma(\rho - a)^2 = n\rho^2 - 2S\rho\Sigma a + \Sigma a^2 = -C,$
$$\rho^2 - 2S\rho\frac{\Sigma a}{n} + \left(\frac{\Sigma a}{n}\right)^2 = \left(\frac{\Sigma a}{n}\right)^2 - \frac{\Sigma a^2}{n} - \frac{C}{n},$$
$$\left(\rho - \frac{\Sigma a}{n}\right)^2 = \left(\frac{\Sigma a}{n}\right)^2 - \frac{1}{n}(\Sigma a^2 + C) = C'.$$

Therefore, by (4) of 210°, the locus of P is a sphere the vector of whose centre is $\frac{\Sigma a}{n}$, its centre consequently being the mean point of the n points.

Section 10

The Cone

217°. To find the equation of a Cone of Revolution whose vertex, O, is the origin.

Let a be a unit-vector along the axis OA, and ρ the vector of any point upon the surface of the cone. Then
$$Sa\rho = -T\rho \cos\theta;$$
θ being the angle POA.
But θ is constant. Therefore,
$$c^2\rho^2 = S^2 a\rho. \quad \ldots \ldots \ldots \quad (1)$$

218°. Had we written the equation of the plane, 105°, as
$$Sa\rho = a^2, \quad \ldots \ldots \ldots \quad (1)$$
and the equation of the sphere as
$$S\beta\rho = \rho^2, \quad \ldots \ldots \ldots \quad (2)$$

we should, by multiplying these two equations together, have obtained the equation of the Cyclic Cone in the form:
$$a^2\rho^2 - S a\rho S \beta\rho = 0, \quad \ldots \ldots \quad (3)$$
instead of $\quad S\dfrac{\rho}{a} S \dfrac{\beta}{\rho} = 1,\ 108°.$

This cone has for its base the circle,
$$Sa\rho = a^2\ ;\ S\beta\rho = \rho^2. \quad \ldots \ldots \quad (4)$$

Let us take a vector with the direction of β and the tensor of a,—$TaU\beta = \overline{OB'}$. The equation of the plane through B' perpendicular to this vector, is
$$0 = S \cdot TaU\beta\, (\rho - TaU\beta) = \dfrac{a}{b} S\beta\, (\rho - \dfrac{a}{b}\beta),$$
or, $\qquad\qquad S\beta\rho = \dfrac{a}{b}\beta^2. \quad \ldots \ldots \quad (5)$

Again, let us take a vector with the direction of a and the tensor of β,—$T\beta Ua = \overline{OA'}$. The equation of a sphere through A' with OA' for a diameter is
$$0 = S\rho\,(\rho - T\beta Ua) = S\rho\,(\rho - \dfrac{b}{a}a),$$
or, $\qquad\qquad Sa\rho = \dfrac{a}{b}\rho^2. \quad \ldots \ldots \quad (6)$

Multiplying (5) and (6) together we get
$$Sa\rho S\beta\rho = \dfrac{a^2}{b^2}\beta^2\rho^2 = \dfrac{-a^2}{b^2}(-b^2)\rho^2 = a^2\rho^2.$$

Therefore, $\qquad (Sa\rho = a^2\ ;\ S\beta\rho = \rho^2)$

and $\qquad\qquad (S\beta\rho = \dfrac{a}{b}\beta^2\ ;\ Sa\rho = \dfrac{a}{b}\rho^2)$

are two different circular sections of the same cyclic cone. Every section of this cone by a plane parallel to the plane $Sa\rho = a^2$, is a circle. For, let c be any constant scalar. Then, 100°, (8), $\qquad Sa\rho = ca^2$

is a plane $\parallel$ to $Sac = a^2$. Substituting this value of $Sa\rho$ in (3), we get
$$\rho_2 - cS\beta\rho = 0.$$
We therefore have for ρ,
$$Sa\rho = c^2a\ ;\ \rho^2 = cS\beta\rho.$$

The locus of P, therefore, is the intersection of the plane through the term of $ca \perp a$, and the sphere with $c\beta$ for a diameter, *i.e.* a circle.

Similarly, any plane parallel to the plane, $S\beta\rho = \dfrac{a}{b}\beta^2$, is a circle.

Therefore the sections of a cyclic cone made by planes perpendicular to either of the Cyclic Normals, a and β, are circles. Both series of planes are consequently perpendicular to the plane OAB. If, then, AD be the intersection of the plane, $Sa\rho = a^2$, with OAB, and AE be the intersection of OAB with a plane through A parallel to $S\beta\rho = \dfrac{a}{b}\beta$;

AD and AE are evidently antiparallel, fig. 46. The two series of circles are consequently called the antiparallel (or subcontrary) sections of the cone.

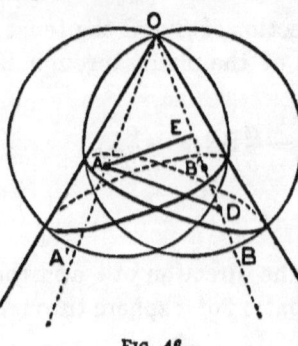

Fig. 46.

The equation of a plane through O parallel to the plane (1) is
$$Sa\rho = 0 ; \quad \quad \quad (7)$$
the equation of a plane through O parallel to the plane (5) is
$$S\beta\rho = 0. \quad \quad \quad (8)$$

These are the equations of the Cyclic Planes.

If the cone, in the first instance, be supposed to have for its base the circle
$$Sa\rho = a^2 ; \; S\beta\rho = \rho^2,$$
it is clear that the cyclic plane (8) is a tangent at the vertex to the circumscribing sphere (2). If, in the second instance, the cone be supposed to have for its base the circle
$$S\beta\rho = \dfrac{a}{b}\beta^2 ; \; Sa\rho = \dfrac{a}{b}\rho^2,$$
the cyclic plane (7) is a tangent at the vertex to the circumscribing sphere (6).

Since $\quad a^2\rho^2 = Sa\rho S\beta\rho = Ta\rho T\beta\rho SUa\rho SU\beta\rho$,

$$SUa\rho SU\beta\rho = T\dfrac{a}{\beta} = \text{constant} ; \quad \ldots \quad (9)$$

or, the product of the cosines of the inclinations of any variable ray, ρ, of an oblique cyclic cone to its two cyclic normals is constant; or, the product of the sines of the inclinations of the same ray to the two cyclic planes is constant. If $a \parallel \beta$, then $\beta = m^2 a$, where m is a constant scalar > 1, and the equation of the cone becomes

$$\frac{a^2}{m^2}\rho^2 = S^2 a\rho ;$$

which is the equation of a cone of revolution, 217° (1).

219°. Of a system of three coinitial and rectangular vectors two are confined to given planes; to find the locus of the third (Professor MacCullagh).

Let π, ρ, σ be the three rectangular vectors. Then, by condition,

$$S\pi\rho = 0 \quad \ldots \ldots \ldots \quad (1)$$
$$S\rho\sigma = 0 \quad \ldots \ldots \ldots \quad (2)$$
$$S\sigma\pi = 0 \quad \ldots \ldots \ldots \quad (3)$$

For the given planes we also have

$$Sa\pi = 0 \quad \ldots \ldots \ldots \quad (4)$$
$$S\beta\rho = 0 \quad \ldots \ldots \ldots \quad (5)$$

It would be impossible generally to eliminate two vectors with less than six given equations. But in the present case, as the tensors are not involved, five are sufficient.

From (3) and (4),
$$\pi = x\mathrm{V}a\sigma ;$$
„ (2) „ (5),
$$\rho = y\mathrm{V}\beta\sigma.$$

Substituting these values of π and ρ in (1),
$$xy\mathrm{S} \cdot \mathrm{V}a\sigma\mathrm{V}\beta\sigma = 0,$$
and, 92° (7),
$$\sigma^2 Sa\beta - Sa\sigma S\beta\sigma = 0 ;$$

the equation of a cyclic cone.

Before concluding, the reader must be reminded that it is not by such geometric applications as the foregoing that the merits of the quaternion method can be adequately illustrated. Its simplicity and power can only be fully shown by physical applications, which can find no place in this, or any other, elementary book. For such applications the reader is referred to the works of Sir W. R. Hamilton and Professor Tait; to the 'Utility of Quaternions in Physics,' by Mr. A. McAulay; and to Dr. Molenbroek's paper, 'Over de Toepassing der Quaternionen op de Mechanica en de Natuurkunde' (Müller, Amsterdam). A perusal of these works will convince most readers that quaternions are 'the natural language of metrical geometry and of physics' (Clifford).

INDEX

The references are to the Pages.
Q. stands for quaternion; V. for vector.

ANGLE-BISECTOR, Expression for, 20
Angle of a Q., Definition of the, 31
Anharmonic Q., Function, Definition of, 149
Anharmonic Ratio, Definition of, 13
Apollonius of Perga, Cyclic Cone of, 109
Apollonius of Perga, Theorem by, 73
Arc, V., Definition of, 86
Area, V., ,, 51
,, of spherical triangle, 143
Axis of a Q., 46

CENTRE, Circum-, of plane triangle, 21
Centre, Ex-, of plane triangle, 21
,, In-, ,, ,, 20
,, Mid-, ,, ,, 21
,, Ortho-, ,, ,, 21
Central Conic, General Equation of, 158
Circle, Equations of, 106, 153
,, Circum-, of spherical triangle, 136
,, In-, of spherical triangle, 134
Circular Harmonic Groups, 152
Cissoid, The, 169
Condition of Equality of two Vs., 2
Condition of Equality of two V. Arcs, 86
Condition of Equality of two Versors, 63

Condition of Equality of two Qs., 63
Condition that four planes meet in a point, 177
Condition that four points may be coplanar, 176
Condition that three vectors may be coplanar, 99
Condition that four vectors may terminate in a plane, 28, 176
Cone, Right, Equation of, 184
,, Cyclic, ,, 109, 185
Conic, General Equation of a, 156
Conical Rotation, 90
Conjugate Functions, Definition of, 127
Conjugate of a Q., 68
,, ,, Scalar, 69
,, ,, V., 69
Conjugates, Isogonal, 22
,, Isotomic, 22
Curvature, Radius of, Expression for the, 171
Cyclic normals of a Cone, 186
,, planes ,, ,, 186
Cycloid, The, 170

DIFFERENTIAL, General Definition of a, 112
Differential of a Q., 117
,, ,, V., 115

EULER, Theorem by, 82

FUNCTION, Anharmonic Q., 149
Functions, Conjugate, 127
,, Self-conjugate, 127

INDEX

GAUSS, Theorem by, 146

HARMONIC Group, Circular, 152
    ,,   Mean, Definition of the, 151
Helicoid, The, 175
Helix, The, 173

i, j, k, Properties of, 37
Index of a right Q., 51
Isogonal conjugates, 22
Isotomic   ,,   22

KEOGH, Theorem by, 144

LOGARITHMIC Spiral, The, 171

MACCULLAGH, Theorem by, 187
Mean point of triangle, 19
  ,,   Harmonic, Definition of, 151
Moivre's Theorem, 55

n-GON inscribed in circle, 153
    ,,   ,,   sphere, 181
Normal, Cyclic, of a cone, 186
  ,,   of Ellipse, 159
  ,,   ,, Hyperbola, 159
  ,,   ,, Parabola, 165
  ,,   Plane of a Curve, Definition of, 174

PLANE, Equations of, 104
  ,,   Radical of two spheres, 183
Points, Inverse, with respect to circle, 72
Polyhedra, Sum of V.-areas of faces of, is zero, 179

QUADRILATERAL, Spherical, A property of, 146
Quaternion, Amplitude of a, 56
    ,,   Angle   ,,   31
    ,,   Definition   ,,   30
Quaternions, Collinear, 66
    ,,   Conjugate, 68
    ,,   Coplanar, 31
    ,,   Diplanar, 31
    ,,   Opposite, 67
    ,,   Reciprocal, 66
    ,,   Right, 37

ternions, Condition of equality of two, 63

RADICAL plane of two spheres, 183
Radius of curvature of the cycloid, 171
Radius of curvature, general expression for, 171
Radius Vector, Distinction between a, and a Vector, 2
Reciprocal of a Q., 66
    ,,   ,,   V., 41
Rotation, Conical, 90
    ,,   Positive and Negative, Definition of, 34

SCALAR, Definition of a, 8
Section, Anharmonic and Harmonic, of Vs., 13
Sections, Antiparallel (or Subcontrary) of cone, 109, 185
Segments, Six, of triangle, 15
Signs of geometric figures, 15
Sphere, Diameter of, circumscribing a tetrahedron, 182
Sphere, Equations of, 107, 181
Spiral, Logarithmic, 171

TENSOR, Definition of a, 8
Theorem by Apollonius of Perga, 73
    ,,   ,, Euler, 82
    ,,   ,, Gauss, 146
    ,,   ,, C. Keogh, 144
    ,,   ,, MacCullagh, 187
    ,,   ,, Moivre, 55
Triangle, Chordal, of a spherical triangle, 145

UNIT V., Definition of a. 8

VECTOR, Definition of a real and actual, 2
Vector, Definition of a null, 2
    ,,   Reciprocal of a, Definition of the, 30
Vector-area, Definition of a, 51
    ,,   -arcs, Circular, 86
    ,,   ,, Condition of equality of two, 86
Versor, Definition of a, 34
    ,,   Right, Definition of a, 37

A CLASSIFIED CATALOGUE

OF

SCIENTIFIC WORKS

PUBLISHED BY

MESSRS. LONGMANS, GREEN, & CO.

LONDON: 39 PATERNOSTER ROW, E.C.

NEW YORK: 15 EAST 16th STREET.

CONTENTS.

	PAGE		PAGE
Advanced Science Manuals	24	Mechanics and Mechanism	5
Agriculture and Gardening	19	Metallurgy	13
Architecture	9	Meteorology	18
Astronomy	14	Mineralogy	13
Biology	18	Navigation	14
Botany	19	Optics	17
Building Construction	9	Photography	17
Chemistry	2	Physics	4
Dynamics	6	Physiography	16
Electricity	10	Physiology	18
Elementary Science Manuals	22	Proctor's (R. A.) Works	15
Engineering	12	Sound	7
Geology	16	Statics	6
Heat	7	Steam and the Steam Engine	8
Health and Hygiene	17	Strength of Materials	12
Hydrostatics	6	Technology	16
Light	7	Telegraphy	10
London Science Class-Books	24	Telephone	10
Longmans' Civil Engineering Series	12	Text-Books of Science	20
		Thermodynamics	7
Machine Drawing and Design	14	Tyndall's (John) Works	11
Magnetism	10	Workshop Appliances	13
Manufactures	16		

CHEMISTRY.

ADDYMAN—Agricultural Analysis. A Manual of Quantitative Analysis for Students of Agriculture. By FRANK T. ADDYMAN, B.Sc. (Lond.), F.I.C. With 49 Illustrations. Crown 8vo. 5s. net.

ARMSTRONG—Organic Chemistry: the Chemistry of Carbon and its Compounds. By H. E. ARMSTRONG, Ph.D. With 8 Woodcuts. Fcp. 8vo. 3s. 6d.

COLEMAN & ADDYMAN—Practical Agricultural Chemistry. For Elementary Students, adapted for use in Agricultural Classes and Colleges. By J. BERNARD COLEMAN, A.R.C.Sc., F.I.C., and FRANK T. ADDYMAN, B.Sc. (Lond.) F.I.C. With 24 Illustrations. Crown 8vo. 1s. 6d. net.

CROOKES—Select Methods in Chemical Analysis, chiefly Inorganic. By WILLIAM CROOKES, F.R.S., &c. With 37 Woodcuts. 8vo. 24s.

EARL—The Elements of Laboratory Work: a Course of Natural Science. By A. G. EARL, M.A., F.C.S., late Scholar of Christ's College, Cambridge. With 57 Diagrams and numerous Exercises and Questions. Crown 8vo. 4s. 6d.

FURNEAUX—Elementary Chemistry, Inorganic and Organic. By W. FURNEAUX, F.R.C.S., Lecturer on Chemistry, London School Board. With 65 Illustrations and 155 Experiments. Crown 8vo. 2s. 6d.

HALL—First Exercises in Practical Chemistry. By A. D. HALL, M.A., Senior Science Master at King Edward's School, Birmingham. Crown 8vo. 1s. 6d.

HJELT—Principles of General Organic Chemistry. By Professor E. HJELT, of Helsingfors. Translated from the German by J. BISHOP TINGLE, Ph.D., Assistant in the Laboratory of the Heriot-Watt College, Edinburgh. Crown 8vo. 6s. 6d.

JAGO—Works by W. JAGO, F.C.S., F.I.C.
—— **Inorganic Chemistry, Theoretical and Practical.** With an Introduction to the Principles of Chemical Analysis Inorganic and Organic. With 196 Experiments, with 49 Woodcuts and numerous Questions and Exercises. Fcp. 8vo. 2s. 6d
—— **An Introduction to Practical Inorganic Chemistry.** Crown 8vo. 1s. 6d.
—— **Inorganic Chemistry, Theoretical and Practical.** A Manual for Students in Advanced Classes of the Science and Art Department. With Plate of Spectra and 78 Woodcuts. Cr. 8vo. 4s. 6d.

KOLBE—A Short Text-Book of Inorganic Chemistry. By Dr. HERMANN KOLBE. Translated and Edited by T. S. HUMPIDGE, Ph.D. With 66 Illustrations. Crown 8vo. 8s. 6d.

MENDELÉEFF—The Principles of Chemistry. By D. MENDELÉEFF, Professor of Chemistry in the University of St. Petersburg. Translated by GEORGE KAMENSKY, A.R.S.M., of the Imperial Mint, St. Petersburg, and edited by A. J. GREENAWAY, F.I.C., Sub-Editor of the Journal of the Chemical Society. With 97 Illustrations. 2 vols. 8vo. 36s.

MEYER—Outlines of Theoretical Chemistry. By LOTHAR MEYER, Professor of Chemistry in the University of Tübingen. Translated by Professors P. PHILLIPS BEDSON, D.Sc., and W. CARLETON WILLIAMS, B.Sc. 8vo. 9s.

MILLER—Introduction to the Study of Inorganic Chemistry. By WILLIAM ALLEN MILLER, M.D., LL.D., F.R.S. With 71 Woodcuts. Fcp. 8vo. 3s. 6d.

NEWTH—Chemical Lecture Experiments. By G. S. NEWTH, Royal College of Science, South Kensington. With 224 Diagrams. Crown 8vo. 10s. 6d.

ODLING—A Course of Practical Chemistry, arranged for the Use of Medical Students, with express reference to the Three Months Summer Practice. By WILLIAM ODLING, M.A. With 71 Woodcuts Crown 8vo. 6s.

OSTWALD—Solutions. By W. OSTWALD, Professor of Chemistry in the University of Leipzig. Being the Fourth Book, with some Additions, of the Second Edition of Ostwald's 'Lehrbuch der Allgemeinen Chemie'. Translated by M. M. PATTISON MUIR, Professor of Gonville and Caius College, Cambridge. 8vo. 10s. 6d.

PAYEN—Industrial Chemistry. A Manual for use in Technical Colleges and Schools, based upon a Translation of Stohmann and Engler's German Edition of PAYEN's 'Précis de Chimie Industrielle'. Edited by B. H. PAUL, Ph.D. With 698 Woodcuts. 8vo. 42s.

REYNOLDS—Experimental Chemistry for Junior Students. By J. EMERSON REYNOLDS, M.D., F.R.S., Professor of Chemistry, University of Dublin; Examiner in Chemistry, University of London. Fcp. 8vo. with numerous Woodcuts.
Part I. Introductory. Fcp. 8vo. 1s. 6d.
Part II. Non-Metals, with an Appendix on Systematic Testing for Acids. Fcp. 8vo. 2s. 6d.
Part III. Metals and Allied Bodies. Fcp. 8vo. 3s. 6d.
Part IV. Carbon Compounds. Fcp. 8vo. 4s.

SHENSTONE—Works by W. A. SHENSTONE, Lecturer on Chemistry in Clifton College.
—— **The Methods of Glass-Blowing.** For the use of Physical and Chemical Students. With 42 Illustrations. Crown 8vo. 1s. 6d.
—— **A Practical Introduction to Chemistry.** Intended to give a Practical Acquaintance with the Elementary Facts and Principles of Chemistry. With 20 Illustrations. Crown 8vo. 2s.

THORPE—A Dictionary of Applied Chemistry. By T. E. THORPE, B.Sc. (Vict.), Ph.D., F.R.S., Treas. C.S., Professor of Chemistry in the Royal College of Science, South Kensington. Assisted by Eminent Contributors. 3 vols. 8vo. Vols. I. & II. 42s. each. Vol. III. 63s.
—— **Quantitative Chemical Analysis.** By T. E. THORPE, Ph.D., F.R.S. With 88 Woodcuts. Fcp. 8vo. 4s. 6d.

THORPE and MUIR—Manual of Qualitative Analysis and Laboratory Practice. By T. E. THORPE, Ph.D., F.R.S.E., and M. M. PATTISON MUIR. With 57 Woodcuts. Fcp. 8vo. 3s. 6d.

TILDEN—Works by WILLIAM A. TILDEN, D.Sc. (Lond.), F.C.S.

—— **Introduction to the Study of Chemical Philosophy.** The Principles of Theoretical and Systematic Chemistry. With 5 Woodcuts. With or without the ANSWERS of Problems. Fcp. 8vo. 4s. 6d.

—— **Practical Chemistry.** The Principles of Qualitative Analysis. Fcp. 8vo. 1s. 6d.

WATTS' Dictionary of Chemistry. Revised and entirely Re-written by H. FORSTER MORLEY, M.A., D.Sc., Fellow of, and lately Assistant-Professor of Chemistry in, University College, London; and M. M. PATTISON MUIR, M.A., F.R.S.E., Fellow, and Prælector in Chemistry, of Gonville and Caius College, Cambridge. Assisted by Eminent Contributors. 4 vols. 8vo. Vols. I. & II. 42s. each (ready). Vol. III., 50s. (ready). Vol. IV., [In the press.

WHITELEY—Works by R. LLOYD WHITELEY, F.I.C., Assistant Lecturer and Demonstrator in Chemistry in the University College, Nottingham.

—— **Chemical Calculations**, with Explanatory Notes, Problems and Answers, specially adapted for use in Colleges and Science Schools. With a Preface by Professor F. CLOWES, D.Sc. (Lond.) F.I.C. Crown 8vo. 2s.

—— **Organic Chemistry.** [Nearly ready.

PHYSICS.

ARNOTT—**The Elements of Physics or Natural Philosophy.** By NEIL ARNOTT, M.D. Edited by A. BAIN, LL.D., and A. S. TAYLOR, M.D., F.R.S. With numerous Woodcuts. Cr. 8vo. 12s. 6d.

COOK—**Physics.** (Specially adapted for Indian Schools and Students.) By J. COOK, M.A., Principal, Central College, Bangalore. With Examination Questions and 206 Illustrations. Crown 8vo. 2s. 6d.

EARL—**The Elements of Laboratory Work:** a Course of Natural Science. By A. G. EARL, M.A., F.C.S. With 57 Diagrams and numerous Exercises, etc. Crown 8vo. 4s. 6d.

GANOT—Works by Professor GANOT. Translated and Edited by E. ATKINSON, Ph.D., F.C.S.

—— **Elementary Treatise on Physics,** Experimental and Applied. With 9 Coloured Plates and 1028 Woodcuts. Crown 8vo. 15s.

—— **Natural Philosophy for General Readers and Young Persons;** a Course of Physics divested of Mathematical Formulæ, expressed in the language of daily life. With 7 Plates, 569 Woodcuts, and an Appendix of Questions. Crown 8vo. 7s. 6d.

GLAZEBROOK and SHAW—**Practical Physics.** By R. T. GLAZEBROOK, M.A., F.R.S., and W. N. SHAW, M.A. 134 Woodcuts. Fcp. 8vo. 7s. 6d.

GUTHRIE—**A Class-Book of Practical Physics.** Molecular Physics and Sound. By F. GUTHRIE, Ph.D. With 91 Diagrams. Fcp. 8vo. 1s. 6d.

HELMHOLTZ—Popular Lectures on Scientific Subjects.
By HERMANN L. F. HELMHOLTZ. Translated by E. ATKINSON, Ph.D., F.C.S., formerly Professor of Experimental Science, Staff College. With 68 Illustrations. 2 vols., crown 8vo. 3s. 6d. each.

—— Contents—Vol. I.—The Relation of Natural Science to Science in General—Goethe's Scientific Researches—The Physiological Causes of Harmony in Music—Ice and Glaciers—The Inter-action of the Natural Forces—The Recent Progress of the Theory of Vision—The Conservation of Force—The Aim and Progress of Physical Science.

—— Vol. II.—Gustav Magnus. In Memoriam—The Origin and Significance of Geometrical Axioms—The Relations of Optics to Painting.—The Origin of the Planetary System—Thought in Medicine—Academic Freedom in German Universities—Herman von Helmholtz. An Autobiographical Sketch.

WORTHINGTON—A First Course of Physical Laboratory Practice. Containing 264 Experiments. By A. M. WORTHINGTON, F.R.S., M.A. With Illustrations. Crown 8vo. 4s. 6d.

WRIGHT—Elementary Physics. By MARK R. WRIGHT., Principal of the Day Training College, Newcastle-on-Tyne. With 242 Illustrations. Crown 8vo. 2s. 6d.

MECHANICS AND MECHANISM.

BALL—A Class-Book of Mechanics. By Sir R. S. BALL, LL.D. 89 Diagrams. Fcp. 8vo. 1s. 6d.

GOODEVE—Works by T. M. GOODEVE, M.A., Professor of Mechanics at the Normal School of Science, and the Royal School of Mines.

—— **Principles of Mechanics.** With 253 Woodcuts and numerous Examples. Crown 8vo. 6s.

—— **The Elements of Mechanism.** With 342 Woodcuts. Crown 8vo. 6s.

—— **A Manual of Mechanics**: an Elementary Text-book for Students of Applied Mechanics. With 138 Illustrations and Diagrams, and 188 Examples taken from the Science Department Examination Papers, with Answers. Fcp. 8vo. 2s. 6d.

GOODMAN—Applied Mechanics. By John Goodman.
[In preparation.

GRIEVE—Lessons in Elementary Mechanics. By W. H. GRIEVE, P.S.A., late Engineer R.N., Science Demonstrator for the London School Board, &c. Stage 1. With 165 Illustrations and a large number of Examples. Fcp. 8vo. 1s. 6d. Stage 2. With 122 Illustrations. Fcp. 8vo. 1s. 6d. Stage 3. With 103 Illustrations. Fcp. 8vo. 1s. 6d.

MAGNUS—Lessons in Elementary Mechanics. Introductory to the Study of Physical Science. Designed for the Use of Schools, and of Candidates for the London Matriculation and other Examinations. With numerous Exercises, Examples, and Examination Questions. With Answers, and 131 Woodcuts. By Sir PHILIP MAGNUS, B.Sc., B.A. Fcp. 8vo. 3s. 6d. Key for the use of Teachers only, price 5s. 3½d. net, *post free, from the publishers only.*

TAYLOR—Theoretical Mechanics, including Hydrostatics and Pneumatics. By J. E. TAYLOR, M.A., Hon. Inter., B.Sc., Central High Schools, Sheffield. With 175 Diagrams and Illustrations, and 522 Examination Questions and Answers. Crown 8vo. 2s. 6d.

THORNTON—Theoretical Mechanics: Section 1. Solids; to cover the Advanced Course of Science and Art Department. By A. THORNTON, M.A. [*In preparation.*

TWISDEN—Works by the Rev. JOHN F. TWISDEN, M.A.

—— **Practical Mechanics**; an Elementary Introduction to their Study. With 855 Exercises and 184 Figures and Diagrams. Crown 8vo. 10s. 6d.

—— **Theoretical Mechanics**. With 172 Examples, numerous Exercises, and 154 Diagrams. Crown 8vo. 8s. 6d.

WARREN—An Elementary Treatise on Mechanics; for the use of Schools and Students in Universities. By the Rev. ISAAC WARREN.
Part I. Statics. Crown 8vo. 3s. 6d.
Part II. Dynamics. Crown 8vo. 3s. 6d.

DYNAMICS, STATICS, AND HYDROSTATICS.

BURTON—An Introduction to Dynamics, including Kinematics, Kinetics, and Statics. With numerous Examples. By CHARLES V. BURTON, D.Sc. Crown 8vo. 4s.

GELDARD—Statics and Dynamics. By C. GELDARD, M.A., formerly Scholar of Trinity College, Cambridge, Mathematical Lecturer under the Non-Collegiate Students' Board, Cambridge. Crown 8vo. 5s.

GROSS—Elementary Dynamics (Kinematics and Kinetics). By E. J. GROSS, M.A., Fellow of Gonville and Caius College, Cambridge. Crown 8vo. 5s. 6d.

MAGNUS—Hydrostatics and Pneumatics. By Sir PHILIP MAGNUS, B.Sc. Fcp. 8vo. 1s. 6d., or, with Answers, 2s.
⁎ The Worked Solutions of the Problems. 2s.

ROBINSON—Elements of Dynamics (Kinetics and Statics). With numerous Exercises. A Text-Book for Junior Students. By the Rev. J. L. ROBINSON, B.A. Chaplain and Naval Instructor at the Royal Naval College, Greenwich. Crown 8vo. 6s.

SMITH—Works by J. HAMBLIN SMITH, M.A., of Gonville and Caius College, Cambridge.

—— **Elementary Statics**. Crown 8vo. 3s.

—— **Elementary Hydrostatics**. Crown 8vo. 3s.

—— **Key to Statics and Hydrostatics**. Crown 8vo. 6s.

WILLIAMSON and TARLETON—An Elementary Treatise on Dynamics. Containing Applications to Thermodynamics, with numerous Examples. By BENJAMIN WILLIAMSON, D.Sc., F.R.S., and FRANCIS A. TARLETON, LL.D. Crown 8vo. 10s. 6d.

WORMELL—The Principles of Dynamics: an Elementary Text-Book for Science Students. By R. WORMELL, D.Sc., M.A. Crown 8vo. 6s.

WORTHINGTON—Dynamics of Rotation.: an Elementary Introduction to Rigid Dynamics. By A. M. WORTHINGTON, M.A., F.R.S., Head Master and Professor of Physics at the Royal Naval Engineering College, Devonport. Crown 8vo. 3s. 6d.

SOUND, LIGHT, HEAT & THERMODYNAMICS.

ALEXANDER—Treatise on Thermodynamics. By PETER ALEXANDER, M.A., Lecturer on Mathematics, Queen Margaret College, Glasgow. Crown 8vo. 5s.

DAY—Numerical Examples in Heat. By R. E. DAY, M.A. Fcp. 8vo. 3s. 6d.

HELMHOLTZ—On the Sensations of Tone as a Physiological Basis for the Theory of Music. By Professor HELMHOLTZ. Royal 8vo. 28s.

MADAN—An Elementary Text-Book on Heat. For the use of Schools. By H. G. MADAN, M.A., F.C.S., Fellow of Queen's College, Oxford; late Assistant Master at Eton College. Crown 8vo. 9s.

MAXWELL—Theory of Heat. By J. CLERK MAXWELL, M.A., F.R.SS., L. & E. With Corrections and Additions by Lord RAYLEIGH. With 38 Illustrations. Fcp. 8vo. 4s. 6d.

SMITH (J. Hamblin)—The Study of Heat. By J. HAMBLIN SMITH, M.A., of Gonville and Caius College, Cambridge. Cr. 8vo. 3s.

TYNDALL—Works by JOHN TYNDALL, D.C.L., F.R.S. See page 11.

WORMELL—A Class-Book of Thermodynamics. By RICHARD WORMELL, B.Sc., M.A. Fcp. 8vo. 1s. 6d.

WRIGHT—Works by MARK R. WRIGHT (Hon. Inter., B.Sc., London).

——— **Sound, Light and Heat.** With 160 Diagrams and Illustrations. Crown 8vo. 2s. 6d.

——— **Advanced Heat.** With 136 Diagrams and numerous Examples and Examination Papers. Crown 8vo. 4s. 6d.

STEAM AND THE STEAM ENGINE, &c.

BALE—A Handbook for Steam Users; being Notes on Steam Engine and Boiler Management and Steam Boiler Explosions. By M. POWIS BALE, M.I.M.E., A.M.I.C.E. Fcp. 8vo. 2s. 6d.

BOURNE—Works by JOHN BOURNE, C.E.

—— A Catechism of the Steam Engine, in its Various Applications in the Arts, to which is added a chapter on Air and Gas Engines, and another devoted to Useful Rules, Tables, and Memoranda. Illustrated by 212 Woodcuts. Crown 8vo. 7s. 6d.

—— Recent Improvements in the Steam Engine. With 124 Woodcuts. Fcp. 8vo. 6s.

CLERK—The Gas Engine. By DUGALD CLERK. With 101 Woodcuts. Crown 8vo. 7s. 6d.

HOLMES—The Steam Engine. By GEORGE C. V. HOLMES, (Whitworth Scholar) Secretary of the Institution of Naval Architects. With 212 Woodcuts. Fcp. 8vo. 6s.

RANSOM—Steam and Gas Engine Governors. By H. B. RANSOM. [*In preparation.*

RIPPER—Works by WILLIAM RIPPER, Member of the Institution of Mechanical Engineers; Professor of Mechanical Engineering in the Sheffield Technical School·

—— Steam. With 142 Illustrations. Crown 8vo. 2s. 6d.

—— Steam and the Steam Engine. An Advanced Course. [*In preparation.*

SENNETT—The Marine Steam Engine. A Treatise for the Use of Engineering Students and Officers of the Royal Navy. By RICHARD SENNETT, R.N., Engineer-in-Chief of the Royal Navy. With 261 Illustrations. 8vo. 21s.

STROMEYER—Marine Boiler Management and Construction. Being a Treatise on Boiler Troubles and Repairs, Corrosion. Fuels, and Heat, on the properties of Iron and Steel, on Boiler Mechanics, Workshop Practices, and Boiler Design. By C. E. STROMEYER, Graduate of the Royal Technical College at Aix-la-Chapelle, Member of the Institute of Naval Architects, etc. With 452 Illustrations. 8vo. 18s. net.

ARCHITECTURE.

GWILT—An Encyclopædia of Architecture. By JOSEPH GWILT, F.S.A. Illustrated with more than 1100 Engravings on Wood. Revised (1888), with Alterations and Considerable Additions, by WYATT PAPWORTH. 8vo. 52s. 6d.

MITCHELL—The Stepping-Stone to Architecture: explaining in simple language the Principles and Progress of Architecture from the earliest times. By THOMAS MITCHELL. With 22 Plates and 49 Woodcuts. 18mo. 1s. sewed.

BUILDING CONSTRUCTION.

Advanced Building Construction. By the Author of 'Rivington's Notes on Building Construction'. With 385 Illustrations. Crown 8vo. 4s. 6d.

BURRELL—Building Construction. By EDWARD J. BURRELL, Second Master of the People's Palace Technical School, London. With 303 Working Drawings. Crown 8vo. 2s. 6d.

SEDDON—Builder's Work and the Building Trade. By Colonel H. C. SEDDON, R.E., Superintending Engineer H.M.'s Dockyard, Portsmouth; Examiner in Building Construction, Science and Art Department, South Kensington. With numerous Illustrations. Medium 8vo. 16s.

RIVINGTON'S COURSE OF BUILDING CONSTRUCTION.

Notes on Building Construction. Arranged to meet the requirements of the Syllabus of the Science and Art Department of the Committee of Council on Education, South Kensington. Medium 8vo.

Part I. First Stage, or Elementary Course. With 552 Woodcuts. 10s. 6d.

Part II. Commencement of Second Stage, or Advanced Course. With 479 Woodcuts. 10s. 6d.

Part III. Materials. Advanced Course, and Course for Honours. With 188 Woodcuts. 21s.

Part IV. Calculations for Building Structures. Course for Honours. With 597 Woodcuts. 15s.

ELECTRICITY AND MAGNETISM.

CUMMING—Electricity treated Experimentally. For the use of Schools and Students. By LINNÆUS CUMMING, M.A., Assistant Master in Rugby School. With 242 Illustrations. Crown 8vo. 4s. 6d.

DAY—Exercises in Electrical and Magnetic Measurements, with Answers. By R. E. DAY. 12mo. 3s. 6d.

DE TUNZELMANN—A Treatise on Electricity and Magnetism. By G. W. DE TUNZELMANN, B.Sc., M.I.E.E. [*In Preparation.*

GORE—The Art of Electro-Metallurgy, including all known Processes of Electro-Deposition. By G. GORE, LL.D., F.R.S. With 56 Woodcuts. Fcp. 8vo. 6s.

JENKIN—Electricity and Magnetism. By FLEEMING JENKIN, F.R.S.S., L. & E., M.I.C.E. With 177 Illustrations. Fcp. 8vo. 3s. 6d.

LARDEN—Electricity for Public Schools and Colleges. By W. LARDEN, M.A. With 215 Illustrations and a Series of Examination Papers with Answers. Crown 8vo. 6s.

POYSER—Works by A. W. POYSER, B.A., Assistant Master at the Wyggeston Schools, Leicester.

—— **Magnetism and Electricity.** With 235 Illustrations. Crown 8vo. 2s. 6d.

—— **Advanced Electricity and Magnetism.** With 317 Illustrations. Crown 8vo. 4s. 6d.

SLINGO and BROOKER—Electrical Engineering for Electric Light Artisans and Students. By W. SLINGO and A. BROKER. With 307 Illustrations. Crown 8vo. 10s. 6d.

TYNDALL—Works by JOHN TYNDALL, D.C.L., F.R.S. *See p.* 11.

TELEGRAPHY AND THE TELEPHONE.

CULLEY—A Handbook of Practical Telegraphy. By R. S. CULLEY, M.I.C.E., late Engineer-in-Chief of Telegraphs to the Post Office. With 135 Woodcuts and 17 Plates. 8vo. 16s.

HOPKINS—Telephone Lines and their Properties. By WILLIAM JOHN HOPKINS, Professor of Physics in the Drexel Institute of Art, Science and Industry, Philadelphia. Crown 8vo. 6s.

PREECE and SIVEWRIGHT—Telegraphy. By W. H. PREECE, F.R.S., M.I.C.E., &c., Engineer-in-Chief and Electrician to the Post Office; and Sir J. SIVEWRIGHT, K.C.M.G., General Manager, South African Telegraphs. With 255 Woodcuts. Fcp. 8vo. 6s.

WORKS BY JOHN TYNDALL,

D.C.L., LL.D., F.R.S.

Fragments of Science: a Series of Detached Essays, Addresses and Reviews. 2 vols. Crown 8vo. 16s.

VOL. I. :—The Constitution of Nature—Radiation—On Radiant Heat in relation to the Colour and Chemical Constitution of Bodies—New Chemical Reactions produced by Light—On Dust and Disease—Voyage to Algeria to observe the Eclipse—Niagara—The Parallel Roads of Glen Roy—Alpine Sculpture—Recent Experiments on Fog-Signals—On the Study of Physics—On Crystalline and Slaty Cleavage—On Paramagnetic and Diamagnetic Forces—Physical Basis of Solar Chemistry—Elementary Magnetism—On Force—Contributions to Molecular Physics—Life and Letters of FARADAY—The Copley Medalist of 1870—The Copley Medalist of 1871—Death by Lightning.—Science and the Spirits.

VOL. II. :—Reflections on Prayer and Natural Law—Miracles and Special Providences—On Prayer as a Form of Physical Energy—Vitality—Matter and Force—Scientific Materialism—An Address to Students—Scientific Use of the Imagination—The Belfast Address—Apology for the Belfast Address—The Rev. JAMES MARTINEAU and the Belfast Address—Fermentation, and its Bearings on Surgery and Medicine—Spontaneous Generation—Science and Man—Professor VIRCHOW and Evolution—The Electric Light.

New Fragments. Crown 8vo. 10s. 6d.

CONTENTS :—The Sabbath—Goethe's 'Farbenlehre'—Atoms, Molecules and Ether Waves—Count Rumford—Louis Pasteur, his Life and Labours—The Rainbow and its Congeners—Address delivered at the Birkbeck Institution on 22nd October, 1884—Thomas Young—Life in the Alps—About Common Water—Personal Recollections of Thomas Carlyle—On Unveiling the Statue of Thomas Carlyle—On the Origin, Propagation and Prevention of Phthisis—Old Alpine Jottings—A Morning on Alp Lusgen.

Lectures on Sound. With Frontispiece of Fog-Syren, and 203 other Woodcuts and Diagrams in the Text. Crown 8vo. 10s. 6d.

Heat, a Mode of Motion. With 125 Woodcuts and Diagrams. Cr. 8vo. 12s.

Lectures on Light delivered in the United States in 1872 and 1873. With Portrait, Lithographic Plate and 59 Diagrams. Crown 8vo. 7s.

Essays on the Floating Matter of the Air in relation to Putrefaction and Infection. With 24 Woodcuts. Crown 8vo. 7s. 6d.

Researches on Diamagnetism and Magnecrystallic Action; including the Question of Diamagnetic Polarity. Crown 8vo. 12s.

Notes of a Course of Nine Lectures on Light, delivered at the Royal Institution of Great Britain, 1869. Crown 8vo. 1s. 6d.

Notes of a Course of Seven Lectures on Electrical Phenomena and Theories, delivered at the Royal Institution of Great Britain, 1870. Cr. 8vo. 1s. 6d.

Lessons in Electricity at the Royal Institution, 1875-1876. With 58 Woodcuts and Diagrams. Crown 8vo. 2s. 6d.

Address delivered before the British Association assembled at Belfast, 1874. With Additions. 8vo. 4s. 6d.

Faraday as a Discoverer. Crown 8vo. 3s. 6d.

LONGMANS' CIVIL ENGINEERING SERIES.

Edited by the Author of 'Notes on Building Construction'.

The following volumes of this new Series are in preparation, and other volumes will follow in due course :—

Tidal Rivers: their Hydraulics, Improvement and Navigation. By W. H. WHEELER, M.Inst.C.E., Author of 'The Drainage of Fens and Low Lands by Gravitation and Steam Power'. With 75 Illustrations. Medium 8vo. 16s. net. [*Ready.*

Notes on Dock Construction. By C. COLSON, M.Inst.C.E. of H.M. Dockyard, Devonport. [*In the press.*

Railway Construction. By W. H. MILLS, M.Inst.C.E., Engineer-in-Chief, Great Northern Railway, Ireland. [*In preparation.*

Calculations for Engineering Structures. By T. CLAXTON FIDLER, M.Inst.C.E., Professor of Engineering in the University of Dundee; Author of 'A Practical Treatise on Bridge Construction'. [*In preparation.*

The Student's Course of Civil Engineering. By L. F. VERNON-HARCOURT, M.Inst.C.E., Professor of Civil Engineering at University College. [*In preparation*

ENGINEERING, STRENGTH OF MATERIALS, &c.

ANDERSON—The Strength of Materials and Structures: the Strength of Materials as depending on their Quality and as ascertained by Testing Apparatus. By Sir J. ANDERSON, C.E., LL.D., F.R.S.E. With 66 Woodcuts. Fcp. 8vo. 3s. 6d.

BARRY—Railway Appliances: a Description of Details of Railway Construction subsequent to the Completion of the Earthworks and Structures. By JOHN WOLFE BARRY, M.I.C.E. With 218 Woodcuts. Fcp. 8vo. 4s. 6d.

DOWNING—Elements of Practical Construction, for the use of Students in Engineering and Architecture. By SAMUEL DOWNING, LL.D. Part I. Structure in direct Tension and Compression. With numerous Woodcuts in the Text, and a folio Atlas of 14 Plates of Figures and Sections in Lithography. 8vo. 14s.

STONEY—The Theory of the Stresses on Girders and Similar Structures. With Practical Observations on the Strength and other Properties of Materials. By BINDON B. STONEY, LL.D., F.R.S., M.I.C.E. With 5 Plates and 143 Illustrations in the Text. Royal 8vo. 36s.

UNWIN—The Testing of Materials of Construction. Embracing the Description of Testing Machinery and Apparatus Auxiliary to Mechanical Testing, and an Account of the most Important Researches on the Strength of Materials. By W. CAWTHORNE UNWIN, B.Sc., Mem. Inst. Civil Engineers. With 141 Woodcuts and 5 folding-out Plates. 8vo. 21s.

Scientific Works published by Longmans, Green, & Co. 13

WORKSHOP APPLIANCES, &c.

JAY and KIDSON—**Exercises for Technical Instruction in** Wood-Working. Designed and Drawn by H. JAY, Technical Instructor, Nottingham School Board. Arranged by E. R. KIDSON, F.G.S., Science Demonstrator, Nottingham School Board. 3 sets, price 1s. each in cloth case. Set I. Plates 1-32. Set II. Plates 33-64. Set III. Plates 65-87.

NORTHCOTT—**Lathes and Turning,** Simple, Mechanical and Ornamental. By W. H. NORTHCOTT. With 338 Illustrations. 8vo. 18s.

SHELLEY—**Workshop Appliances,** including Descriptions of some of the Gauging and Measuring Instruments, Hand-cutting Tools, Lathes, Drilling, Planing and other Machine Tools used by Engineers. By C. P. B. SHELLEY, M.I.C.E. With 292 Woodcuts. Fcp. 8vo. 4s. 6d.

UNWIN—**Exercises in Wood-Working** for Handicraft Classes in Elementary and Technical Schools. By WILLIAM CAWTHORNE UNWIN, F.R.S., M.I.C.E. 28 Plates. Fcp. folio. 4s. 6d. in case.

MINERALOGY, METALLURGY, &c.

BAUERMAN—Works by HILARY BAUERMAN, F.G.S.
— **Systematic Mineralogy.** With 373 Woodcuts and Diagrams. Fcp. 8vo. 6s.
— **Descriptive Mineralogy.** With 236 Woodcuts and Diagrams. Fcp. 8vo. 6s.

BLOXAM and HUNTINGTON—**Metals**: their Properties and Treatment. By C. L. BLOXAM and A. K. HUNTINGTON, Professors in King's College, London. With 130 Woodcuts. Fcp. 8vo. 5s.

GORE—**The Art of Electro-Metallurgy,** including all known Processes of Electro-Deposition. By G. GORE, LL.D., F.R.S. With 56 Woodcuts. Fcp. 8vo. 6s.

LUPTON—**Mining.** An Elementary Treatise on the Getting of Minerals. By ARNOLD LUPTON, M.I.C.E., F.G.S., etc., Mining Engineer, Professor of Coal Mining at the Victoria University, Yorkshire College, Leeds. With 596 Illustrations. Crown 8vo. 9s. net.

MITCHELL—**A Manual of Practical Assaying.** By JOHN MITCHELL, F.C.S. Revised, with the Recent Discoveries incorporated. By W. CROOKES, F.R.S. With 201 Illustrations. 8vo. 31s. 6d.

RUTLEY—**The Study of Rocks;** an Elementary Text-Book of Petrology. By F. RUTLEY, F.G.S. With 6 Plates and 88 Woodcuts. Fcp. 8vo. 4s. 6d.

VON COTTA—**Rocks Classified and Described: A Treatise** on Lithology. By BERNHARD VON COTTA. With English, German, and French Synonyms. Translated by PHILIP HENRY LAWRENCE, F.G.S., F.R.G.S. Crown 8vo. 14s.

MACHINE DRAWING AND DESIGN.

LOW AND BEVIS—A Manual of Machine Drawing and Design. By DAVID ALLAN LOW (Whitworth Scholar), M.I. Mech. E., Headmaster of the Technical School, People's Palace, London; and ALFRED WILLIAM BEVIS (Whitworth Scholar), M.I. Mech.E., Director of Manual Training to the Birmingham School Board. With over 700 Illustrations. 8vo. 7s. 6d.

LOW—Improved Drawing Scales. By DAVID ALLAN LOW (Whitworth Scholar), Headmaster of the Technical School, People's Palace, London. 4d. in case.

LOW—An Introduction to Machine Drawing and Design. By DAVID ALLAN LOW, Headmaster of the Technical School, People's Palace, London. With 97 Illustrations and Diagrams. Crown 8vo. 2s.

UNWIN—The Elements of Machine Design. By W. CAWTHORNE UNWIN, F.R.S., Professor of Engineering at the Central Institute of the City and Guilds of London Institute. Part I. General Principles, Fastenings and Transmissive Machinery. With 304 Diagrams, &c. Crown 8vo. 6s. Part II. Chiefly on Engine Details. With 174 Woodcuts. Crown 8vo. 4s. 6d.

ASTRONOMY AND NAVIGATION.

BALL—Works by Sir ROBERT S. BALL, LL.D., F.R.S.

—— Elements of Astronomy. With 136 Figures and Diagrams, and 136 Woodcuts. Fcp. 8vo. 6s.

—— A Class-Book of Astronomy. With 41 Diagrams. Fcp. 8vo. 1s. 6d.

BŒDDICKER—The Milky Way. From the North Pole to 10° of South Declination. Drawn at the Earl of Rosse's Observatory at Birr Castle. By OTTO BŒDDICKER. With Descriptive Letterpress. 4 Plates, size 18 in. by 23 in. in portfolio. 30s.

BRINKLEY—Astronomy. By F. BRINKLEY, formerly Astronomer Royal for Ireland. Re-edited and Revised by J. W. STUBBS, D.D., and F. BRUNNOW, Ph.D. With 49 Diagrams. Crown 8vo. 6s.

CLERKE—The System of the Stars. By AGNES M. CLERKE. With 6 Plates and numerous Illustrations. 8vo. 21s.

HERSCHEL—Outlines of Astronomy. By Sir JOHN F. W. HERSCHEL, Bart., K.H., &c. With 9 Plates and numerous Diagrams. Crown 8vo. 12s.

MARTIN—Navigation and Nautical Astronomy. Compiled by Staff-Commander W. R. MARTIN, R.N. Royal 8vo. 18s.

MERRIFIELD—A Treatise on Navigation for the use of Students. By JOHN MERRIFIELD, LL.D., F.R.A.S., F.M.S. Crown 8vo. 5s.

PROCTOR—Works by Richard A. Proctor.

Old and New Astronomy. 12 Parts, 2s. 6d. each. Supplementary Section, 1s. Complete in 1 vol. 4to. 36s.

Myths and Marvels of Astronomy. Crown 8vo. 5s. Silver Library Edition. Crown 8vo. 3s 6d.

The Moon: Her Motions, Aspect, Scenery, and Physical Condition. With many Plates and Charts, Wood Engraving, and 2 Lunar Photographs. Crown 8vo. 5s.

The Universe of Stars: Researches into, and New Views respecting, the Constitution of the Heavens. With 22 Charts (4 coloured) and 22 Diagrams. 8vo. 10s. 6d.

Other Worlds than Ours: the Plurality of Worlds Studied under the Light of Recent Scientific Researches. With 14 Illustrations; Map, Charts, &c. Crown 8vo. 5s. Silver Library Edition. Crown 8vo. 3s. 6d.

Treatise on the Cycloid and all Forms of Cycloidal Curves, and on the Use of Cycloidal Curves in dealing with the Motions of Planets, Comets, &c. With 161 Diagrams. Crown 8vo. 10s. 6d.

The Orbs Around Us: Essays on the Moon and Planets, Meteors and Comets, the Sun and Coloured Pairs of Suns. Crown 8vo. 5s.

Light Science for Leisure Hours: Familiar Essays on Scientific Subjects, Natural Phenomena, &c. 3 vols. Cr. 8vo. 5s. each.

Our Place among Infinites: Essays contrasting our Little Abode in Space and Time with the Infinites around us. Crown 8vo. 5s.

The Expanse of Heaven: Essays on the Wonders of the Firmament. Cr. 8vo. 5s.

New Star Atlas for the Library, the School, and the Observatory, in Twelve Circular Maps (with 2 Index-Plates). With an Introduction on the Study of the Stars, Illustrated by 9 Diagrams. Crown 8vo. 5s.

Larger Star Atlas for Observers and Students. In Twelve Circular Maps, showing 6000 Stars, 1500 Double Stars, Nebulæ, &c. With 2 Index-Plates. Folio, 15s.; or the Twelve Maps only, 12s. 6d.

The Stars in their Seasons: an Easy Guide to a Knowledge of the Star Groups. In 12 Large Maps. Imperial 8vo. 5s.

The Star Primer: showing the Starry Sky, Week by Week. In 24 Hourly Maps. Crown 4to. 2s. 6d.

Lessons in Elementary Astronomy; with Hints for Young Telescopists. With 47 Woodcuts. Fcp. 8vo. 1s. 6d.

WEBB—Celestial Objects for Common Telescopes. By the Rev. T. W. WEBB, M.A., F.R.A.S. Fifth Edition, Revised and greatly Enlarged, by the Rev. T. E. ESPIN, M.A., F.R.A.S. 2 vols. Vol. I. now ready. With Portrait and a Reminiscence of the Author. 2 Plates, and numerous Illustrations. Crown 8vo. 6s.

16   Scientific Works published by Longmans, Green, & Co.

MANUFACTURES, TECHNOLOGY, &c.

ARNOLD—Steel Manufacture. By J. O. ARNOLD. [*In preparation.*

MORRIS AND WILKINSON—Cotton Spinning. By JOHN MORRIS and F. W. WILKINSON. [*In preparation,*

SHARP—The Manufacture of Bicycles and Tricycles. By ARCHIBALD SHARP. [*In preparation.*

TAYLOR—Cotton Weaving and Designing. By JOHN J. TAYLOR, Lecturer on Cotton Weaving and Designing in the Preston, Ashton-under-Lyne, Chorley, and Todmorden Technical Schools, &c. With 373 Diagrams. Crown 8vo. 7s. 6d. net.

WATTS—An Introductory Manual for Sugar Growers. By FRANCIS WATTS, F.C.S., F.I.C., Assoc. Mason Coll., Birmingham, and Government Chemist, Antigua, West Indies. With 20 Illustrations. Crown 8vo. 6s.

PHYSIOGRAPHY AND GEOLOGY.

BIRD—Works by CHARLES BIRD, B.A., F.G.S., Headmaster of the Rochester Mathematical School.

—— **Elementary Geology.** With Geological Map of the British Isles, and 247 Illustrations. Crown 8vo. 2s. 6d.

—— **Advanced Geology.** [*In preparation.*

GREEN — Physical Geology for Students and General Readers. With Illustrations. By A. H. GREEN, M.A., F.G.S., Professor of Geology in the University of Oxford. 8vo. 21s.

LEWIS—Papers and Notes on the Glacial Geology of Great Britain and Ireland. By the late HENRY CARVILL LEWIS, M.A., F.G.S., Professor of Mineralogy in the Academy of Natural Sciences, Philadelphia, and Professor of Geology in Haverford College, U.S.A. Edited from his unpublished MSS. With an Introduction by HENRY W. CROSSKEY, LL.D., F.G.S.

THORNTON—Work by JOHN THORNTON, M.A., Headmaster, Clarence Street Higher Grade School.

—— **Elementary Physiography:** an Introduction to the Study of Nature. With 10 Maps and 173 Illustrations. New Edition, with Appendix on Astronomical Instruments and Measurements. Crown 8vo. 2s. 6d.

—— **Advanced Physiography.** With 6 Maps and 180 Illustrations. Crown 8vo. 4s. 6d.

HEALTH AND HYGIENE.

BRODRIBB—Manual of Health and Temperance. By T. BRODRIBB, M.A. With Extracts from Gough's 'Temperance Orations'. Revised and Edited by the Rev. W. RUTHVEN PYM, M.A. Crown 8vo. 1s. 6d.

BUCKTON—Health in the House; Twenty-five Lectures on Elementary Physiology in its Application to the Daily Wants of Man and Animals. By CATHERINE M. BUCKTON. With 41 Woodcuts and Diagrams. Crown 8vo. 2s.

CORFIELD—The Laws of Health. By W. H. CORFIELD, M.A., M.D. Fcp. 8vo. 1s. 6d.

FRANKLAND—Micro-Organisms in Water, their Significance, Identification, and Removal. Together with an Account of the Bacteriological Methods involved in their Investigation. Specially Designed for those connected with the Sanitary Aspects of Water Supply. By Professor PERCY FRANKLAND, Ph.D., B.Sc. (Lond.), F.R.S., and Mrs. PERCY FRANKLAND.

POORE—Essays on Rural Hygiene. By GEORGE VIVIAN POORE, M.D. Crown 8vo. 6s. 6d.

WILSON—A Manual of Health-Science: adapted for use in Schools and Colleges, and suited to the Requirements of Students preparing for the Examinations in Hygiene of the Science and Art Department, &c. By ANDREW WILSON, F.R.S.E., F.L.S., &c. With 74 Illustrations. Crown 8vo. 2s. 6d.

OPTICS AND PHOTOGRAPHY.

ABNEY—A Treatise on Photography. By Captain W. DE WIVELESLIE ABNEY, F.R.S., late Instructor in Chemistry and Photography at the School of Military Engineering, Chatham. With Woodcuts. Fcp. 8vo. 3s. 6d.

GLAZEBROOK—Physical Optics. By R. T. GLAZEBROOK, M.A., F.R.S., Fellow and Lecturer of Trin. Coll., Demonstrator of Physics at the Cavendish Laboratory, Cambridge. With 183 Woodcuts of Apparatus, &c. Fcp. 8vo. 6s.

WRIGHT—Optical Projection: a Treatise on the Use of the Lantern in Exhibition and Scientific Demonstration. By LEWIS WRIGHT, Author of 'Light: a Course of Experimental Optics'. With 232 Illustrations. Crown 8vo. 6s.

PHYSIOLOGY, BIOLOGY, &c.

ASHBY—Notes on Physiology for the Use of Students preparing for Examination. By HENRY ASHBY, M.D. With 141 Illustrations. Fcp. 8vo. 5s.

BARNETT—The Making of the Body: a Reading Book for Children on Anatomy and Physiology With Illustrations and Examples. By Mrs. S. A. BARNETT. [*In the press.*

BIDGOOD—A Course of Practical Elementary Biology. By JOHN BIDGOOD, B.Sc., F.L.S. With 226 Illustrations. Crown 8vo. 4s. 6d.

BRAY—Physiology and the Laws of Health, in Easy Lessons for Schools. By Mrs. CHARLES BRAY. Fcp. 8vo. 1s.

FURNEAUX—Human Physiology. By W. FURNEAUX, F.R.G.S. With 218 Illustrations. Crown 8vo. 2s. 6d.

HUDSON and GOSSE—The Rotifera, or 'Wheel-Animalcules'. By C. T. HUDSON, LL.D., and P. H. GOSSE, F.R.S. With 30 Coloured and 4 Uncoloured Plates. In 6 Parts. 4to. 10s. 6d. each; Supplement, 12s. 6d. Complete in 2 vols. with Supplement, 4to. £4 4s.

MACALISTER—Works by ALEXANDER MACALISTER, M.D., Professor of Anatomy, University of Cambridge.

—— **Zoology and Morphology of Vertebrata.** 8vo. 10s. 6d.

—— **Zoology of the Invertebrate Animals.** With 59 Diagrams. Fcp. 8vo. 1s. 6d.

—— **Zoology of the Vertebrate Animals.** With 77 Diagrams. Fcp. 8vo. 1s. 6d.

MORGAN—Animal Biology: an Elementary Text-Book. By C. LLOYD MORGAN, Professor of Animal Biology and Geology in University College, Bristol. With numerous Illustrations. Cr. 8vo. 8s. 6d.

THORNTON—Human Physiology. By JOHN THORNTON, M.A. With 258 Illustrations, some of which are coloured. Crown 8vo.

METEOROLOGY, &c.

ABBOTT—Elementary Theory of the Tides: the Fundamental Theorems Demonstrated without Mathematics, and the Influence on the Length of the Day Discussed. By T. K. ABBOTT, B.D., Fellow and Tutor, Trinity College, Dublin. Crown 8vo. 2s.

JORDAN—The Ocean: a Treatise on Ocean Currents and Tides, and their Causes. By WILLIAM LEIGHTON JORDAN, F.R.G.S. 8vo. 21s.

SCOTT—Weather Charts and Storm Warnings. By ROBERT H. SCOTT, M.A., F.R.S., Secretary to the Meteorological Council. With numerous Illustrations. Crown 8vo. 6s.

BOTANY.

AITKEN—Elementary Text-Book of Botany. For the use of Schools. By EDITH AITKEN, late Scholar of Girton College. With over 400 Diagrams. Crown 8vo. 4s. 6d.

BENNETT and MURRAY—Handbook of Cryptogamic Botany. By ALFRED W. BENNETT, M.A., B.Sc., F.L.S., Lecturer on Botany at St. Thomas's Hospital ; and GEORGE MURRAY, F.L.S., Senior Assistant Department of Botany, British Museum. With 378 Illustrations. 8vo. 16s.

EDMONDS—Elementary Botany. Theoretical and Practical. By HENRY EDMONDS, B.Sc., London. With 319 Diagrams and Woodcuts. Crown 8vo. 2s. 6d.

KITCHENER—A Year's Botany. Adapted to Home and School Use. With Illustrations by the Author. By FRANCES ANNA KITCHENER. Crown 8vo. 5s.

LINDLEY and MOORE—The Treasury of Botany ; or, Popular Dictionary of the Vegetable Kingdom : with which is incorporated a Glossary of Botanical Terms. Edited by J. LINDLEY, M.D., F.R.S., and T. MOORE, F.L.S. With 20 Steel Plates and numerous Woodcuts. 2 Parts. Fcp. 8vo. 12s.

McNAB—Class-Book of Botany. By W. R. McNAB. 2 Parts. Morphology and Physiology. With 42 Diagrams. Fcp. 8vo. 1s. 6d. Classification of Plants. With 118 Diagrams. Fcp. 8vo. 1s. 6d.

THOMÉ and BENNETT—Structural and Physiological Botany. By Dr. OTTO WILHELM THOMÉ and by ALFRED W. BENNETT, M.A., B.Sc., F.L.S. With Coloured Map and 600 Woodcuts. Fcp. 8vo. 6s.

WATTS—A School Flora. For the use of Elementary Botanical Classes. By W. MARSHALL WATTS, D.Sc., Lond. Cr. 8vo. 2s. 6d.

AGRICULTURE AND GARDENING.

ADDYMAN—Agricultural Analysis. A Manual of Quantitative Analysis for Students of Agriculture. By FRANK T. ADDYMAN, B.Sc. (Lond.), F.I.C. With 49 Illustrations. Crown 8vo. 5s. net.

COLEMAN and ADDYMAN—Practical Agricultural Chemistry. For Elementary Students, adapted for use in Agricultural Classes and Colleges. By J. BERNARD COLEMAN, A.R.C.Sc., F.I.C., and FRANK T. ADDYMAN, B.Sc. (Lond.), F.I.C. Crown 8vo. 1s. 6d.

LLOYD—The Science of Agriculture. By F. J. LLOYD. 8vo. 12s.

TEXT-BOOKS OF SCIENCE—*Continued.*

Workshop Appliances, including Descriptions of some of the Gauging and Measuring Instruments—Hand-Cutting Tools, Lathes, Drilling, Planing, and other Machine Tools used by Engineers. By C. P. B. SHELLEY, M.I.C.E. With 291 Woodcuts. Fcp. 8vo. 4s. 6d.

Elements of Machine Design. By W. CAWTHORNE UNWIN, F.R.S., B. Sc., M.I.C.E.
Part I. General Principles, Fastenings, and Transmissive Machinery. 304 Woodcuts. 6s.
Part. II. Chiefly on Engine Details. 174 Woodcuts. Fcp. 8vo. 4s. 6d.

Structural and Physiological Botany. By Dr. OTTO WILHELM THOMÉ, and A. W. BENNETT, M.A., B.Sc., F.L.S. With 600 Woodcuts. Fcp. 8vo. 6s.

Plane and Solid Geometry. By H. W. WATSON, M.A. Fcp. 8vo 3s. 6d.

ELEMENTARY SCIENCE MANUALS.

Written specially to meet the requirements of the ELEMENTARY STAGE OF SCIENCE SUBJECTS *as laid down in the Syllabus of the Directory of the* SCIENCE AND ART DEPARTMENT.

Practical Plane and Solid Geometry, including Graphic Arithmetic. By I. H. MORRIS. Fully Illustrated with Drawings prepared specially for the Book. Crown 8vo. 2s. 6d.

Geometrical Drawing for Art Students. Embracing Plane Geometry and its Applications, the Use of Scales, and the Plans and Elevations of Solids, as required in Section I. of Science Subject I. By I. H. MORRIS. Crown 8vo. 1s. 6d.
Being the First Part of Morris's Practical Plane and Solid Geometry.

Text-Book on Practical, Solid, or Descriptive Geometry. By DAVID ALLEN Low (Whitworth Scholar). Part I. Crown 8vo. 2s. Part II. Crown 8vo. 3s.

An Introduction to Machine Drawing and Design. By DAVID ALLEN Low (Whitworth Scholar). With 97 Illustrations and Diagrams. Crown 8vo. 2s.

Building Construction. By EDWARD J. BURRELL, Second Master at the Technical School of the People's Palace, London. With 308 Illustrations and Working Drawings. Crown 8vo. 2s. 6d.

An Elementary Course of Mathematics. Containing Arithmetic ; Euclid (Book I. with Deductions and Exercises) ; and Algebra. Crown 8vo. 2s. 6d.

Theoretical Mechanics. Including Hydrostatics and Pneumatics. By J. E. TAYLOR, M.A., Hon. Inter. B.Sc. With numerous Examples and Answers, and 175 Diagrams and Illustrations. Crown 8vo. 2s. 6d.

ELEMENTARY SCIENCE MANUALS—Continued.

A Manual of Mechanics: an Elementary Text-Book for Students of Applied Mechanics. With 138 Illustrations and Diagrams, and 188 Examples taken from the Science Department Examination Papers, with Answers. By T. M. GOODEVE, M.A. Fcp. 8vo. 2s. 6d.

Sound, Light, and Heat. By MARK R. WRIGHT (Hon. Inter. B.Sc. London). With 160 Diagrams and Illustrations. Crown 8vo. 2s. 6d.

Physics. Alternative Course. By MARK R. WRIGHT, Author of 'Sound, Light, and Heat'. With 242 Illustrations. Crown 8vo. 2s. 6d.

Magnetism and Electricity. By A. W. POYSER, M.A. With 235 Illustrations. Crown 8vo. 2s. 6d.

Inorganic Chemistry, Theoretical and Practical. With an Introduction to the Principles of Chemical Analysis. By WILLIAM JAGO, F.C.S., F.I.C. With 49 Woodcuts and numerous Questions and Exercises. Fcp. 8vo. 2s. 9d.

An Introduction to Practical Inorganic Chemistry. By WILLIAM JAGO, F.C.S., F.I.C. Crown 8vo. 1s. 6d.

Practical Chemistry: the Principles of Qualitive Analysis. By WILLIAM A. TILDEN, D. Sc. Fcp. 8vo. 1s. 6d.

Elementary Inorganic Chemistry. By W. S. FURNEAUX, F.R.G.S., Crown 8vo. 2s. 6d.

Elementary Geology. By CHARLES BIRD, B.A., F.G.S. With Coloured Geological Map of the British Islands, and 247 Illustrations. Crown 8vo. 2s. 6d.

Human Physiology. By WILLIAM S. FURNEAUX, F.R.G.S. With 218 Illustrations. Crown 8vo. 2s. 6d.

Elementary Botany, Theoretical and Practical. By HENRY EDMONDS, B.Sc., London. With 319 Woodcuts. Crown 8vo. 2s. 6d.

Steam. By WILLIAM RIPPER, Member of the Institution of Mechanical Engineers. With 142 Illustrations. Crown 8vo. 2s. 6d.

Elementary Physiography. By J. THORNTON, M.A. With 10 Maps and 173 Illustrations. With Appendix on Astronomical Instruments and Measurements. Crown 8vo. 2s. 6d.

Agriculture. By HENRY J. WEBB, Ph.D., Agricultural College, Aspatria. With 34 Illustrations. Crown 8vo. 2s. 6d.

A Course of Practical Elementary Biology. By J. BIDGOOD, B.Sc. With 226 Illustrations. Crown 8vo. 4s. 6d.

ADVANCED SCIENCE MANUALS.

Written specially to meet the requirements of the ADVANCED STAGE OF SCIENCE SUBJECTS as laid down in the Syllabus of the Directory of the SCIENCE AND ART DEPARTMENT.

Magnetism and Electricity. By ARTHUR WILLIAM POYSER, M.A., Trinity College, Dublin. With 317 Diagrams. Crown 8vo. 4s. 6d.

Inorganic Chemistry, Theoretical and Practical. A Manual for Students in Advanced Classes of the Science and Art Department. By WILLIAM JAGO, F.C.S., F.I.C. With Plate of Spectra, and 78 Woodcuts. Crown 8vo. 4s. 6d.

Physiography. By JOHN THORNTON, M.A. With 6 Maps, 180 Illustrations, and Coloured Plate of Spectra. Crown 8vo. 4s. 6d.

Heat. By MARK R. WRIGHT, Principal of the Normal Department, Durham College of Science, Hon. Inter. B.Sc. (Lond.). With 136 Illustrations and numerous Examples and Examination Papers. Crown 8vo. 4s. 6d.

Building Construction. By the Author of 'Rivington's Notes on Building Construction'. With 385 Illustrations, and an Appendix of Examination Questions. Crown 8vo. 4s. 6d.

Geology. By CHARLES BIRD, B.A. [In preparation.

Human Physiology. By JOHN THORNTON, M.A. With 258 Illustrations, some of which are coloured. Crown 8vo. 6s.

Theoretical Mechanics: Section 1., SOLIDS. By A. THORNTON, M.A.
  [In preparation.

THE LONDON SCIENCE CLASS-BOOKS.

Edited by G. CAREY FOSTER, F.R.S., and by Sir PHILIP MAGNUS, B.Sc., B.A., of the City and Guilds of London Institute.

Astronomy. By Sir ROBERT STAWELL BALL, LL.D., F.R.S. With 41 Diagrams. 1s. 6d.

Mechanics. By Sir ROBERT STAWELL BALL, LL.D., F.R.S. With 89 Diagrams. 1s. 6d.

The Laws of Health. By W. H. CORFIELD, M.A., M.D., F.R.C.P. With 22 Illustrations. 1s. 6d.

Molecular Physics and Sound. By FREDERICK GUTHRIE, F.R.S. With 91 Diagrams. 1s. 6d.

Geometry, Congruent Figures. By O. HENRICI, Ph.D., F.R.S With 141 Diagrams. 1s. 6d.

Zoology of the Invertebrate Animals. By ALEXANDER McALISTEP M.D. With 59 Diagrams. 1s. 6d.

Zoology of the Vertebrate Animals. By ALEXANDER McALISTER, M.D. With 77 Diagrams. 1s. 6d.

Hydrostatics and Pneumatics. By Sir PHILIP MAGNUS, B.Sc., B.A. With 79 Diagrams. 1s. 6d. (To be had also with Answers. 2s.) The Worked Solution of the Problems. 2s.

Botany. Outlines of the Classification of Plants. By W. R. McN M.D. With 118 Diagrams. 1s. 6d.

Botany. Outlines of Morphology and Physiology. By W. R. Mc M.D. With 42 Diagrams. 1s. 6d.

Thermodynamics. By RICHARD WORMELL, M.A., D.Sc. Wi Diagrams. 1s. 6d.

www.ingramcontent.com/pod-product-compliance
Lightning Source LLC
Chambersburg PA
CBHW022013220426
43663CB00007B/1062